ANCESTORS

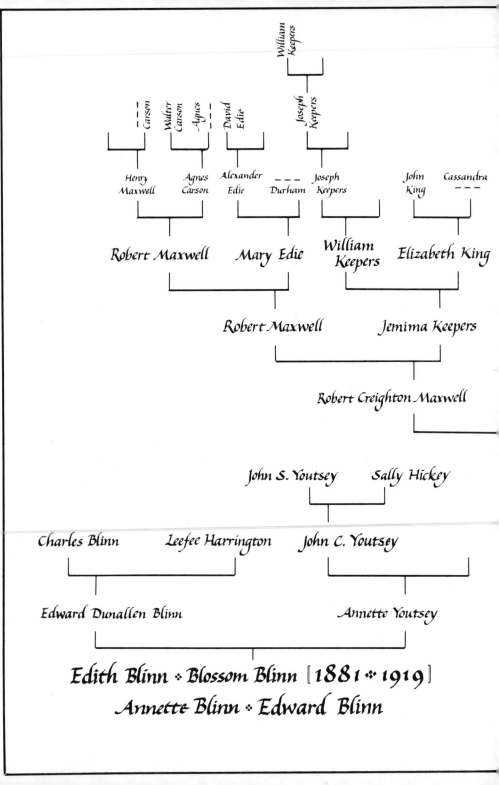

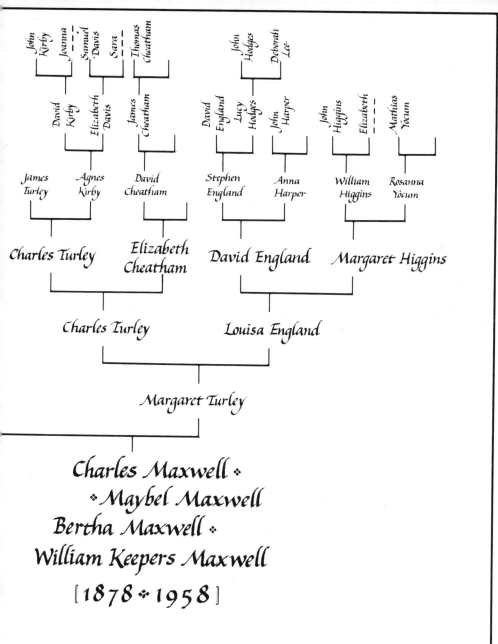

Also by William Maxwell

ANCESTORS

A Family History

by

William Maxwell

NONPAREIL BOOKS
David R. Godine, Publisher
BOSTON

This is a *Nonpareil Book* published in 1985 by
DAVID R. GODINE, PUBLISHER, INC.
306 Dartmouth Street
Boston, Massachusetts 02116

Acknowledgment for the epigraphs is made to Alfred A. Knopf, Inc.,
for the quotation from *A World of Love* by Elizabeth Bowen
to W. W. Norton & Company, Inc., for the quotations from
The Letters of Rainer Maria Rilke 1892–1910.

Library of Congress Cataloging in Publication Data

Maxwell, William, 1908–
Ancestors.

(A Nonpareil book ; 38)
Reprint. Originally published: New York : Knopf, 1971.
1. Maxwell family. I. Title. II. Series.
C S71.M465 1985   929'.2'0973   85-869
I S B N 0-87923-574-8 (pbk.)

First printing

Printed in the United States of America

ANCESTORS

||

My Grandfather Maxwell was a lawyer in Lincoln, Illinois, and one of his clients, out of affection for him, brought back from a visit to Scotland a sepia photograph of Caerlaverock Castle. This ruined fortress is the ancestral seat of a Scottish family of some importance, members of which have held the titles of earl of Morton, earl of Nithsdale, Lord Maxwell, and Lord Herries. I don't know what place of honor the photograph occupied in my grandfather's house or office, for he died before I was born. During my childhood it hung over the horsehair couch in my Aunt Maybel's sitting room. When I was tired of reading I used to lie on the couch and stare at it. Steeped in storybooks, I expected history to show, like emotion on a human face, and it did not seem possible that any splendor had ever fallen on these particular castle walls. Instead of a proper drawbridge there was a light wooden bridge, painted white, with railings, as if it were a building in a public park. The castle itself appeared to be damp and mouldy and in the middle of nowhere, and I found it hard to imagine anyone living in it. It was referred to in the family as the Maxwell castle—proudly, but also as if that was all there was to know about it. I didn't think to ask somebody where it was.

My ignorance lasted about forty-five years, until my daughter Kate at the age of ten took *The Scottish Chiefs* out of her school library and when she was a few pages into it raised her head to ask a question about Scottish history. I had been watching her with pleasure. At about that same age I read and reread this rather stilted and old-fashioned novel, which is about a lost cause—the insurrection led by Sir William Wallace against the English king, Edward I. The moment he was successful—at one point he drove the English entirely out of Scotland—the Scottish nobles either deserted his banner or divided his councils by their jealousy. They perjured themselves, they changed sides again and again. Even Robert the Bruce. Most of all Robert the Bruce. Wallace alone never wavered, a boy's hero that no historian has ever had to apologize for.

I got up and went to the bookcase and took down Volume I of Green's *A Short History of England*. As I was turning the pages of the section on the conquest of Scotland, to my astonishment I came upon the Maxwell castle. There was no mistaking it, even though the castle in the engraving was only an inch and a half high and it was not the view in the photograph but from the other side. Furthermore, since the caption under the engraving read, "After J. M. W. Turner," I was obliged to conjure up a little man with a hook nose, in an ill-cut brown tailcoat, with very small hands and feet, setting up his easel where there was a good view of the castle and the plain.

Someone I know went to Caerlaverock Castle two or three years ago and, discovering later that I was interested in it, dug up the *Ministry of Public Building and Works Official Guidebook* sold at the castle gate. From this I learned, for the first time, that Caerlaverock is triangular in shape—the photograph didn't show it—with four big round towers and two moats, one inside the other. It stands on a peninsula of the Solway, which in Medieval times was one of the main highways into Scotland. It was built toward the end of the 13th century, probably by the English to use against the Scots, but fell into their hands. In 1300 Edward I led an English army into Scotland for the siege of Caerlaverock. There exists a rhyming account of this incident, in Old French, and I am indebted to the *Guidebook* for the following passage from it. Even though it is a translation, it has an eerie quality. It is not just a written description but a voice speaking, from such a remote past, and in the special and highly characteristic language of that past: "Caerlaverock was so strong a castle that it feared no siege before the king came there, for it would never have had to surrender, provided it was well supplied, when the need arose, with men, engines and provisions. In shape it was like a shield, for it had but three sides round it, with a tower at each corner, but one of them was a double one, so high, so long and so wide, that the gate was underneath it, well made and strong, with a drawbridge and a sufficiency of other defenses. And it had good walls, and good ditches filled to the brim with water. And I think you will never see a more finely situated castle, for on the one side can be seen the Irish Sea, towards the west, and to the north the fair moorland, surrounded by an arm of the sea, so that no creature can approach it on two sides, without putting himself in danger of the sea. On the south side it is not easy, for there are many places difficult to get through because of woods and marshes and ditches hollowed out by sea where it meets the river."

Though in theory the castle could have held out forever against Edward I, he took it without much difficulty, and it remained an English stronghold until after he died. When it became clear that there was less reason to be afraid of Edward II, the keeper of the castle for the English, Sir Eustace Maxwell, declared for Robert the Bruce. He was besieged at Caerlaverock but held out. Later on (it being Bruce's policy to deny the English any stronghold that might prove useful to them in a later campaign) the castle wall was pulled down in places, so that it could not be defended. By 1347 the castle was again fortified and being lived in, and Herbert of Maxwell delivered hostages there, after submitting to Edward III, and in return had letters of protection "to himself and to his men and to the castle, with its armor, victuals and other goods, and the cattle which were in it." A good deal of the present castle was built at this time. It went on figuring prominently in the Scottish wars for the next three hundred years, until it capitulated to the Covenanters in 1640. They made an uninhabitable ruin of it.

There is no evidence that any ancestor of mine ever lived in Caerlaverock Castle, even in the capacity of a kitchen boy or swineherd. Tenant farmers commonly took the surname of their landlord, and so it does not follow that every Maxwell is a blood relative of every other person of that name. The nobility and the gentry, who would have come by their names directly and not through adoption, didn't emigrate to America. But the photograph was all the proof the older generation required that the loins from which they had sprung were ultimately aristocratic, and if it ever occurred to them that their religious affiliations were with those who stripped the castle of its furnishings and pulled down the roofs and made a breach in the walls, they kept this unsatisfactory thought to themselves.

Without the photograph it is doubtful if my first cousin, William Maxwell Fuller, would have gone to the trouble of making a genealogy of his (and my) Grandfather Maxwell's family. His mother, my Aunt Bert, was my father's favorite sister. I loved her, but Max I hardly knew at all. He was ten years older than I was, and grew up in a different place. I saw him from time to time at family gatherings, and talked to him alone only once, when he was in his late thirties. He had a brokerage business in Cincinnati, and was married, with a twelve-year-old daughter. I was living in Greenwich Village, and he came east on a business trip and took me to dinner at an expensive restaurant on lower Fifth Avenue. We were beautifully at cross purposes all evening. I thought he had called me out of a sense of duty, whereas in fact it was because something—that I was a misfit introverted child, that he was fond of my mother and father, that I represented the younger brother he wished he had had—made him interested in me. All I know for sure, and I wish I had known it on that occasion, is that he was immensely pleased and proud of me because I had published a couple of novels.

I can see us now so clearly, in that lime-green hotel dining room—his face across the table from me, and his double-breasted dark-blue pin-stripe suit, and his courteous manner of speaking, and his habit of lighting one cigarette from another—that it almost seems possible to live the evening over again the way it ought to have gone.

At first, in our efforts to lift the relationship to where it seemed to belong, we were not quite natural with each other. As people go, we weren't much alike, but it wasn't true either that we had nothing in common. He was named for my father and so was I. Max spent the early part of his childhood and I spent all of mine in a small town in the dead center of Illinois. We both went to high school in Chicago. My father felt that Max had failed in his responsibilities to his mother, but we could hardly talk about that. When other relatives got around to speaking of my writing, it was to point out kindly that there were novels which did sell—historical novels with lots of action in them, and plot. And that were afterwards bought by the movies for a considerable amount of money. It was not a conversation I wanted to repeat with Max. I had been in Cincinnati once, overnight, and hadn't called him. So we couldn't talk about Cincinnati. I had never met his wife and daughter. And I didn't own any stocks and bonds. Meeting my eyes over the top of his menu, he urged me to have turtle soup with him. I don't think I did. I can't remember what I had. But when his soup came he summoned the headwaiter grandly and demanded a glass of sherry to put in it, and I wondered how he knew that this was what you were supposed to do.

As we ate, he asked one question after another. I have done it myself so many times since with somebody who was younger and not very talkative. It is the only thing you can do. He asked about my job, and about what it was like living in New York, and I saw how attentively he listened to everything I said. He was like an imaginary older brother —interested, affectionate, perceptive, and more securely situated in a world of his own making. I liked him very much, but I went on answering his questions with a single statement that obliged him to think up some new question —instead of saying to him, "I was living in a rooming house on Lexington Avenue and I had dinner with somebody from the office one night who said there was a vacant apartment in the building where he lived, so I went home with him, and the door was unlocked but there weren't any light bulbs, and I took it because I liked the way it felt in the dark. The rent is thirty-five dollars a month. You go past an iron gate into a courtyard with gas streetlamps. It was built during the Civil War, I think. Anyway, it's very old. And my apartment is on the third floor, looking out on a different courtyard, with trees in it. Ailanthus trees. I like having something green to look at. Technically it's a room and a half. The half is a bedroom just big enough for a single bed, and I never sleep there because it's too like lying in a coffin. I sleep on a studio couch in the living room. The fireplace works. And once when I had done something I was terribly ashamed of, I went and put my forehead on the mantelpiece. It was just the right height.

"The kitchen is tiny, but it has a skylight that opens, and by putting one foot on the edge of the sink and the other on top of the icebox I can pull myself up onto the roof, and I sit there sometimes looking at the moon and the stars. In the morning, when I'm shaving, I hear the prostitutes being brought to the women's prison. Shouting and screaming. Though I'm on a courtyard, it's never really quiet in New York the way it is in the country. Just as I'm drifting off at night I hear a taxi horn. Or I hear the Sixth Avenue el, and try to fall asleep before the next one comes. The building directly across from my windows is some kind of a factory, and in the daytime the workmen come out and stand on the fire escape talking, and when the doors are open I can hear the clicking of the machinery. At night there is a cat that sits on the fire escape and makes hideous sounds like a baby having its throat cut, until I get up and throw beer bottles at it. If I don't get any sleep I'm no good at my job. It's an interesting job and I like it and I'm lucky to have it, but I have to deal with so many people all day long that when night comes I don't want to see anybody. When the telephone rings, which isn't very often, I don't answer it. I let it ring and ring and finally it stops, and the silence then is so beautiful. I read, or I walk the streets until I'm dead tired and come home hoping to fall asleep. At the far end of the courtyard there's an intern from St. Vincent's Hospital who never pulls his shades. I see his light go on about eleven. He has a girl—she is so nice— she brought him a balloon when he was sick. But there is another girl she doesn't know about who sleeps with him too. Next to the factory, on the second floor, there is a young married couple. In the morning when I'm drinking my coffee by the window, the sunlight reaches far enough into their apartment for me to see the shapes of their bodies under the bedclothes. Sometimes she comes to the window in her nightgown or her slip and stands brushing her hair. You can tell they're in love because their movements are so heavy. As if they were drugged. And once I saw him sitting in his undershorts putting on his socks. Everything they do is like a painting.

"I tried to get a job in New York once before, in 1933, before my first book was published, and couldn't. It was like trying to climb a glass mountain. The book had two favorable reviews but it didn't cause any commercial excitement whatever, so I went home, and started another novel, and when that petered out I started another, and made my savings stretch as far as possible, and took help from friends. Not money. Room and board, in exchange for doing things for them that they were perfectly able to do for themselves. This was so I wouldn't feel obligated. When I finished the second book I came back here and this time I managed to stay. But my job takes up so much of my energy that I write less and less. I can do stories, but that's all. And not many of them.

"I've fallen in love three times in my life, and each time it was with someone who wasn't in love with me, and now I can't do it any more. I have friends. There's a place uptown where I can go when I feel like being with people, and the door is never locked, you just walk in and go through the apartment till you find somebody, and they set an extra place at the dinner table for me without asking, and so I don't feel nobody cares whether I live or die. But I can't sleep at night because when I put out my hand there isn't anybody in the bed beside me, and it's as if I'd exchanged one glass mountain for another, and I don't know what to do . . ."

We left the restaurant together, and shook hands under a street light, and that was the last I ever saw of him.

If I had put my cards on the table, would he then have laid his down too? Perhaps. And perhaps not. I really don't know. Usually what triggers this response is the similarity of two experiences, and ours were not at all similar. Shortly after he was born, his mother divorced his father and so far as I know never saw him again. Max spent the early part of his childhood in my Grandfather Maxwell's house, and then in my Aunt Maybel's. That as a boy he lay on that horsehair couch looking up at the picture of Caerlaverock Castle there can be no doubt. When he was six years old, his mother remarried. She divorced that husband too. Around the turn of the century it was not common for women to extricate themselves from marital difficulties. Rather than be exposed to public criticism, they dramatized their misery or cultivated what they referred to as their nerves. My aunt didn't go in for either one. She was high-spirited and strong-willed and at close quarters unmanageable. She was also very pretty, and so fond of a good joke—or even a bad one—and she doubtless could have gone on marrying and divorcing, but instead she went to work in a corset factory in Chicago.

Once I asked my father what Max's father was like, and he said, in the indirect way grown people answer children's questions, that Bert liked the wrong kind of men. I interpreted this to mean that my aunt liked men who wore loud checks and spent their time at the racetracks, and it may well have been true. Since I was very fond of her, I would have excused an even greater lapse from good judgment. Two of the men who wanted to marry her, my father said, were, later on, very successful in business. If she'd married either one of them—but she wouldn't have them. And he considered this a further evidence of her perversity. His own character was straightforward and uncompromising and cautious, and he tended to view human behavior in rather simple, old-fashioned (even for his period) terms; that is, he thought everybody was at all times able to distinguish between right and wrong, and when they got into trouble it was largely their own doing. Though he considered that his sister had mismanaged her life, he stood by her faithfully, offering financial help when it was needed, and I used to suspect him of taking a melancholy pleasure in the thoroughness with which she pulled the house down on her head. She named her only child for him, and when my father was in trouble she came running.

As a small child, Max Fuller was so beautiful that photographs of him, in a girl's petticoat, with his bare legs crossed at the ankle and an expression of innocence on his exquisite androgynous face, were framed by the yard. There was a set in our upstairs hall, under the gas night-light, and my Aunt Maybel, my father's older sister, had another. It was a period that admired sweetness above all other qualities in art.

How Max felt about those pictures may be deduced from the fact that, as a grown man, he parted his hair in the middle and plastered it flat to his head. Even so, he'd have looked like the Arrow collar ads that were everywhere at the time, except that he lacked the proper physical complacency.

From snapshots pasted in my Grandmother Maxwell's scrapbook it appears that as a boy Max was properly clothed, that he had friends, male and female, that he was sent to a boys' camp, that he played football, that he knew how to sit on a horse, that he was not afraid to dive from high places. Since there were no Socialists in the family, the corset factory in Chicago was not referred to as a sweat shop, but surely that's what it was. Moving back one stage from the man who knew about putting sherry in turtle soup, I arrive at a nice-looking boy of seventeen, whose face was without any color and whose expression, especially about the eyes, reminded me of a nervous animal. Nothing that I ever heard about my Aunt Bert's second husband would have led one to believe that he was a wicked man, but the ground on which my aunt obtained a divorce from him was "that the said defendant had been guilty of habitual drunkenness for the space of two successive years prior to the filing of this Bill of Complaint . . ." This cannot have been pleasant for my aunt, or for Max. His stepfather had a daughter by a previous marriage, who lived with them, and she and Max did not get on well. My aunt's second marriage lasted about ten years, after which it was too late for Max to start over again on a different and better childhood.

The scrapbook contains a number of undated postcards and letters from him, including this:

Dearest Grandmother:

I received your nice letter and am trying to live to your desires and be a credit to the Maxwell family. I have plenty of confidence and know I will make good. Mother and I are happy now and wish you would come up and see us. I like my work fine and I still attend Sunday school. With lots of love to you,

Maxwell

Sixteen or seventeen, he must have been, for, clearly, there is no longer a man in the house. The happiness, like all happiness, was fragile. Later on, by her mournful way of speaking of him, and sometimes more explicitly, my Aunt Bert led people to think that Max did not love her. Or at least that he did not love her the way he should. At eleven years old I didn't know enough about life to question it, though it was, of course, highly questionable and self-indulgent behavior. Who is to say how much Max loved his mother except Max? How much did she love him? He was not an unfeeling man, and it doesn't make sense, any of it, except as an example of how a grave disappointment can be transferred from the real cause, about which one can do nothing, to some other, more sensitive area.

Before this happened, there was a change in the circumstances of her life. She had a run of good luck. Her natural flair with ribbons and laces and artificial flowers was recognized by the people she worked for. They put her in the designing department and then offered her a job taking orders from merchants in small towns around the state. She used our house as her headquarters because it was convenient and because my father needed her at that point. And for a short while she was very successful. But then the family doctor told her that she had to have her appendix removed, and in performing the operation he cut something he shouldn't have. Or so my father said. With the result that my aunt could no longer carry heavy sample cases and had to retire from the road. It was too sudden and complete a reversal. It had meant so much to her to be out in the world, doing well, and making a good salary. During her convalescence she put on weight. And she did not feel at all well. For the first time in her life her body was a burden to her. But she had to do something. Through a business connection she got a job as a substitute teacher in a coal-mining town in southern Illinois. It was a stopgap. She did not want to live down there, and she wasn't sure how long she would be physically able to go on dealing with unruly seventh-graders. One day a big box of hats arrived at our house from southern Illinois, every one of them fetching. And reasonably priced. Within twenty-four hours they were all sold. Another box arrived and went just as quickly. Before my aunt could send a third, my father got a letter from the secretary of the local Chamber of Commerce. Nate Landauer, the owner of a ladies' ready-to-wear shop on the courthouse square, had complained that my father (who didn't know one end of a lady's hat from the other) was operating a millinery shop out of his house in Park Place. My father would have liked to tell them both to go to hell, but he didn't. In some obscure way they had him. He wrote my Aunt Bert that she wasn't to send any more hats.

This blow was one more proof, which she didn't really need, that her luck had deserted her. But she still had Max. If she was forced by ill health to give up her job she could go and keep house for him. He didn't even have a house at this time—he was an engineering student at the University of Cincinnati. But people do not go to school forever.

Max upset his mother's plans by getting married, when he was only five months out of college, to a girl from a well-to-do family in Cincinnati. My aunt did not disapprove of his wife but of his marrying at all, when his first duty was to her. She saw this as something unarguable, a moral obligation he had failed to meet. The older generations would have unhesitatingly agreed with her, but hers was the last that was able to entertain such an idea. Max was a child of the twenties, and it was not a period that went in for ancestor worship. If I were to suggest to my own children that their first duty was to their mother or me, not to themselves, they would be astonished.

Max and his mother had a falling out, of a lasting kind. He continued to write to her, and from time to time she went to Cincinnati for a visit. Her daughter-in-law and her granddaughter figured in her conversation. But the awkwardness persisted.

If Max's mother could not or would not abandon her grievance against him, there was somebody who was always waiting to receive him with open arms: my Aunt Maybel. He loved her also, for she had helped bring him up, and he didn't hold it against her that she lived in the 19th century, not the 20th. During his boyhood, her house, where nobody ever came home drunk and knocked over the furniture, or for that matter even so much as drank a glass of beer on a hot night, was a haven of refuge his mind must often have dwelt on. She was totally unlike his mother physically and in every other way. She always did what she said she was going to do. And most of all she took him and all his concerns seriously.

She took everything seriously, including the solemn business of proving that she had a right to be a member of the

D.A.R. And she managed to interest Max in genealogy. He was a lot brighter and better educated and more thorough than she was, and he went at it in a businesslike fashion, reading out-of-the-way books and carrying on a lively correspondence with county clerks. He and my Aunt Maybel wrote back and forth about whether the one who died in 1771 could have been a son of John, d. 1756, not the first James . . . Gibberish unless you put your mind to it quite firmly.

At no time in his life was my cousin as securely situated as I thought when I was having dinner with him. His marriage was happy, but even a happy marriage requires having your wits about you, and Max's situation was not uncomplicated. The world he married into was socially a cut—several cuts—above the one he was born into. His father-in-law was the head of the Cincinnati traction system and a public figure. Max's wife was ambitious for him and it was probably her influence that led him to give up engineering, a field in which advancement was likely to be slow, in favor of starting a brokerage business. My Aunt Maybel and my Grandmother Maxwell loaned him the money to open an office, and he did well enough but not spectacularly—I mean he wasn't a millionaire at twenty-seven. At first they lived with his wife's family, then on the second floor of a duplex; his wife had a miscarriage, which in turn produced an emotional crisis, and they ended up living with Max's father-in-law as before. When their daughter was born, Max's wife kept the baby in her room, and Max moved up to the attic. This arrangement must have lasted for quite some time, for Max's daughter remembers her father coming down to the second floor in his bathrobe to shave. But eventually he asserted himself and they lived in their own house again.

Max's father-in-law's interest and affection were so centered on his own son, who did not turn out well, that he was not much aware of Max, who did. The relation was cordial but not close. I think of my relations with my father —of how consistently I resisted his opinions, from the age of fifteen, and at the same time believed that he offered the only possible model of decent behavior. And then I think of Max, of what it was like for Max with no father to ape or take issue with.

At the age I was then, I never asked personal questions, but I wish I had somehow given him a chance to say what it was that he hoped to gain for himself as he went about collecting facts having to do with births, deaths, and marriages of several generations of self-respecting, not very well-educated, for the most part devout men and women nobody has ever heard of.

The genealogy was never finished. Outlying branches of the family did not always take the trouble to answer Max's letters. Or if they did, the facts they supplied him with were jumbled. Or mystifying. Or irrelevant. In order to get the information he needed, he'd have had to devote years of his life to poring over old records and church registers—years that it turned out he did not have. In his early forties he developed Buerger's disease, which is defined in the medical dictionary as an inflammation of the innermost wall of a blood vessel, with a clot formation. It is a form of gangrene, and it occurs generally in the lower arteries and veins of the leg. It is an allergy, related to chain-smoking. My gentle, kind cousin stoically endured the amputation of a leg, and was thought to be out of danger when a new clot formed.

At some point during his illness he and his mother were reconciled. It would have been monstrous of her to go on holding the past against him when he had no future. She stopped grieving because he did not love her and grieved instead over the disaster that had overtaken her only child.

After he died, she added a few facts about my generation and the one after it, and my father had the genealogy typed for her, and carbon copies were sent around to everybody in the family. My copy instantly went into a desk drawer, where it stayed for fifteen years. One day I came on it while I was looking for something else, and began to read it, beginning with my father's generation and following the not always distinct trail back through the 19th century into the middle and early part of the 18th.

The fact that the genealogy does not go back to the Norman Conquest and that nobody appears to have been socially distinguished makes me feel that what is there, though incomplete, is nevertheless reliable.

Max's daughter inherited his taste for antiquarian research. Living in a later period, with more leisure and a more professional approach, she succeeded in running down facts he had failed to come by. His notes, with her corrections and additions, were Xeroxed for me—a boxful of names, dates, and mysteries. For at certain points she too found herself blocked. As she explained, "Southern county clerks love to remind someone from Massachusetts that many records were destroyed during the Civil War—only they don't call it that or state it so directly. They say, 'Sorry, our records begin in 1865.' One wrote that there was 'a small fire' in 1865. All this makes genealogical research in Virginia a bit tricky."

The first page of Max's genealogy (which he doesn't even call that but, instead, a "working outline") reads:

SOME OF THE DESCENDANTS

OF

HENRY MAXWELL

COMPILED BY

WILLIAM MAXWELL FULLER

January 22nd, 1940

Henry Maxwell was born in Scotland about 1730. Born where? And to whom? I don't know the answer to either question. One can speculate, but what would be the point? It is like looking out over the ocean in the dark and trying to make out something, a cliff, a stretch of coastline, when you know perfectly well that even in the daytime the other side is too far away for human eyes to see.

2

I have always liked my name. This may be because of the people I was surrounded with as a child. When they used my name, or my brother's, or for that matter one another's, it was almost always with affection, which somehow rubbed off on the name itself. William Maxwell—to hold it off at arm's length—is not a common name and neither is it exactly uncommon. It turns up in the *Waverley* novels, in Scottish and English and American history, in the juvenilia of Charlotte Brontë, in all sorts of places. When Boswell has supper with his cousin, Sir William Maxwell, at Howell's in Half Moon Street, I know that it is not me, that it has nothing to do with me, but, irrationally, I am pleased.

Or perhaps the real reason I like my name is that it is Scottish. When I was six years old my mother took me to Bloomington, thirty miles away, to hear Harry Lauder. And when we arrived at the theater there were two bagpipers— huge men, over six feet—in kilts, walking up and down and making those squealing noises and my heart began to pound with excitement. Since that moment everything Scottish— kilts, plaid, bagpipe music, the accent, the coloring—produces a mysterious, unthinking pleasure in me.

The use of last names was introduced into Scotland by the Normans in about 1100. The first people to acquire them were the nobles and the great landowners, who called themselves after the lands they possessed. According to George F. Black's *The Surnames of Scotland*, the name *Maxwell* is "derived from a salmon pool on the Tweed, near Kelso Bridge, still locally known as 'Max-wheel.' Maccus, son of Undewyn, a Saxon lord, in the reign of David I, obtained a grant of land on the Tweed before 1150, and from the fishery attached thereto, called Maccus's Wiel (OE. *wael*, a pool, whirlpool), the lands obtained their name."

Maxwell is a Lowland name, common in Dumfriesshire but not limited to it. In a book * my cousin unearthed, Henry Maxwell's sons are said to be from Wigtonshire and Kirkcudbrightshire. Since they were born in America, what this means is that their father's people lived in those two Lowland counties, which are side by side in the extreme southwest of Scotland. Kirkcudbrightshire is mountainous, sloping down to the rugged coast of the Solway Firth. It is cattle-raising country, dotted with ruined abbeys and castles. Wigtonshire is hilly moorland, about half of it under cultivation. It has a great many lakes, and hill forts, standing stones, Pictish crannogs, and other vestiges of pre-Roman Britain.

Assuming that Henry Maxwell's father was a tenant farmer, he was born in a stone shanty with a turf or a thatched roof and with straw, heather, or moss stuffed in the cracks between the stones. A stone house built without mortar could be pulled apart by a raiding party in the morning and by nightfall be intact once more. The fire was in the middle of the floor, and the smoke escaped through holes in the roof —some of the smoke. The cattle were tethered at one end of the only room and the family lay down to sleep at the other, on piles of heather. Smallpox and skin disease were prevalent throughout the countryside.

* Charles B. Hanna: *Historical Recollections of Harrison County in the State of Ohio* (New York, 1900).

If the Lowland farmer spoke with an uncouth accent, dressed in rags, lived in a miserable hovel, and fed on the same grain he fed his animals, it was not because he was a savage but because the relentless marauding of the English left him with very little choice. As for why he didn't simply cut his throat, the answer is that he was a Presbyterian and did not expect much in the way of earthly happiness.

A granddaughter of Henry Maxwell, when she was an old woman, said that he and his uncle, Walter Carson, fled from Scotland to Ireland to escape persecution. Walter Carson was a Quaker, which meant that he would not bear arms or take an oath in courts of law and elsewhere or attend the established church or pay tithes, and so he was in several kinds of trouble at once. After two years in Ireland they sailed for America, Walter Carson's family being with them, and settled in Pennsylvania. Because of its policy of religious toleration it had become a refuge for European immigrants of persecuted sects. Walter Carson doubtless went there for that reason. And to be among people who believed, as he did, that one can receive whatever understanding and guidance in divine truth he may need from the "inward light" placed in his own heart by the Holy Spirit.

As for Henry Maxwell, what seems most likely is that he was an orphan left in the care of his mother's brother.

The old woman said that if her grandfather had any brothers or sisters, she had never heard them spoken of. She also said that he was highly educated and came of a well-to-do family in Scotland, and brought money with him to this country, which he changed into "Congress money"— that is to say, money issued by the Continental Congress— soon after his arrival, thereby impoverishing himself. Henry Maxwell was eleven or twelve years old when he left Ireland, and I like very much the idea of an erudite boy arriving in America with a trunk full of pound notes. Unfortunately it isn't true. It can't be. By 1741 Walter Carson was already living in what was then Lancaster County and is now York County, Pennsylvania, and the first issue of Continental money was made in 1775. Possibly two different stories got crossed in the old woman's mind. If that boy wasn't rich, at least he could read and write, for Scotland, unlike England, had had free public schools since the 16th century.

The known facts about him are: He married his cousin, Agnes Carson, and worked at the weaver's trade. He had seven sons and no daughters. He fought in the American Revolution; he was a private in the Fifth Regiment of the Pennsylvania Line. He is listed in the tax rolls of 1783 as owning one horse and two horned cattle, for which he paid a tax of five shillings, seven pence; and in the 1790 census, under the name of Harry Maxwell—unless Harry Maxwell is another man, living in the same township, which is unlikely. And he died sometime before January 19, 1792, when his estate was administered.

If Henry Maxwell owned any land, no documentary evidence of this fact has ever been uncovered by any of the family antiquarians. But the land was there, not being used by anybody, and he may just not have bothered about taking title to it. In 1741 Walter Carson acquired from the Commonwealth of Pennsylvania one hundred acres on Big Bottom, near Conewago Creek, on the east side of the Susquehanna. In 1743, a hundred and fifty acres at Three Springs. In 1744 two hundred acres on Great Conewago. And that same year he and his wife, Agnes, bought two hundred acres more, on Conewago Creek, from John Steel. This was all cheap land, beyond the Quaker farms that ringed Philadelphia, and his neighbors were mostly Germans from the Palatinate and illiterate but resourceful Scotch-Irish who had given up farming as a bad job and turned to hunting and trapping. With that much land to be dealt with in one way or another, one can say—it is not a question of having to imagine—that Henry Maxwell as a boy had to clear brush and cut timber, was set to pulling stumps, rounded up the cows and milked them. The look of the sky, which was so very different from the sky at home or in Ireland, and the direction of the wind told him what the next day's weather would be like. A halo round the moon meant a lengthy slow rain inside of eight hours. Smoke that did not rise meant that a storm was on the way. A heavy dew at night meant a fair day for drying hay. Sometimes he and his uncle went haying at night, by the light of the moon or the stars, because it was cooler. Bats and swallows flying near the ground meant rain, and so did the increased odor of swamps and ditches.

The sound of a bell coming over the woods and fields meant a church service, a funeral, or an Indian attack. In the fall of the year his hands were stained from husking black walnuts. In winter, so they would be warm when he put them on in the morning, he pushed his clothes down to the bottom of the bed with his bare feet, and slept with his head under the covers. While he was waiting his turn at the mill he got into a fight with a boy who was a head taller than he was, and afterward they were friends. They fished and set snares together, and rode one behind the other, bareback, on the same old white horse. Compared with all this, what is a trunk full of pound notes? What, even, is erudition?

It is possible that his uncle asked him to keep the accounts. To make brown ink you boiled walnut shells, vinegar, and salt. For black ink you added indigo or lamp black.

As his uncle had been strict with him, so he was strict with his sons, and taught them how to read and write, how to use a gun, how to set up the loom for him. He inculcated in them (by knocking their heads together if necessary) respect for their father and mother, and a proper devotion to the Almighty God, who ruled their lives. I see them sitting down at a rude table—seven long-legged, shaggy-haired, hungry boys. What are they having for supper? Fried perch, possibly. Or bear meat. Or hog and hominy. Whatever could be cooked in an iron pot or a long-handled skillet or in the ashes of the huge hearth. Very likely there is a flintlock rifle within reach as they eat. (A trader on Middle Creek, after getting drunk in the company of some Indians, murdered them in their sleep—four men and two women. And in the morning he and his nineteen-year-old servant-boy threw the bodies in the creek and then went upstream to the cabin of one of the Indians and killed another Indian woman and two girls and a child. And now nobody was safe.) If Henry Maxwell heard an owl or a sound like a twig snapping, the inside of his mouth turned dry, for they were totally unprotected. In the fall of the year, he left his family and drove from farm to farm, with his loom in his cart. And the women brought out great masses of carded wool and flax, and he opened his pattern book before them. From time to time he was able to send word where he was, and from this they judged when he would be home.

Though he grew up among Quakers, Henry Maxwell never became one. The proof of this is that he bore arms against the British. So did his oldest son, James. In 1776 Henry Maxwell was in his late forties. Soldiers in that ill-fed, ill-clothed, undisciplined and perpetually dissolving army did not have to be young; only able-bodied. He had just turned sixty when he died, during the first administration of George Washington. I don't know what he looked like.

As for his seven sons, James married *blank*; Walter married Rachel *blank*; Thomas married Jane Dixon; Samuel, John, and Henry again married *blank*; Robert married Mary Edie. Gone to graveyards every one, but not in any great hurry. They all died in their seventies except the youngest, Robert, who lived to be eighty-one and was my great-great-grandfather.

He was a shoemaker by trade, but it was by no means his only occupation. For a number of years, he and his brother Thomas were Indian scouts in the service of the Federal Government. In a book of reminiscences published in 1837, a certain Thomas R. Crawford states that the earliest visit of white men to what is now Harrison County, Ohio, was in the fall of 1793, and that five men, Indian scouts and spies, were sent out from Fort Thomas (which was built on the site of the present city of Wheeling, West Virginia), and that Robert Maxwell was one of them. They made their way "from the mouth of Wheeling Creek up the dividing ridge and crossed over on the evening of the second day. After they left the river, they proceeded to the headwaters of the Stillwater, venturing rather far into the interior for so small a force." They were attacked by Indians during a night's camping, and not all of them managed to return to the fort.

My great-great-grandfather was twenty-six at the time of the expedition from Fort Thomas. Within a year he had moved north, and settled in Brooke County, in what is now the extreme northern part of the state of West Virginia, a little way down the thin wedge that separates southern Pennsylvania from Ohio. Though it was part of Virginia until the Civil War, the reader must think of a hilly country with small farms and few slaves, and of a frontier society very different from that of the great plantations of the Tidewater. Here Robert Maxwell met and married the daughter of a Scotch-Irish frontiersman named Alexander Edie, who was exceedingly given to pulling up stakes and trying somewhere new. He had lived all over the western part of Pennsylvania and the eastern part of Ohio, farming and trading in land, and moving on whenever other settlers began to crowd in on him. He married twice and had two girls and six boys by each wife, and with that many people under his own roof I do not wonder that he wasn't more gregarious. My great-great-grandmother, Mary Edie, was his second child by his first wife, a Miss Dunbar. One of his sons became a doctor and another served in the Virginia legislature. Alexander Edie was sufficiently well-regarded by his fellow citizens to serve as foreman of the first grand jury of Washington County, Pennsylvania, and he seems to have witnessed a good many wills. On petition of the town of Washington, he and four others were appointed to view and if necessary lay out a road from Catfish Camp to the Presbyterian meeting house. He secured by deed from the Commonwealth of Virginia a tract of a thousand acres on the Ohio River near Steubenville. On this land there was a large blockhouse, half fort and half dwelling, where the people of the community took refuge during Indian raids. He went security for a friend who got into trouble, and when the man fled, Alexander Edie had to pay the bond of £5,000, which all but ruined him.

Standing in my grandmother's bedroom, with a distant look in her eyes, as if she saw it all happening, Max Fuller's mother told me a story that I now know was about the frontiersman's daughter, Mary Edie. In the early spring, Robert Maxwell, having told his wife he would return at a certain time, went farther west, into Ohio, in search of better land, in a valley that was reasonably flat and fertile. He found land that he liked the look of, but the crop had to go in at once, so he stayed and planted before he started back. When he did not return at the time he said he would, his wife decided that something had happened to him, for he always did what he said he would do. She waited a week while she made him a pair of trousers and parched a bag of corn, and then, with the baby in her arms, wrapped in a shawl, she set out on foot, along a footpath through the forest. The trees frequently had trunks five or six feet thick, and almost no sunlight penetrated their dense foliage. The virgin forest was gloomy and oppressively silent. She could have twisted her ankle and been unable to go on or turn back. She could have been overtaken by a drunken hunter who had been too long without a woman. She could have met up with a party of Indians and been scalped and the baby's brains dashed out against the trunk of a tree. She could have lost her way and starved to death. Instead, after many days, she met my great-great-grandfather coming home.

Apart from their gravestones, which their descendants soon lost track of, the people who settled in the wilderness did not leave lasting memorials; they left stories instead. The music of Beethoven's *Fidelio* always rises up in my mind when I think of that meeting in the forest, and my throat constricts with an emotion that is, I'm afraid, purely factitious—unless feelings are more a part of our physical inheritance than is commonly believed, in which case it is Mary Edie's joy, unquenchable, passed on, and then passed on again, generation after generation, along with the color of eyes and the shape of hands and characteristic habits of mind and temperament.

In 1800 Robert Maxwell took out a patent for land lying along Indian Short Creek. In that same book about the early days of Harrison County, there are a good many references to him. The scouting party is mentioned, and the fact that he and his brother Thomas were among the first white settlers and came before the roads were built. In 1805 Robert Maxwell was paid $1 for a wolf's scalp. In 1810 he was elected constable and held this office for nine years. He served as a private in the War of 1812. At about this time he was elected county commissioner and squire—a title of office and courtesy usually given to justices of the peace. In 1824 and 1830 he took title to more land. From 1834 to 1840 he was an associate justice of the Court of Common Pleas.

His oldest daughter, the same old woman I spoke of, said that he was a man of clear, cool, and calculating mind, self-made and self-educated; that he had endured many hard-

ships and was deeply religious; that when angered he would
not allow himself to speak until he had regained control of
his feelings; that he was stern, severe, and sarcastic, and
boasted that no one had ever said anything to which he could
not make a satisfactory retort; that he was a kind husband
and father, and his children revered and honored him.

A child's view.

As it happens, I do know what my great-great-grand-
parents looked like. A pair of oval photographs, made from
daguerreotypes and considerably retouched, has come down
in the family. The rather elegant tailoring of his coat and
waistcoat suggests a man of some position, but he was not
affluent. As for the face, you could not possibly mistake him
for anything but a Scot. Looking at the photograph I feel I
almost know what his voice sounded like. And even what he
would say. For this rather mournful letter, written to his
brother Henry during the War of 1812—at which time my
great-great-grandfather was forty-seven or forty-eight—
brings his personality into sharp focus: ". . . we had a
Daughter Born to us on the Seventeenth of June last which
makes the Seventh Daughter we have now living we have
had likewise two Sons Born Since we come out here which
makes our family now ammount to Eleven and thanks be to
the giver they are all in pretty good health at present Mary
is not yet got very Stout Since she has had the little one but
She has been generally in good health Since we come out I
my Self had a very sore Spell last Fall a year ago and was
even Dispaired of by the Doctor that waited on me and
weakly as I was before I have been more so since indeed I
am very often almost unfit for any Business but as I still do
the business of Constable and as Sister is in the Township in
which I live we are inabled to get along pretty well for so far
grain has been very scarce here indeed, it has been almost
impossible to git atall but I hope it soon will be plenty
enough we are now in great Expectations of gitting a Min-

ister placed ammongst us Shortly. Mr. Walden's Congregation has become weak as not to be able to keep him any longer
and We are about putting in a Call for him which all expect
he will except. Brother Thomas and family are well I expect he will perhaps write therefore I will leave his Concerns
to to himself we have Rumors ammongst us about the downf
of Bonaaparte if true I am afraid it will operate much against
us as it will give the British an opertunity of bringing there
whole force bouth by Sea and land against us which in our
present divided State may have very Serious Consequences
The Federalists ammongst us opin they are about it what
your Sentiments about the present war is unknownt to me
but I hope the name of Tory will never be anexed that of
Maxwell at least that Carries the same Blood in there veins
that I do we have no Maxwell Tories in this part."

The portrait of Mary Edie shows a woman in late middle
age, with a linen cap over her dark hair, a sunken mouth, and
large dark eyes in which I think I read trust in the will of the
Lord and patience and resignation with regard to the ways
of her husband.

Robert Maxwell and Mary Edie had fifteen children, of
whom my great-grandfather, also named Robert, was the
eleventh. They were all born between 1794 and 1818, which
means that for twenty-five years there was always a baby in
the house. Jeannot Creighton, Henry, Elizabeth Stevenson,
Alexander Edie, Agnes Carson, Polly Ann, Jacintha, Mary
Atkinson, Euphemia, William, Robert, Martha, Walter
Carson, Agnes Carson (the first one having died in infancy), and Thomas.

My great-great-grandfather was brought up a Presbyterian, and for twenty years served as an elder. The nearest
Presbyterian church was eight miles away, in Cadiz. He had
one horse, and Mary Edie would not ride to church and

have her husband walk. A nursing baby could not be left at home while she walked that distance, sat through a long service in the morning and another in the afternoon, and walked back again. She was not strong enough to go on foot with the baby in her arms. The dilemma was resolved by her oldest daughter, Jeannot Creighton (my source is again that same old woman, only now it was herself she was telling about), who loved her mother and father so well that she thought it an honor to do for and wait upon them. On Sunday morning she would milk the cow and do up the housework and then carry the baby eight miles to Cadiz, and if it fretted during the service she took it from her mother and, sitting on a log outside, dandled it on her knee.

All this was recounted by Jeannot Creighton Maxwell to my Grandfather Maxwell's sister Sarah, a great while later, and found its way into a letter dated April 2, 1876. In the same letter, my grandfather's sister wrote, "I will speak of Aunt Jane's visit [to Uhrichsville, Ohio] now. I wish you could have seen and conversed with her. She is very intelligent, and has a splendid memory. It does not seem the least impaired by age or ill health, and she reads a great deal. . . . I like her very much, she seemed so like father and looked like him. I was sorry for the poor old soul. Her days of usefulness are over, and no one wishes to be troubled with the care of her. She thinks all young folks should marry. She stayed single to please and care for an aged and feeble father. He gave all he had to Uncle Walter to take care of her, but his wife makes it so unpleasant for her that she cannot stay there in peace any longer." *

* In a letter to Max Fuller, my Aunt Maybel said that my grandfather, whose name was Robert Creighton Maxwell, helped himself to the Creighton when he was so small he could not say it, and that he called himself "Tate." This my grandfather must have told her himself. Jeannot Creighton Maxwell was his aunt, and perhaps he took the name because he was fond of her. Or he may just have liked her middle name. Creighton is a

Shunted from one relative to another, Jeannot Creighton Maxwell died ten years later, in Iowa, on a visit to the widow of Sam Dixon Maxwell, who was her cousin. In going through her effects they found "some very ancient books, letters, and papers of various kinds"—including the letter written by Robert Maxwell to his brother Henry during the War of 1812, and a volume of sermons with the name "David Maxwill" on the flyleaf. There is no David Maxwell among the descendants of Henry Maxwell. He must have brought this book with him when he came to America, the one clue to the family in Scotland he sprang from.

Walter Maxwell's unpleasant wife who drove his sister out of the house was born Moriah Shipton. Mary Atkinson Maxwell married Samuel McBarnes, William married Sarah McGraw, and the second Agnes Carson married John Lock. Elizabeth Stevenson and Polly Ann married Robert and James Gibson, who may have been brothers, and Alexander Edie and Robert married Sarah and Jemima Keepers, who were sisters. Keepers is a Welsh name, and came down through my father to me.

This is the place where I stop being totally dependent on family archives and can speak from experience and memory —that is, from photographs that were around me during my childhood, and remarks in which as much information was conveyed by the speaker's tone of voice as by what was said. The sense of distance is greatly diminished.

I hear my father's voice, saying, "Jemima Keepers was a remarkable woman." He never lied about anything, and so it doesn't occur to me to treat this statement skeptically.

---

variant spelling of Crighton—a Scottish border family that lived in the same general area as the Maxwells. Who the Creightons were that she was named after nobody knows. My grandfather was never called by his first name. The Creighton was usually shortened to "Creight."

"The Keeperses were a very fine family," he says. But here, though I accept what he says, I am far from sure what he means. And I can't ask him because he has gone to join the people he was talking about. I don't think he meant that they were socially important. Jemima Keepers' father, William Keepers, had an iron forge. Before that, the Keepers men were farmers in Maryland. My father may have meant only that they didn't use conspicuously bad grammar or owe anybody a dime; he attached great importance to financial probity. Or he could have meant that they were people of intelligence and character. In any case, he was speaking from first-hand knowledge. My Grandfather Maxwell took him on a family visit to Ohio when my father was a little boy, and he met several of his uncles and undoubtedly his grandmother as well, for she was alive at that time.

I'm sure they didn't ride in a sleeping car—it would have cost too much. And that they brought something to stay their hunger: thick meat sandwiches. Pickles. Pie. And cake. And that my father had a great deal to say, for he was the youngest and it was the first time in his life that he had enjoyed his father's undivided attention all through a day and a night. Perhaps he was lucky and had a whole seat to stretch out on, facing the one where my grandfather sat, bolt upright, in the dimly lighted coach. If the train was crowded, he slept with his head in his father's lap. And woke in the night at mysterious wayside stations, and saw greenish-white lights, and heard voices and mysterious clanking sounds, and asked still another question about what it was like in Ohio, and fell back into sleep the moment the wheels began to turn.

In the morning they got off the train and walked directly across the street to the hotel. And in the hotel lobby my grandfather put the satchel down and told my father to stand right there and keep an eye on it, while he went to the desk. It was a big dark room, with a high ceiling and lots of polished brass, and potted palms, and marble statues, and numerous cuspidors, and my father had never seen anything like it. He was busy taking it all in, when suddenly he heard his name being called. A big boy in a uniform with his hair slicked down was going through the lobby calling his name. My father went up to him and said, "I'm William Keepers Maxwell," and a tall, lean, broad-shouldered man with a mustache, who had turned up at the same instant, said, *"I'm William Keepers Maxwell."* Then, looking down at my father, "Why, you must be Creight's boy!" The pleasure was mutual and lasting.

Judging by Jemima Keepers' portrait, my father got not only her last name but also her nose, and my daughter Kate got her forehead. And nobody that I know inherited her high cheekbones and beautifully sculptured upper eyelids. She is wearing a velvet dress with a lace collar, and she seems to have forgotten that she is sitting for her portrait. This air of melancholy preoccupation may be only that she carried a burden of sadness that was habitual and lasting and showed even when she was attending to other matters. She did not have an easy life.

The portrait of my great-grandfather is of a much younger man, with thick dark hair and eyebrows, widely spaced eyes, and a square jaw. It has been so retouched that it looks like a photograph of a drawing by a not very accomplished amateur, and that may be what it is. His clothes are much more simply cut than his father's. He looks forthright and honest and unreal. He was a marble engraver, which I take to mean that he carved inscriptions on tombstones. My great-grandparents moved from Stillwater, Ohio, to Uhrichsville about 1840, and fourteen years later they moved to Waynes-burg, Pennsylvania, where, that same year, my great-grand-father died, very suddenly, at the age of forty-two. His nuncupative will reads: "On the morning of the 14th day of September A.D. 1854, Robert Maxwell called upon us the undersigned in his dwelling house in the Borough of Waynesburg Greene County Penn in the last extremity of his last illness, to notice the following disposition of his property, to wit. William A. Porter Esqu. asked him if he was aware of the fact that he was soon going to die? The Testator answered, that he was. Mr. Porter then asked him what request he had to make?—he said, first he wished all his just debts to be paid out of his estate. Second he wished his wife Jemima to have all the residue of his Estate both real and personal—he said that there was a judgment in the state of Ohio in his favor, which he wished his wife to have also, he said he would like to make some other arrangements but could not talk and called upon us to take particular notice that this was his wish and desire. Shortly after, to the best of our knowledge, about one hour, the said Robert Maxwell died."

What happened after that is told in a letter to Max Fuller from a cousin of his mother's. "My mother, Mary Maxwell, was born seven months after the sudden death of her father from dysentery. He was a well-to-do man, living in Uhrichsville, Ohio; Aunt Sade considered him a most remarkable man—very stern, and very considerate, if you can understand that combination. He never broke his word, but was quite slow giving it, she said. After his death, his partner asked for some papers which grandmother gave him, and when the estate was settled, it was found that there was nothing left, but the partner had suddenly become well to do. Grandmother farmed out her five children, and went to her sister to await the birth of my mother. The mortgage on their home was foreclosed. An old friend, Judge somebody, I cannot remember the name, bought in the property, and gave grandmother a deed. One of the choicest stories in our family is that when the sons were grown, they repaid the amount to the old Judge. Mother always rejoiced in telling that. Later grandmother had some of her children with her, and always my mother; but never your grandfather; he had the hardest lot of all of them, and was I fancy the most ambitious, or he would never have done so well as he did with all the handicaps he had."

In my Grandmother Maxwell's scrapbook, under the heading "Maxwell Fuller's Own Grandfather," there is an account of his life, in her handwriting. It is maddening. She must have known something about his early years, but what she put down is what she found in print (as if that alone was dependable) in a history of Logan County, published in 1886.

My copy came down to me through the other side of the family, accidentally, in the same box with a dozen big black bound volumes of the *Century* magazine I had asked for. The spine is missing and the cover hangs by a few threads, but the pages are edged, top, sides, and bottom, with gilt, the type is of a good size, the paper hasn't turned brown after eighty-five years, and the lithographic portraits are of men and women who clearly believed that since God knew exactly what they were like, there was no point in trying to deceive the photographer.

The paragraph about my Grandfather Maxwell begins: "Robert Creighton Maxwell, attorney at law, Lincoln, Illinois, is a native of Ohio, born in Uhrichsville, Tuscarawas County, August 6, 1849. His parents were Robert and Jemima (Keepers) Maxwell, the former a native of Virginia, of Scotch descent, and the latter of Ohio, of Welsh descent. His parents moved to Waynesburg, Pennsylvania, where the father died in 1854. His mother then returned to Ohio, where she is still living. After the father's death the family was broken up and our subject found a home with strangers."

My grandfather was barely five years old when his father

died. He was the fourth child; he had an older sister and two older brothers and a brother who was two years younger. Was it chance that he had the hardest lot of all of them? Or was it because his mother knew that he was the one who was most able to stand up to adversity?

Simple hard work or even being worked to the limit of his strength I do not think would have been considered, in that period, a hard lot. He must have been harshly treated (though the writer of that letter could have meant merely that he was cut off from all family affection).

It is only partly clear what happened. Jemima Keepers, having no home of her own, and expecting another child, went to live with her sister, but couldn't keep her other children with her and so they were divided up, probably among her relatives. There was no one who was able, or willing, to take my grandfather, and she had no choice but to entrust him into the keeping of strangers. Though a bookish man, my grandfather knew enough about farming to do it competently for several years before he took up the practice of law. My guess is that he was handed over to a farmer and worked for his keep from the time he was five years old, and the farmer got all the work out of him he possibly could. But my father and my aunts never spoke about it, nor my grandmother—from which I conclude that my grandfather himself never spoke about it, perhaps because he could not bear to speak about it. Or because it was gone, left behind when he left Ohio.

The history continues: "He mainly supported and educated himself, attending the school of Uhrichsville till seventeen years of age. In 1866 he left Ohio and came to Illinois."

The history doesn't tell how my grandfather got from Ohio to Illinois, but I know, anyway: he bought a pair of shoes and started walking. About six hundred miles. Somewhere between a month and six weeks of steady walking. If it was the early part of the summer, as it is only reasonable to suppose, he was not seventeen but sixteen. In 1866 there was a railroad that would have taken him where he wanted to go, but walking was cheaper. No details of this journey have survived—only the fact that he made it, the year after the Civil War ended. And so it can be assumed that men in uniform trudged along beside him with their discharge papers in their pockets. For a good part of the journey he must have followed the National Road, which at that time extended from Cumberland, Maryland, to Vandalia, Illinois. The roadbed was thirty feet wide, and the eastern section was paved with an inch of crushed stone and gravel. The western section was not paved with anything. Tree stumps eighteen inches high were left in the road but trimmed and rounded with an axe so that carriages could safely pass over them. The National Road was used by a steady stream of two-wheeled carts, Conestoga wagons, farm wagons, men on horseback, men on foot, men driving cattle, hogs, horses, and mules. Now choking on clouds of dust, now with his new shoes caked with mud, my grandfather moved among them.

When he had the good fortune to arrive at a log cabin or a farmhouse at nightfall, I expect they took him in. But in 1866 the Great Prairie was not densely populated, and so, many times, when evening came there was not a house of any kind in sight, and he went into an oak grove, out of the wind, and made a bed of leaves beside a fallen log. In his knapsack, or if he didn't have a knapsack then in his coat pocket, he carried a Bible, which I see him reading from as he walks along. It is too late in the day for him to be surprised by hostile Indians in Ohio or Indiana, but he could have been murdered by a white man for whatever was in his pockets. Such crimes were not common but they did occur.

His first sight of the prairie he must always have remembered. The vast illimitable plain spreading in all directions.

Timber and grass, grass higher than his head and undulating in the wind like the long swells of ocean. The Virgilian cloud shadows following one on another. The meeting of earth and sky. The feeling of being exposed. The unreality—for part of what he saw was a mirage and would fade from sight, only to reappear in its actuality half an hour later when he reached the crest of that farther ridge.

I know what my grandfather looked like at the time of this journey, because I have a tintype of him, given to me by my Aunt Bert. It was taken when he was still a very young man. The face is not that of somebody given to feeling sorry for himself. The photographer is probably responsible for the cheerful, upward tilt of the head, but the set of the narrow jaw is surely his own, and what it suggests is granite. Even so, it's a long walk from Ohio to Illinois.

When he had crossed the Indiana line and was about fifteen miles northeast of Springfield, destiny prompted him to stop in a farmyard and ask for a drink of water. The farmer inquired where he was going, and my grandfather explained that he was looking for a job teaching school. "Can you teach singing?" the farmer asked, and my grandfather said that he could. "You can stay here, then," the farmer said.

The house was clean and neat, the stock well cared for. In the fields the grain was ripe for the harvest, and it may have made him think of the Bible. It was land Jehovah might have given Abraham for his descendants. There were five sons and four daughters in the family. The oldest was just back from the war. The youngest was a little girl of three whom everybody petted. They were twelve when they sat down to eat. What I think happened, though nobody ever said it did happen, is that when they got up from the table he picked out a hoe and went into the corn patch. On Sunday he walked beside them to church, but as they went in he held back, because of the condition of his clothes, and one of the boys saw this and motioned that he was to sit with them. When Saturday came around, the farmer's wife asked him to try on a shirt that was still warm from the iron, and when it fit she said he was to keep it and wear it on Sunday. One day when he sat down and held her skein of wool for her to wind, she said, "Have you written to your mother?" and he knew that he was accepted.

They were gentle, soft-voiced people, and treated him with a kindness he was not accustomed to. And he was careful not to seem better educated than they were, though in fact he was. What he couldn't conceal was how happy he was. When he rode off to singing school on the farmer's horse, the oldest daughter, Maggie, rode behind him, with her arms around his waist. Two years later, they were married, on Christmas Eve, 1868.

3

With a Middle Western American family, no sooner do you begin to perceive the extent of the proliferation of ancestors backward into time than they are lost from sight. Every trace of them disappears, through the simple erosion of human forgetfulness. They were in movement in a new country. The women were committed to drudgery and died young. The men had no proper tools to farm with, and weren't good farmers anyway. They used up the land by improper practices. Wild animals broke into their fields. Their horses were half-starved, and their cattle sometimes actually did starve, before there was any grass in the spring. In the mountains of Virginia they listened thoughtfully to tales of how easy life was in Kentucky, and from Kentucky, when they had to sell out, or were sold out, to pay their debts, they moved on into Illinois. With their minds always on some promised land, like the Old Testament figures they so much resembled, they did not bother to record or even remember the place of their origin.

My Grandmother Maxwell's mother's maiden name was Louisa England, and my grandmother accepted as gospel truth something that probably was not true—namely, that she was descended on her mother's side from a little boy who wandered on board a sailing ship and was given the name of England because that was where he came from and all anybody knew about him.

In an effort to find out something more about this branch of the family (and before I had access to my cousin's papers, which would have told me all there was to know) I entered into correspondence with the Reverend Stephen J. England, of Enid, Oklahoma, who once lived in central Illinois. His name was given to me by the minister of a church on Park Avenue, when I went there to borrow a history of the Disciples of Christ from the church library. It could hardly have been more roundabout.

Dr. England had never heard the story of the little boy who wandered onto a sailing ship, and thought it apocryphal. But he knew something about his own ancestry, going back to a David England who lived on the James River in Virginia at the time of the American Revolution. Dr. England's line of descent was through one of David England's sons, and he thought it likely that mine was through another, Stephen England, who was, he said, a great preacher of the frontier and a towering figure in the. early history of the Christian Church.

The minister of the Park Avenue Christian Church had already suggested this, and I said, "No, that couldn't possibly be."

Dr. England recommended that I write to a Mrs. Lloyd Robert Geist, of Maryville, Missouri, who was descended from Stephen England and had a good deal of information about that branch of the England family. It turned out that Mrs. Geist's great-grandmother and Louisa England, my grandmother's mother, were sisters. And the great preacher of the frontier was their grandfather. Mrs. Geist supplied me with a genealogy going back past Stephen England to his father, David England, and *his* father, William England, who had a plantation in Goochland County, thirty or forty miles up the James River from Richmond, and died in 1768.

Among Max Fuller's papers there was a photostat of my Aunt Maybel's application for membership in the D.A.R. On one page she stated that the England family "could hardly be traced as my great-great-grandfather when a boy of 4 years old went onto a ship docked in English water at or near England and the ship left shore and they were so far out before they discovered the boy and would not go back so brought him on to America and gave him the name of England, as he could not tell his name."

What kind of a four-year-old boy doesn't know his own name? Was she claiming descent from a mental defective?

On another page of the same application she said that her great-great-grandfather, Stephen England, was born in Virginia in 1774. Neither side of my family has ever had the slightest difficulty in entertaining two contradictory ideas at once.

Max was unable to go back beyond William England. There were several Englands who received Royal Land Patents or Land Grants in the 17th century, but no one has been able to connect William England with any of them. William England left his second son, David, half the plantation and the best featherbed and furniture. David England was fourteen when he came into his inheritance. He married Lucy Hodges. Her father, John Hodges, signed his will with an *x*. Lucy Hodges, on a deed of 1779, also had recourse to an *x*, but ten years later had learned to write her own name. It was no reflection on a farmer's wife not to be able to read and write, and the fact that she was not content to remain illiterate suggests that her husband may have been a gentleman and a farmer, or that she herself had a hitherto unencouraged inclination to use her mind for something besides carding wool and beating wet clothes with a club to get the dirt out.

David England was a private in the Continental Army. It wasn't a glorious experience, judging by a petition he and several other soldiers addressed to the Governor of Virginia and the Honorable Members of the Council. The Goochland Militia marched to Hillsborough in divisions and there, soon after, sustained a disgraceful rout, "being raw and ignorant of discipline and under officers generally as undisciplined as your petitioners, who being ordered not to fire until they had the word, and then to advance with charged Bayonetts, occasioned the confusion that followed." The men arrived at Hillsborough destitute, "without a shirt to shift to," and applied for leave to go home and procure such supplies as their families could furnish, and were refused. With the connivance of their officers, some of them went home anyway, and hurried back, to be told that they were sentenced as deserters to eight months additional service in the Continental Army. The petitioners stated that "they did not wish to repine of the Lott, in performing a Tour of duty in so good a cause, but most of them being very poor men with families of small children unable to labour, must inevitably loose a great part of their stocks by the shortness of their present crops, when then must be the distress of their helpless families the ensuing year, should they be deemed soldiers eight months longer." The petition passed through various hands and ended up with the following bleak sentence attached to it: "I have no power to remit the sentence of the law, nor do I know any power which can, except the General Assembly, unless the Commander-in-chief to the Southward should think proper to discharge the petitioners at any certain point of time short of eight months, which it does not appear probable to me he will do. Thomas Jefferson, 10–7–1780."

Either because of what happened while he was soldiering or because the soil was worn out from too much planting of tobacco, David England left the land that was bequeathed to him and to his heirs forever and settled in eastern Kentucky, where he died in 1801. The forests of Kentucky were magnificent (there is a record of a sycamore tree with a trunk twelve feet in diameter) and the lowlands offered good pasture. There were more deer and buffalo here than anywhere east of the Mississippi River, and therefore more of the wild animals that preyed on them. The Indians thought so highly of Kentucky that they refused to live in it. They used it as a hunting ground, and crossed over from Ohio and Indiana and Tennessee. The white men were not so delicate, of course, and within twenty-five years of the time they began moving in in large numbers, game had become scarce. That David England contributed to this mindless and improvident slaughter and to the destruction of the forests there is no reason to doubt. To each of his sons, in his will, he left five hundred acres of the Indians' hunting ground.

The oldest, Stephen England, my great-great-great-grandfather, was a Baptist preacher in Kentucky until he met and became friends with Barton Warren Stone. Their friendship has been giving off reverberations ever since, for more than a hundred and fifty years now. This book is one of them.

Stephen England could have been a General Baptist, in which case he held the Arminian belief that the atonement of Christ is not limited to the elect only but is general; or he could have been a Particular Baptist and believed that atonement is particular and for the few. Probably he was the second, because the pioneers who settled the southern mountains after the American Revolution mostly were of this persuasion. To accept placidly or with satisfaction the damnation throughout eternity of the greater part of mankind requires a harsher nature than, from all accounts, Stephen England had. And what I think is that in his preaching he had come up against a high wall of some kind, from which Barton Stone delivered him.

Where did they see each other? In the forest, probably, sitting on a log. Someplace where they wouldn't be disturbed. Of the two, Stone was infinitely better educated, a man of genuine intellectuality. My great-great-great-grandfather was, when he descended from the pulpit, a farmer, and a simple man.

I know that it is possible to consider history wholly in the context of ideas—the rise of this abstraction, the pressure exerted by that—because people do. And are impatient and even enraged if you suggest that human personality enters into it. But that isn't the way my mind works. I have to get out an imaginary telescope and fiddle with the lens until I see something that interests me, preferably something small and unimportant. Not Lee's surrender at Appomattox but two men, both in their late thirties, whose eyes are locked, as if to look up at the sky or at an oak leaf on the ground would break the thread of their discourse. One of them is wearing very small old-fashioned spectacles, which he has pushed up off his face. In the rush and complexity of his logic he sometimes stutters. Both men are nagged by the knowledge that the sun is low on the hills and there are chores that must be done before dark and they would so much rather go on talking about whether faith precedes repentance or follows it.

My father's family—and particularly my Aunt Maybel and her husband and my grandmother—were not like everybody else and I cannot explain what they were like without going into the history of the religious movement that not only shaped them but that possessed them heart and soul. I assumed that five or six pages would dispose of the subject. Because I was familiar with the inside of the Christian Church in Lincoln, I thought I understood the form of worship practiced there. It turned out that I had almost everything wrong. Surprised to find that it was not something that sprang from the mind of some narrow-minded Scottish Calvinist, that it was not even Scottish and certainly not Calvinist, I went on, and then on, and on, drawn by the excitement and pleasure of what I found. If the telescope is focused properly, ideas are caught in it as well as people. And people do not have sawdust in their heads but, more often than not, passionate convictions, the strangest and most passionate being what they believe the Lord of the Universe expects of them.

At the end of his life Stone wrote a seventy-nine-page auto-biography * for his children and his friends. The engraved portrait in the front of this book shows a thin-faced man with very fine eyes and very small old-fashioned spectacles, pushed into the curls above a noble forehead. The lips are chiseled and the mouth is slightly askew in relation to the formidable nose. Looked at under a magnifying glass, the face is alive and ready to begin a conversation. Stone's little book is meant to be a work of pure edification, and for the mid-19th century reader no doubt it was. The 20th century reader is more likely to be struck by the wonderful eye for absurdity, the extreme sensibility, the candor, a literary tone not at all characteristic of religious writing of the period, and the gift for placing people in a scene. For example: "My horse being put away, I went into the house and sat down in silence. The old lady and daughter were busily spinning, and the old gentleman in conversation with another aged man. One of them observed to the other that a discovery had been lately made, that if the logs of the house be cut in the full moon of February, a bed-bug would never molest that house."

And this: "My colleague, J. Anderson, having preached through the settlements of West Tennessee, determined to visit Kentucky. We had our last apointment in Thomas Craighead's congregation, in which neighborhood we had often preached. As we expected a large and intelligent

---

* *The Biography of Elder Barton Warren Stone written by himself, with Additions and Reflections by Elder John Rogers* (Cincinnati, 1847).

audience, we endeavored to prepare discourses suitable to the occasion. My companion, Anderson, first rose to preach from these words: 'Without holiness no man shall see the Lord.' I shall never forget his exordium, which, in fact, was also his peroration. Holiness, said he, is a moral quality —he paused, having forgotten all his studied discourse. Confused, he turned with staring eyes to address the other side of his audience, and repeated with emphasis—Holiness is a moral quality—and after a few incoherent words, he paused again, and sat down. Astonished at the failure of my brother, I arose and preached. He declared to me afterwards, that every idea had forsaken him; that he viewed it as from God, to humble his pride; as he had expected to make a brilliant display of his talent to that assembly. I never remembered a sermon better, and to me it has been very profitable; for from the hint given, I was led to more correct views of the doctrines of original sin, and of regeneration."

The old bookseller who exclaimed, "Mr. Stone's books ought all to be put in a pile, and burned, and he in the middle of them," had never laid eyes on him. He gave off—his temperament gave off—a kind of fragrance. Because of it, everybody around him felt at ease. He saw no reason not to be affectionate with strangers, and he never hesitated to say what was on his mind or heart. "Brother Crihfield," he exclaimed, "is this *you?* From your writings I had expected to see a little, ugly, black-headed, dark-skinned ill-natured fellow; but if it is you, behold I am mistaken! For I see a genteel looking man." After sitting through a sermon that was full of ginger and salt, he shook hands with the minister and then said, "Brother Brown, you speak too harshly of people's errors. Dear brother, when you find a stone across the path of truth, just carefully roll it away, but don't try to spat the man that laid it there." When his wife apologized for the skimpy fare at her table, Stone looked around at the unexpected guests and with his face shining with hospitality said, "What of all these good things shall I help you to?" He was like a house with all the doors and windows thrown wide open; anything and anybody could penetrate to the center of his being. And his words as they came from his mouth had a kind of natural beauty.

Stone was born in 1772, in the Tidewater district of Maryland. He was a lineal descendant of William Stone, the first Protestant governor of Maryland, during whose term of office the Maryland Toleration Act of 1649 was enacted, granting protection to all Christians who believed in the Trinity. When Barton Stone was still a child, his father died and his mother moved her large family of children and servants to the backwoods of Virginia, about eighty miles below the Blue Mountain. The Revolutionary War was sometimes remote and sometimes not. On the day Nathaniel Greene met Cornwallis at Guilford Courthouse, when the whole countryside was in a great anxiety and bustle, Stone's mother sent him with his two older brothers to conceal the horses in a brush thicket, lest they be taken by scouting parties. Hiding in the woods, the boys heard the roar of the artillery thirty miles away and "awfully feared the results."

After the war was over, the soldiers brought back with them to this quiet backwater many vices almost unknown there before—"as profane swearing, debauchery, drunkenness, gambling, quarreling and fighting. For having been soldiers, and having fought for liberty, they were respected and caressed by all. . . . Their influence in demoralizing society was very great." Many of the parsons had gone back to England when their salaries were discontinued, and the churches stood empty, until Baptist preachers turned up and began to preach. They preached in a tuneful or singing voice, and huge crowds came to hear them, and to see people immersed, for the practice was novel in those parts.

"I was a constant attendant," Stone says, "and was particularly interested to hear the converts giving in their experience. Of their conviction and great distress for sin, they were very particular in giving an account, and how and when they obtained deliverance from their burdons. Some were delivered by a dream, a vision, or some uncommon appearance of light—some by a voice spoken to them, 'Thy sins are forgiven thee'—and others by seeing the Saviour with their natural eyes."

Stone prayed in secret, morning and evening, hoping for a voice or a vision. But then Methodist preachers came, their conduct grave, holy, meek, plain, and humble, and their preaching quite as electrifying as the Baptists'. The Baptists said that the Methodists were the locusts of the Apocalypse. Unable to decide between them and feeling sorry for the Methodists, who were few in number and persecuted, Stone quit praying and went back to playing hopscotch or the colonial equivalent.

The village schoolmaster pronounced him a finished scholar, after four or five years of reading, writing, and arithmetic, and he left home, at eighteen, to attend an academy in Guilford. It was his intention to become a barrister. In order to get on more rapidly with the study of Latin grammar, he lived chiefly on milk and vegetables, and never allowed himself more than six or seven hours' sleep, and so lowered his resistance to the religiosity that was working its way through the school. Thirty of the students had recently been converted by the popular Presbyterian revivalist, James McGready, and each morning before classes they assembled in a private room and engaged in singing and praying. In their general behavior they evinced a piety and happiness that made Stone uneasy, for he believed that religion would impede his progress in learning and be frowned on by his family and companions. He therefore associated with the students who made light of divine things and joined in with them in their jokes at the expense of the pious. For this his conscience upbraided him when he was alone, with the result that he could not enjoy the company of the devout or the ungodly. He decided to pack his things and move on to a new school, and was prevented from doing this by the weather. Remaining in his room all day, he came to the conclusion that he should pursue the study of Latin grammar and let others go their own way. But then his roommate persuaded him to walk out into the country to hear McGready, who had returned to the neighborhood. His appearance was not prepossessing, his gestures were the reverse of elegance, he had small piercing eyes and a coarse tremulous voice. But he so powerfully propounded the doctrine that mankind, being totally depraved, could not believe, or repent, or obey the gospel except through the immediate intervention of the Holy Spirit that for a solid year Stone was "tossed on the waves of uncertainty—laboring, praying, and striving to obtain saving faith—sometimes desponding, and almost despairing, of ever getting it."

He went to a meeting on Sandy River and the president of Hampden-Sidney College described a broken and contrite heart. Stone felt that it was so like his own that he could allow himself a gleam of hope, and for the first time took communion. But that evening McGready spoke. He took as his text "*Tekel*, thou art weighed in the balance and found wanting," and went through all the legal works of the sinner, all the hiding places of the hypocrite, all the resting places of the deceived. Before he finished, Stone had descended into an indescribable apathy. McGready paid him a visit and labored to arouse him from his torpor by a further description of the terrors of God and the horrors of Hell. Stone told him that it was useless, that he was entirely callous, and McGready left him in this despairing state without one encouraging word.

Stone's mother got wind of what was going on and sent for him, was distressed at his altered appearance, and wept when he told her all he had been through. Shortly afterward, being awakened to a sense of her own dangerous condition, she left the Church of England and united with the Methodists.

Stone went back to the academy, and at another meeting—for he could not keep away from them—heard a strange young preacher, William Hodge, speak with much animation and with many tears of the love of God to sinners and what that love had done for them. "The discourse being ended, I immediately retired to the woods alone with my Bible. Here I read and prayed, with various feelings, between hope and fear. But the truth I had just heard, 'God is love,' prevailed. Jesus came to seek and save the lost—'Him that cometh unto me, I will in no wise cast out.' I yielded and sunk at his feet a willing subject. I loved him—I adored him—I praised him aloud in the silent night,—in the echoing grove around. I confessed to the Lord my sin and folly in disbelieving his word so long—and in following so long the devices of men. I now saw that a poor sinner was as much authorized to believe in Jesus at first, as at last—that *now* was the accepted time, and the day of salvation."

It was a turning point in his spiritual life, but it did not solve his other problems. His expenses for board, clothes, tuition, and books were greater than he had anticipated, he had used up his small patrimony, and it was with great difficulty that he finished his course of study. Also, he had lost all interest in the study of law. He revealed to the headmaster of the school his great desire to preach the gospel, and that he had no assurance of being divinely called and sent. When this did not prove an insurmountable obstacle, he began to study theology, and soon ran afoul of the doctrine of the Trinity. "Witsius would first prove that there was but one God, and then that there were three persons in this one God, the Father, Son, and Holy Ghost—that the Father was unbegotten—the Son eternally begotten, and the Holy Ghost eternally proceeding from the Father and the Son—that it was idolatry to worship more Gods than one, and yet equal worship must be given to the Father, the Son, and Holy Ghost. He wound up all in uncomprehensible mystery. My mind became confused, so much confused that I knew not how to pray. Till now, secret prayer and meditation had been my delightful employ. It was a heaven on earth to approach my God and Saviour; but now this heavenly exercise was checked, and gloominess and fear filled my mind." Fortunately he heard of a treatise by Dr. Watts on the same subject, read it, and found his mind at rest. For the time being. The subject was to plague him all his life.

With other candidates, Stone was examined before the Presbytery. The examiner was very short and indefinite on the subject of the Trinity, and didn't go into the peculiarities of the system—"Doubtless," Stone says, "to prevent debate on the subject in Presbytery, and to maintain peace among its members."

Before the next session, at which time Stone would be licensed to preach, he was again in a depressed state. He had totally run out of money, and none of his relatives was willing to help him. His mind was "embarrassed by many abstruse doctrines, which I admitted as true; yet could not satisfactorily reconcile with others which were plainly taught in the Bible." He decided to give up the idea of preaching, and collected his last resources of money—amounting to fifteen dollars—and started alone for the state of Georgia, where he had a brother. Halfway in his journey he was seized with a violent fever. Being scarce of money and among strangers, he decided to keep on. The fever rose so high that he became delirious and was found by a philanthropist—that is to say, a kind man—sitting on his horse,

which was feeding by the side of the road. The philanthropist took him home and put him to bed, and the next
morning Stone resumed his journey, and arrived at his
brother's house in Oglethorpe County, where he was sick
for several months.

Through the influence of his brother he got a job as
professor of languages in a Methodist school. "Men of
letters were few at that time, especially in that part of the
world, and were regarded with more than common respect.
The marked attention paid me by the most respectable
part of the community was nearly my ruin"—meaning that
he went to parties and so enjoyed himself that he found
suddenly that his religious devotion was cold and his communion with God much interrupted. So he took up, instead,
with a Mr. Springer, a very zealous Presbyterian preacher,
whose discourses made Stone begin to feel a strong desire
again to preach the gospel. A great many Frenchmen who
had fled from the Reign of Terror landed in Georgia and
one of them was teaching in the school. Stone resumed his
study of French. It was characteristic of him that while the
passionate side of his nature was attempting to deal with
his religious uncertainty, another side proceeded quietly
along, learning because he liked to. Later on, when a similar
opportunity presented itself, he picked up a reading knowledge of Hebrew.

Having finished the year out, he went back to North
Carolina, appeared before the Presbytery, and was licensed
to preach. Stone and a friend named Foster rode off together,
both with appointments to preach in the southern part of the
state, but before the first Sunday came around, Foster confessed that he did not feel qualified for the solemn work of
preaching the gospel and had decided not to do it any more.
Hearing his own doubts expressed by someone he considered
in every way his superior was too much for poor Stone. He
waited until Foster was out of the house and then got on

his horse and started for Florida, where nobody would know him. After a few miles he turned aside from this journey to attend a meeting, and there he met an acquaintance—an opinionated old lady, who suspected his intentions, told him plainly that she feared he was acting the part of Jonah, solemnly warned him of the danger, and advised him, since he disliked the southern part of North Carolina, to go over the mountains, to the West.

That evening when he went back to the meeting, there was Foster in the congregation. Though he had given up preaching, he had not given up hearing others do it. After upbraiding Stone for leaving him, Foster decided to go west also. They were in the country of strangers, on the other side of the mountain, and both in a very low state of mind, when a man ran out of a small house on the road to Fort Chiswell and hailed them. It was another acquaintance, from North Carolina, and nothing would do but that the two young men must arrest their journey long enough to preach at the Presbyterian meetinghouse. Both refused, but agreed to stay and attend the meeting. Stone was prevailed on to ascend the pulpit. While singing and praying, he found that his mind was happily relieved and that he was enabled to speak with boldness, and with profit to the people.

This congregation and several others in the vicinity were without anybody to preach to them, and they entreated Stone to abide with them a while. He lingered, preaching, through May and June, and then started west again. At Knoxville he went to the house of rendezvous for travelers journeying through the wilderness to Nashville, and found only two men there, waiting for company. Against his better judgment he started off with them. One was a large, coarse backwoodsman and Indian fighter of great courage. The other was the greatest coward Stone had ever seen. Crossing the Clinch River at sunset, they were discovered by fifteen or twenty Indians about a hundred yards away, on the edge of a canebreak. The Indians sprang up, and the travelers spurred their horses and did not stop till they were at the foot of Cumberland Mountain. Here they turned off the road, and in the thick brushwood tied their horses and lay down on their blankets. "Being much fatigued I slept so soundly that I did not perceive a shower of rain, which had awakened the other two, and driven them off to seek shelter. At length I awoke, and missed my company. Everything was profoundly silent, except the wolves and foxes in the mountain. My feelings were unpleasant. I almost concluded that the Indians had surprised them, and that they had fled. I remembered that the same God who had always protected me, was present, and could protect me still. To him I humbly commended myself, laid down again, and securely slept through till day, when I saw my companions about a hundred yards off, sheltered by a large tree. I blamed them for leaving me thus exposed to the ravening beasts around."

He soon had another and more substantial reason to blame them. In climbing the mountain that morning, Stone's horse lost a shoe, and went lame. He asked the backwoodsman to let him ride his pack horse and put the pack on Stone's. The request was refused. Stone trotted after his horse, until he was overcome by weariness. The other two rode off, leaving him alone in the wilderness. Taking his time and driving the horse in front of him, he arrived at a settlement, where he was kindly received and rested several days and then he proceeded to Shiloh, where he found many old friends and fellow students lately come home from North Carolina. With one of them Stone made an agreement to travel and preach "through all the settlements of Cumberland." This didn't take very long, for the settlements were all within a few miles of Nashville, which was at that time a village. The two young men went on to Kentucky, and there continued their itinerant preaching until winter set in. The united congregations at Cane Ridge and Concord, in Bourbon County, were at that time vacant, and Stone preached to them. He was invited to settle. Though he was young, his preaching was correct and interesting. And he himself was very much liked. He endeavored to preach the truth as he found it in the Bible, and seldom made any direct allusion to or attack on the sentiments or doctrines of those who differed from him. When he was not preaching he applied himself closely to reading and study. Within a few months he had added fifty members to the congregation at Concord and thirty at Cane Ridge, and he concluded that it was better to stay in one place than to exhort here and there, among strangers.

In the fall of 1798 a call from his two congregations was presented to him through the Presbytery of Transylvania, and he accepted, knowing that the Presbytery would have to pass on his suitability, and also would require him to agree to the Westminster Confession of Faith as the system of doctrines taught in the Bible. The Westminster Confession is the official creed of the Church of Scotland and, with some changes, of most Presbyterian churches and also of Congregationalists. It is the work of an assembly of divines, examined and approved in 1647 by the General Assembly of Scotland, and ratified by Act of Parliament in 1649. It begins in grandeur, as one would expect of a serious prose work of the mid-17th century. "There is but one only living and true God, who is infinite in being and perfection, a most pure spirit, invisible, without body parts or passions, immutable, immense, eternal, incomprehensible, Almighty, most wise, most holy, most free, most absolute . . ." But after a few pages the harsh climate, the mists, and the dampness of Calvinism begin to pervade both the thinking and the language. "All those whom God hath predestined into life, and those only, he is pleased in his appointed and accepted time effectually to call by his word and Spirit, out of that state of sin and death in which they are by nature . . . Others not elected, although they may be called by the

ministry of the word, and may have some common operation
of the spirit; yet they truly never come to Christ, and therefore cannot be saved: much less can men not possessing the
Christian religion, be saved in any other way whatsoever,
be they never so diligent to frame their lives according to
the light of nature, and the laws of that religion they do
possess, and to assert and maintain, that they may, is very
pernicious and to be detested."

Stone began to study the Confession carefully, and, as
usual he stumbled at the doctrine of the Trinity. Doubts
also arose in his mind on the doctrines of election, reproba-
tion, and predestination. "I had before this time learned
from my superiors the way of divesting those doctrines of
their hard, repulsive features, and admitted them as true,
yet unfathomable mysteries. Viewing them as such, I let
them alone in my public discourses, and confined myself to
the practical part of religion, and to subjects within my
depth. But in reexamining these doctrines, I found the
covering put over them could not hide them from a discern-
ing eye with close inspection. Indeed, I saw they were necessary to the system without any covering."

Before the Presbytery convened, Stone took two of the
members aside and "made known to them my difficulties,
and that I had determined to decline the ordination at that
time. They labored, but in vain, to remove my difficulties
and objections. They asked me how far I was willing to receive the confession? I told them, as far as I saw it consistent
with the word of God. They concluded that was sufficient.
I went into Presbytery and when the question was proposed,
'Do you receive and adopt the Confession of Faith, as containing the system of doctrine taught in the Bible?' I
answered aloud, so that the whole congregation could hear,
'I do, as far as I see it consistent with the word of God.'
No objection being made I was ordained."

He was twenty-four years old.

He continued to be nagged by doubts, which he labored to repel as Satanic temptations. Nevertheless, as he was addressing his congregations on the doctrine of total depravity and the necessity of the physical power of God to produce faith, and at the same time urging them to repent and believe the gospel, his zeal would be chilled at the contradiction. *For how could they believe? How could they repent unless it was God's sovereign will and pleasure that they should repent? How could they do impossibilities? And how could they be guilty in not doing them?* "Such thoughts would almost stifle utterance, and were as mountains pressing me down to the shades of death." He tried to take refuge in the distinction between natural and moral ability and inability, but by whatever name it was called that inability was in the sinner, and therefore he could not believe, or repent, but must be damned.

4

Stone resolved not to declare his views publicly until he felt able to defend them. He read the Bible. He retired to the solitude of the woods and sank down on his knees. At the thought of a God who, professing great love for his children, would punish them for not carrying out impossible commands, blasphemy rose in his heart and he was tempted to utter it. Sweat burst from the pores of his body. He prayed for the ruined world.

In his parish and in the rest of Kentucky, life went on quietly. His own passionate feelings met with no response. Preaching from the pulpit at Cane Ridge or at Concord, he was aware of a universal apathy, as if the powers of religion had disappeared and even the form of it was fast waning away.

At the end of the 18th century the Protestant church was completely given over to sectarianism. There were five kinds of Baptists and six kinds of Presbyterians—in the American wilderness, where congregations were small and poor and widely scattered and for the most part dependent on itinerant preachers. Only one person in ten belonged to any church whatever. Among the Presbyterians, a minister of one branch was not acceptable to any of the other five, and weeks passed during which it was impossible to hold a service or take communion. The presbyteries and synods were powerful and suspicious, and the slightest deviation from the Westminster Confession was sufficient to bring about a minister's expulsion from the church.

Faith and reason being of no avail, the scrupulous person waited, often in vain, for convincing proof—a dream, a vision, a voice, an uncommon appearance of light—that he had arrived at belief through the direct action of God. In his autobiography Stone cries out, "Let me here speak when I shall be lying under the clods of the grave. Calvinism is among the heaviest clogs on Christianity in the world. It is a dark mountain between heaven and earth . . ." Suddenly a way around the mountain was revealed—the tidal wave of religious interest and excitement that in later years came to be known as the Great Western Revival. It began about 1800, lasted three years, and was confined almost entirely to Kentucky and Tennessee. The meetings had to be held out of doors, at some church rather than in it, for no church was large enough. And the guiding spirit and principal evangelist was that beady-eyed, gravel-voiced Presbyterian, James McGready, whose preaching had so upset Stone in his youth.

In Mrs. Trollope's *Domestic Manners of the Americans* there is an account of a Methodist camp meeting in the backwoods of Indiana, in 1829, that in appearance and in spirit would not have been very different from those a generation earlier. "The spot chosen was the verge of an unbroken forest, where a space of about twenty acres appeared to have been partially cleared for the purpose. Tents of different size were pitched very near together in a circle round the cleared space; behind them were ranged an exterior circle of carriages of every description, and at the back of each were fastened the horses which had drawn them thither. . . . The first glance reminded me of Vauxhall, from the effect of the lights among the trees, and the moving crowd below them; but the second showed a scene totally unlike anything I ever witnesed. Four high frames, constructed in the form of altars, were placed at the four corners of the enclosure; on these were supported layers of earth and sod, on which burned immense fires of blazing pinewood. On one side a rude platform was erected to accommodate the preachers, fifteen of whom attended this meeting, and . . . preached in rotation, day and night, from Tuesday to Saturday."

Stone was returning to Kentucky from North Carolina when the first news of the revival reached him. He was traveling in the company of a Dr. Hall, and they were met by some men from Tennessee who had letters for Hall. "We stopped in the woods. The doctor began to read silently; but soon cried out aloud, and burst into a flood of tears. At first we were at a loss for the cause; but soon learned from the bearer of the letters, and from the letters themselves, that which equally affected us all. It was an account of a wonderful meeting at Shiloh in Tennessee—that many had been struck down as dead, and continued for hours apparently breathless, and afterwards rose, praising God for his saving mercy—that the saints were all alive— and sinners all around weeping and crying for mercy—and that multitudes were converted and rejoicing in God."

In the spring of 1801 Stone made a journey of two hundred miles across the state of Kentucky to attend a camp meeting on the edge of the prairie, and what he saw there astonished and moved him. No longer content with frightening people out of their wits, McGready was now bent on inducing the direct action of the Holy Spirit, through what were spoken of as "exercises"—seizures that looked like an epileptic fit, and were, of course, not that but men, women, and children declaring the wonderful works of God and the glorious mysteries of the gospel. Falling down as though slain in battle, they continued in that state for hours, sometimes exhibiting signs of life by a deep groan, or a piercing shriek, or a prayer for mercy most fervently uttered. After which they would rise shouting deliverance, and address the surrounding multitude, and many more would fall down in the same state from which the speakers had just been delivered. Stone sat patiently for hours beside the unconscious body of a man he knew to be a careless sinner, and observed everything that passed from the beginning to the end, and was convinced that it was the work of God. "So low had religion sunk, and such carelessness universally had prevailed, that I have thought that nothing common could have arrested the attention of the world; therefore these uncommon agitations were sent for this purpose."

The agitations were very uncommon indeed. There was the falling exercise: "The subject . . . would generally, with a piercing scream, fall, like a log . . . and appear as dead." And the jerks: "When the head alone was affected, it would be jerked backward and forward, or from side to side, so quickly that the features of the face could not be distinguished. When the whole system was affected, I have seen a person stand in one place and jerk backward and forward, in quick succession, their hands nearly touching the floor behind and before." And the dancing exercise. And the laughing exercise—while giving way to loud hearty laughter (which excited laughter in no one else) the subject appeared rapturously solemn. And the running exercise, and the barking exercise, and most remarkable of all, the singing exercise: "The subject, in a very happy state of mind, would sing most melodiously, not from the mouth or nose, but entirely in the breast. . . . Such music silenced everything and attracted the attention of all. It was most heavenly. None could ever be tired of hearing it. Doctor J. P. Campbell and myself were together at a meeting, and were attending to a pious lady thus exercised, and concluded it to be surpassing any thing we had known in nature."

As one would expect, Mrs. Trollope carried away a rather different impression: "When we arrived, the preachers were silent; but we heard issuing from every tent mingled sounds of praying, preaching, singing, and lamentation. . . . At midnight a horn sounded through the camp, which, we were told, was to call the people from private to public worship; and we presently saw them flocking from all sides to the front of the preachers' stand. . . . One of the preachers began in a low nasal tone . . . and assured us of the enormous depravity of man as he comes from the hands of his Maker, and of his perfect sanctification after he had wrestled sufficiently with the Lord to get hold of him, *et caetera*. The admiration of the crowd was evinced by almost constant cries of 'Amen! Amen!' 'Jesus! Jesus!' 'Glory! Glory!' and the like. But this comparative tranquility did not last long: the preacher told them that 'this night was the time fixed upon for anxious sinners to wrestle with the Lord;' that he and his brethren 'were at hand to help them,' and that such as needed their help were to come forward into 'the pen.' . . . The crowd fell back . . . and for some minutes there was a vacant space before us. The preachers came down from their stand and placed themselves in the midst of it, beginning to sing a hymn, calling upon the penitents to come forth. As they sung they kept turning themselves round to every part of the crowd, and, by degrees, the voices of the whole multitude joined in chorus. . . . The combined voices of such a multitude, heard at dead of night, from the depths of their eternal forests . . . did altogether produce a fine and solemn effect . . . but ere I had well enjoyed it, the scene changed, and sublimity gave way to horror and disgust. . . . Above a hundred persons, nearly all females, came forward, uttering howlings and groans, so terrible that I shall never cease to shudder when I recall them. They appeared to drag each other forward, and on the word being given, 'let us pray,' they all fell on their knees; but this posture was soon changed for others that permitted greater scope for the convulsive movements

sobbings, convulsive groans, shrieks and screams the most
appalling, burst forth on all sides. . . . The preachers
moved among them, at once exciting and soothing their
agonies. I heard the muttered 'Sister! dear sister!' . . .

"A very pretty girl, who was kneeling . . . immediately
before us, amongst an immense quantity of jargon, broke
out thus: 'Woe! woe to the backsliders! hear it, hear it,
Jesus! when I was fifteen my mother died, and I backslided,
Oh Jesus, I backslided! take me home to my mother, Jesus!
take me home to her, for I am weary! Oh John Mitchell!
John Mitchell!' and after sobbing piteously behind her
raised hands, she lifted her sweet face again, which was pale
as death, and said, 'Shall I sit on the sunny bank of salvation
with my mother? my own dear mother? Oh Jesus, take me
home, take me home!'

"Who could refuse a tear to this earnest wish for death
in one so young and so lovely? But I saw her, ere I left the
ground, with her hand fast locked, and her head supported
by a man who looked very much as Don Juan might, when
sent back to earth as too bad for the regions below.

"One woman near us continued to 'call on the Lord,' as
it is termed, in the loudest possible tone, and without a moment's interval, for the two hours that we kept our dreadful
station. She became frightfully hoarse, and her face so red
as to make me expect she would burst a blood-vessel. . . .

"The stunning noise was sometimes varied by the
preachers beginning to sing; but the convulsive movements
of the poor maniacs only became more violent. At length
the atrocious wickedness of this horrible scene increased to a
degree of grossness, that drove us from our station; we returned to the carriage at about three o'clock in the morning,
and passed the remainder of the night in listening to the
ever increasing tumult at the pen. To sleep was impossible.

At daybreak the horn again sounded, to send them to private devotion; and in about an hour afterwards I saw the whole camp . . . joyously and eagerly employed in preparing and devouring their most substantial breakfasts."

The worship of the Golden Calf in the backwoods of Indiana is what it seems most like, but my Grandmother Maxwell spoke of attending camp meetings as casually as we would speak of going to the movies.

When Stone went home and reported what he had seen, many of the congregation at Cane Ridge left the church weeping. He hurried over to Concord to preach that night and "two little girls were struck down under the preaching of the word, and in every respect were exercised as those were in the south of Kentucky." He had an appointment to preach the next day at William Maxwell's, and as he arrived at the gate, his friend Nathaniel Rogers, "a man of the first respectability and influence in the neighborhood," saw him and shouted aloud the praises of God and the two men rushed into each other's arms, Rogers still praising the Lord aloud. In twenty minutes from the time Stone started preaching, scores of people had fallen to the ground. Others tried to flee from the scene and couldn't. An intelligent deist of the neighborhood went up to Stone and said, "Mr. Stone, I always thought before that you were an honest man; but now I am convinced that you are deceiving the people." Stone spoke a few words to him mildly, and the deist "fell as a dead man, and rose no more till he confessed the Saviour."

McGready and the other revivalists moved north with the spring weather. Every Sunday all through May and June there were meetings at the churches around Lexington, and the attendance got larger and larger. Between five and six thousand people thronged to Stone's church at Concord. The whole countryside appeared to be in motion.

In July, Stone was married to Elizabeth Campbell, the daughter of a colonel and the granddaughter of General William Russell of Virginia. She was a pious woman, and much engaged in religion. After the ceremony they hurried up from Muhlenberg County, where her mother lived, to Cane Ridge, to be in readiness for what turned out to be the most famous of all the great camp meetings.

It began on the seventh of August, and lasted six days and nights. The attendance was estimated at twenty thousand—ten per cent of the entire white population of Kentucky at that time. Stone says, "The numbers converted will be known only in eternity. Many things transpired there, which were so much like miracles, that if they were not, they had the same effects as miracles on infidels and unbelievers; for many of them were by these convinced that Jesus was the Christ, and bowed in submission to him." Presbyterian, Methodist, and Baptist ministers preached, sometimes simultaneously, at different stations throughout the woods.

It was not Stone's meeting, nor did it take place at his church, but he was not merely an interested spectator. "Since the beginning of the excitement I had been employed day and night in preaching, singing, visiting and praying with the distressed, till my lungs failed, and became inflamed, attended with a violent cough and spitting of blood. It was feared to be the beginning of consumption."

His doctor forbade him to preach any more, and he felt himself fast descending to the tomb. "Viewing this event near, and that I should soon cease from my labors, I had a great desire to attend a camp meeting near Paris."

At this meeting, in a shady grove a few miles from Cane

Ridge, for the first time a Presbyterian preacher spoke out against the work of the revivalists. He also insisted that the assembled multitude leave the camp and continue the meeting in town, in a church that wouldn't hold half of them. They couldn't do this without leaving their tents and wagons exposed, which a great many were unwilling to do. The consequence was, the meeting was divided. "Infidels and formalists triumphed at this supposed victory, and extolled the preacher to the skies; but the hearts of the revivalists were filled with sorrow. Being in a feeble state, I went to the meeting in town. A preacher was put forward, who had always been hostile to the work, and seldom mingled with us . . . I felt a strong desire to pray as soon as he should close. He at length closed, and I arose and said, let us pray. At that very moment another preacher of the same cast with the former, rose in the pulpit to preach another sermon. I proceeded to pray, feeling a tender concern for my fellow creatures, and expecting shortly to appear before my Judge. The people became much affected, and the house was filled with cries of distress. Some of the preachers jumped out of a window back of the pulpit, and left us. Forgetting my weakness, I pushed through the crowd from one to another, pointed them the way of salvation, and administered to them the comforts of the gospel. My good physician was there, came to me in the crowd, and found me wet with sweat. He hurried me to his house, and lectured me severely on the impropriety of my conduct. I immediately put on dry clothes, went to bed, slept comfortably, and rose next morning relieved from the disease which had baffled medicine, and threatened my life."

In the eyes of orthodox Presbyterians, it was all ignorant profanation, a parody of Divine Grace. They were just as offended by the fact that preachers of different denominations took part in the same meeting as they were by the men who circulated through the outskirts of the crowd selling whiskey. But the greatest outrage of all, and no doubt what made the formalists jump out of the window, was the doctrine that Jesus died for all and salvation depended only on believing in Him. It was simply not what Calvin said.

Three months later, at a special session of the Washington (Kentucky) Presbytery, which included churches on both sides of the Ohio River, a lay elder arose and entered a verbal complaint against one of the most conspicuous figures at the Cane Ridge meeting, Richard McNemar, as a propagator of false doctrines. There were so many revivalists ready to come to his defense that his accusers were reluctant to force the question to a vote. The investigation was dragged out for two years, and then, without ever giving McNemar a hearing, the Presbytery concluded that his views amounted to Arminianism and were hostile to the interests of all true religion. A copy of this judgment was sent to every church under the supervision of the Washington Presbytery, and, at the same time, McNemar was appointed to preach among the vacant congregations as usual. It is the sort of logic that *Alice in Wonderland* is so full of.

The Synod of Kentucky looked into the matter, and after censuring the Presbytery for various irregularities, it went on to try two of the Cane Ridge evangelists on charges of its own. It was also looking into the opinions and statements of Stone and three other revivalists—Marshall, Thompson, and Dunlavy. "The four of us well knew what would be our fate," Stone says, "for it was plainly hinted to us, that we would not be forgotten by the Synod. We waited anxiously for the issue, till we plainly saw it would be adverse to McNemar and consequently to us all. We then withdrew to a private garden where, after prayer for direction . . . we drew up a protest against the proceedings of the Synod in McNemar's case, and a declaration of our independence, and of our withdrawal from their jurisdiction, but not from their communion. This protest we immediately presented to the Synod through their Moderator—it was altogether unexpected by them, and produced very unpleasant feelings; and a profound silence for a few minutes ensued. We retired to a friend's house in town, whither we were quickly followed by a committee from the Synod, sent to reclaim us." Old father David Rice reminded them "that every departure from Calvinism was an advance to atheism. The grades named by him were, from Calvinism to Arminianism—from Arminianism to Pelagianism—from Pelagianism to deism—from deism to atheism. This was his principal argument, which could have no effect on minds ardent in the search of truth."

In Scotland it had happened many times that a group of Presbyterians had withdrawn from the general organization of the church and continued to be Presbyterians. What was unprecedented here was that they were repudiating the church's right to determine the doctrines set forth in the Bible. After several more tactful attempts to win the evangelists over, the Synod suspended them for departing from the standards of the church, declared their pulpits vacant, and appointed substitutes to take over their churches. The evangelists published a hundred-page pamphlet, in which they stated their objections to the Westminster Confession and all other confessions and creeds.

The main body of Stone's two congregations adhered to him, and asked him to continue as their pastor. He informed them that he would continue to preach among them, though not in the relation that had previously existed, and in their presence he tore up the contract by which they had obligated themselves for his support.

His only means of making a living now was his farm. But he preached every night and frequently in the daytime,

and since he had emancipated his two slaves and had no
money to pay hired hands, he often found that the weeds
were getting ahead of his corn. Though he was fatigued
in body, his mind was, he said, as happy and calm as a
summer evening. He took pen and ink with him to the corn-
field, and as thoughts worthy of note occurred, he stopped
plowing and committed them to paper, and so accumulated
matter for a pamphlet on the doctrine of Atonement.

The five evangelists formed a presbytery of their own—
or what they called a presbytery; there were no officers, or
any lay members, or any churches which the Springfield
Presbytery could be said to represent. They were merely
an unorganized group of independent Presbyterian ministers
with a common purpose of reform. Other ministers, convinced by their arguments, united with them. Though they
went about enthusiastically preaching and printing pamph-
lets against everything the Presbyterian Church stood for,
they innocently hoped to remain an independent unit of it,
and when they were not allowed to, they dissolved their
"presbytery" and thereafter went by the name of the
Christian Church. The action was announced in an ironic
document of considerable importance—"The Last Will
and Testament of the Springfield Presbytery." As Stone
explains, quoting Scripture, where a testament is, there
must of necessity be the death of a testator, otherwise it is
of no strength at all. Except a corn of wheat fall into the
ground, and die, it abideth alone; but if it die it bringeth
forth much fruit.

The Testament begins: "The Presbytery of Springfield,
sitting at Cane Ridge, in the county of Bourbon, being,
through a gracious Providence, in more than ordinary
bodily health, growing in size and strength daily; and in
perfect soundness and composure of mind; and knowing
that it is appointed for all delegated bodies once to die; and
considering that the life of every such body is very uncer-

tain, do make and ordain this our last Will and Testament, in manner and form following, viz.:

"*Imprimis.* We *will,* that this body die, be dissolved, and sink into union with the Body of Christ at large; for there is but one body, and one Spirit, even as we are called in one hope of our calling.

"*Item.* We *will,* that our name . . . be forgotten . . .

"*Item.* We *will,* that our power of making laws for government of the church, and executing them by delegated authority, forever cease . . .

"*Item.* We *will,* that candidates for the Gospel ministry henceforth study the Holy Scriptures with fervent prayer, and obtain license from God to preach the simple Gospel, *with the Holy Ghost sent down from Heaven,* without any admixture of philosophy, vain deceit, traditions of men, or the rudiments of the world. And let none henceforth take *this honor to himself, but he that is called of God as was Aaron.*

"*Item.* We *will,* that the church of Christ . . . resume her native right of internal government . . .

"*Item.* We *will,* that each particular church . . . choose her own preacher, and support him by a free will offering without a written *call* or *subscription*—admit members— remove offenses; and never henceforth delegate her right of government to any man or set of men whatever.

"*Item.* We *will,* that the people henceforth take the Bible as the only sure guide to heaven; and as many as are offended with other books, which stand in competition with it, may cast them into the fire if they choose . . .

"*Item.* We *will,* that preachers and people, cultivate a spirit of mutual forbearance; pray more and dispute less . . .

"*Item.* We *will,* that our weak brethren, who may have been wishing to make the Presbytery of Springfield their king, and wot not what is now become of it, betake themselves to the Rock of Ages, and follow Jesus for the future.

"*Item.* We *will,* that the Synod of Kentucky examine every member, who may be *suspected* of having departed from the Confession of Faith, and suspend every such suspected heretic immediately; in order that the oppressed go free, and taste the sweets of gospel liberty. . . ."

This mixture of piety and cheerful impudence acted, Stone says, "like fire in a dry stubble. The sparks lighting in various parts of the field would quickly raise as many blazes all around."

Most of the churches for which the revivalists had preached joined them, and new churches were organized. This is what happened when Stone preached to a group of Baptists in southwestern Ohio: "The result was, that they agreed to cast away their formularies and creeds, and take the Bible alone for their rule of faith and practice—to throw away their name Baptist and take the name 'Christian'—and bury their association and to become one with us in the great work of Christian Union. Then they marched up in a band to the stand where Mr. Stone was preaching, shouting the praises of the Lord, and proclaiming what they had done."

In a short while, all but two of the Presbyterian churches in southwestern Ohio had become Christian churches. Soon there were hundreds, all through Kentucky, Tennessee, southern Ohio, and Indiana.

There was also trouble. In 1805 the Shakers sent missionaries to Kentucky. "They informed us that they had heard of us in the East," Stone says, "and greatly rejoiced in the work of God among us—that as far as we had gone we were right; but we had not gone far enough into the work—that they were sent by their brethren to teach the way of God more perfectly, by obedience to which we should be led into perfect holiness. They seemed to understand all the springs and avenues of the human heart. They delivered their testimony, and labored to confirm it by the Scriptures—promised the greatest blessings to the obedient, but certain damnation to the disobedient. They urged the people to confess their sins to them, especially the sin of matrimony, and to forsake their wives, wives their husbands. This was the burden of the testimony. They said they could perform miracles, and related many as done among them. But we could never persuade them to try to work any miracles among us. . . . They had new revelations, superior to the Scriptures, which they called the old record, which were true, but superseded by the new. When they preached to the world, they used the old record, and preached a pure gospel, as a bait to catch the unwary; but in the close of their discourse they artfully introduced their testimony. In this way they captivated hundreds and ensnared them in ruin."

Among the captivated were two of the original five ministers who left the Presbyterian Church together—McNemar and Dunlavy. And they were indeed ensnared in ruin, for Dunlavy "died in Indiana, raving in desperation for his folly in forsaking the truth for an old woman's fable," and the Shakers had a revelation given to them to remove McNemar from their village and take him to Lebanon, Ohio, and set him down in the streets, and leave him there destitute, in his old age.

Two more of the five ministers, Marshall and Thompson, disliking so much freedom of theological opinion, returned to the Presbyterian Church.

Through all this, Stone went about preaching and converting with undiminished enthusiasm. If he preached in a house, it was full to overflowing. If he preached out of doors at some country crossroads, men, women, and children walked six or seven miles to hear him. "The darkest nights did not prevent them; for as they came to meeting, they tied up bundles of hickory bark, and left them by the way at convenient distances apart; on their return they lighted these bundles, which afforded them a pleasant walk. Many have I baptized at night by the light of these torches."

From Kentucky the pioneers streamed out into other states—into Illinois, Missouri, and Iowa—taking the Christian Church with them. And Stone found himself in charge of a loose association of eighty churches, with thirteen thousand members, thirty-eight elders, and thirteen unordained preachers, over all of whom he denied having any authority. But through a magazine, the *Christian Messenger*, which he edited and published, and through his firmness of character, he had become the most influential personality of his church, and to all intents and purposes its leader.

5

In the absence of statistics, the pioneers believed what some-body told them, and it was said at this time that in Ohio such wheat, rye, oats, and corn grew in the river bottoms as had never been seen before, and that if you threw a hen into a field of grain there was no chance of its ever getting out. Also that when the women went for roasting ears, they needed an ax to cut down the cornstalks.

In 1813 Stephen England moved north into Ohio, taking his wife and ten children and two sons-in-law with him, and lived there for five years. Then a disease broke out among the cattle. Calves were aborted, the cows gave only a quarter of the usual amount of milk. The disease was of unknown origin, and highly contagious, and had no cure. From drinking the milk of infected cows, human beings developed a fever and other symptoms, such as a headache and sweating, and lost all desire to move. This lasted about two weeks, stopped, and then started up again.

One day the blackbirds flitting from branch to branch observed a different kind of activity in the clearing. The carpenter's tools and cooking utensils, the hoes and the log chain, the mattock, the axes, the bedding, the spinning wheel and the big wheel, the churn, the looking glass and the loom and the Bible were stowed away in the wagons. The teams were backed up to the traces. The women and children were disposed, by families and by age. And, leaving the doors of their cabins standing open and the grain nodding in the fields they had cleared with so much labor, my great-great-great-grandfather and his sons-in-law headed for the Territory of Illinois.

They arrived at Edwardsville, in Madison County, which is a little east of St. Louis, in the fall of 1818, a few weeks before Illinois was admitted as a state of the Union. They didn't like it here—why I don't know. It appears not to have been poor country. The first white man to visit the locality was James Gillham, twenty-five years before. He came here in search of his wife and three children, who had been taken captive from their home in Kentucky by a band of Indians. French traders told him that his family was being held for ransom in the Kickapoo village on Salt Creek, near the present site of Lincoln—as far away again as he was from Kentucky—and, with two Frenchmen as interpreters and an Irishman as an intermediary, he managed to get them back. He was so impressed with the beauty and fertility of the region around Edwardsville that he settled here. Perhaps the reason Stephen England and his sons-in-law didn't like it was that they no longer had the choice of the best land. Glowing reports of the country farther north induced them to set out in the middle of winter on a hundred-mile journey of exploration.

The contour of the land in the San-ga-mo country amazed them. In Ohio and in southern Illinois there were hills and valleys, as at home. Here it was as flat as a table top and the sky was like an inverted bowl over their heads. As they passed through what is now Springfield, the county seat and the state capital, they saw no signs of human habitation; only the tracks of wild animals. On the south bank of the Sangamon River, a short distance from the southwest corner of what is now Logan County, a man named William Higgins had just built a cabin. They stayed overnight with him. Next morning they crossed to the north side of the river and there paced out, in the timber and prairie, the dimensions of their new farms. To prevent others who might come after from choosing the same ground, they cut some logs, laid them across each other in three piles, and each man cut his initials on a tree to show that the land was claimed. Then they went back to their families. In March they returned, bringing Stephen England's son David, who was still a boy, with them. A foot of snow fell the night they arrived. Homespun, deerhide, whatever they had on, offered almost no protection against the cold that blows across that country in the wintertime. Three of them were grown men and better acquainted with physical hardship, and what they experienced was only what they expected. They dismissed the cold from their minds, as they did the howling of the wolves. The boy, lying in the shelter of a fallen tree, with his father's heavy arm around him, was close enough to childhood to be surprised that life was so unkind.

Stephen England and his son felled trees and cut logs for a cabin sixteen by eighteen feet, and soon had the walls up and the door and the chimney place cut out. Andrew Cline and Wyatt Cantrell still had their materials on the ground when the melting snow warned them that they must start south at once or they wouldn't be able to get their wagons across the river. They tried to bring their families north immediately, but the teams weren't equal to drawing the heavy wagons through the mud and slush. They gave it up. Taking two of Stephen England's grown daughters with them to do the cooking, they went back to Sangamon County in April, completed their cabins, cleared land, and planted crops.

The first week in June, William Higgins' wife and two daughters heard the crack of whips and the creaking of heavy wagon wheels. The dogs started to whine and bark. The women came out into the sunshine and stood with their hands shading their eyes, ready to greet their new neighbors. That same spring, other families settled nearby and, "the people having planted their crops, wished to have religious services, so Mr. England announced that he would preach at his own house late in June. . . . Everybody in the entire settlement came. Two women walked five miles through the grass, which was almost as high as their heads. The husband of one of them walked and carried their babe. That was the first sermon ever preached north of the Sangamon River in this county and probably in Central Illinois." *

The first year, the three families who settled on the north bank of the Sangamon River got about half a crop, but the following year the yield was nearly sixty bushels an acre. The flies would sometimes so trouble the horses and the oxen that they had to be driven into the timber and a fire kindled to drive the insects away. In the fall nearly everybody suffered from the shakes. You got it from walking through the wet grass. It had a fixed beginning and end, and came generally on alternate days. It was followed by a burning fever, and when that abated, the victim felt "entirely woebegone, disconsolate, sad, poor, and good for nothing." A woman who went back to Tennessee reported that Illinois was a good place for men and horses, but it was hell on oxen and women.

Stephen England continued to call the settlers together and preach to them. When the benches and stools were all taken and there was no longer even a place to stand, the women would take their shoes off and get up on the beds— eight to ten of them on a single bed. As my great-great-great-grandfather warmed to his subject he would pull his coat off. Sometimes there were Indians present. What they made out of the service is rather hard to imagine. The Bible presented no difficulties. It was right there in front of them,

---

* Nathaniel S. Haynes: *History of the Disciples of Christ in Illinois* (Cincinnati, 1915).

and the medicine man made magic with it. But the doctrine
of saving faith? Baptism? the doctrine of Atonement? the
right of the individual congregation to govern itself? and
the Holy Ghost eternally proceeding from the unbegotten
Father and the eternally begotten Son? Was it perhaps
simply that the Indians were by nature gregarious, and until
they met with a sufficient amount of discouragement from
the white men couldn't see a gathering of any kind without
adding themselves to it?

In 1820 Stephen England formed a church, with himself, his wife, two other men and five other women as members, all of whom signed this agreement: "We, members
of the church of Jesus Christ, being providentially moved
from our former place of residence from distant part, and
being baptized on the profession of faith and met in the
house of Stephen England, on a branch of Higgins Creek,
in order to form a constitution, having first given ourselves
to the Lord and then to one another, agree that our constitution shall be on the Holy Scriptures of the Old and New
Testaments, believing them to be the only rule of faith and
practise." Three years later they built a log meetinghouse,
and Stephen England continued to serve as minister until he
died, of a cancer in one of his ankles. He preached the
gospel as long as he could stand, and delivered his last
sermon sitting in a chair.

The inscription on his tombstone reads:

ELDER STEPHEN ENGLAND

PIONEER MISSIONARY

Born in Virginia, June 12, 1773

Died Sept. 26, 1823

Settled in Sangamon County in 1819

He preached the first sermon and organized

the first church and performed the first

marriage ceremony in Sangamon County

On his way to this wedding he passed through a field where a neighbor was plowing and borrowed a pair of shoes from him for the occasion.

The reason I was so sure I couldn't be descended from Stephen England was that the Christian Church was the abiding interest of my Grandmother Maxwell's life. Surely if she was descended from the man Dr. England referred to as a towering figure in the early days of the Christian Church, I'd have heard about it over and over as I was growing up—not only from her, but also from my Aunt Maybel. I still find it hard to believe, though it is a simple fact. I was eighteen when my grandmother died, and so the explanation is not that she did speak of Stephen England and I was just too young to remember or be interested in matters of this kind. What she had to say about later preachers—Brother Hatfield and Brother Cannon, Brother Holton and other men whose sermons she had sat through—did not interest me but I remember their names, even so.

In a letter to Max Fuller, my Aunt Maybel says, "I am glad you enjoyed the Maxwell genealogy and will be glad to give the letters to you, will put them in an envelope and mark your name on them so should anything happen to me they will be yours. Blinn [my younger brother] is the only other interested in such so will want you to share what you find with him, he has been very interested in my D.A.R. About this *Exema*, Maxwell, I feel quite sure you never had anything like that but if you remember when you came home from Laurel, Mississippi, you had eaten so much salt pork, your stomach was upset and your skin was very rough but we soon cured that up with proper food . . ."

My cousin's eczema is neither here nor there, but the very breath of her being is in that expression of concern and I could not bring myself to shut her up when I should have.

My brother was in high school when this letter was written, and his interest in antiquarianism did not survive the pressures of a busy law practice. My older brother, with his passionate pleasure in horses and guns, is too much a displaced pioneer himself to have much romantic curiosity about them. My aunt's statement was correct in so far as it applied to me: at that period I was not "interested in such." Stories, yes, but not dry facts and especially not genealogical details and speculations that would open the portals of the D.A.R. But why did they keep me in such total ignorance?

Some time in the 1930's, in Illinois, there was a reunion of the living descendants of Stephen England, at which fifteen hundred people were present. I learned about it from Dr. England. One would almost think they conspired to keep me from finding out about my ancestors. Though my grandmother and my Aunt Maybel and my Aunt Bert and my father all had their secrets, like everyone else, they were not of a conspiring disposition. There must be some other explanation.

The only explanation I can offer is hurt feelings. My father did not much care who he was descended from. He was by nature forward looking, and disliked everything that was old—old houses with windows that didn't fit properly and let the cold in, antique furniture that you had to be careful how you sat on, and music not written in his lifetime. "Oh, that's ancient history," he would say, about something that was not remote but merely in the past; what happened in the past was of no possible interest to anyone. It is conceivable that my grandmother and my aunt, not liking to have their toes stepped on, stopped speaking of genealogical matters in his presence. Or I may have said something that made them think I shared his prejudice. I don't think I did, though. The truth is, I am not convinced by any of this reasoning. Their failure to speak of Stephen England remains mysterious to me.

. . .

The other line of descent in my Grandmother Maxwell's family begins with a James Turley who was born in Fairfax County, Virginia, and who served as a private in the Continental Army when he was sixteen. He married Agnes Kirby, in Virginia, and they had fourteen children, seven boys and seven girls. If he was anything but a farmer there is no record of it. When he was thirty-one he moved to South Carolina. Four years later he moved again—to Kentucky this time, with two of the children in baskets slung on either side of a steady pack horse.

After twenty years in Kentucky he crossed over into southern Illinois and settled in Union County, which is on the Mississippi River, below St. Louis. Five years later he moved north to Sangamon County, where several of his sons joined him and where he died fifteen years later at the age of seventy-one. The *Logan County History* says that among the Indians he was a sort of arbitrator, and known as the "Big Chief" and "Big Bostony." What does the name mean? The list of his goods and chattels offered up for auction includes seven horses, thirty-nine head of cattle, twenty-three sheep, and sixty-five head of hogs. At this auction his son Charles, who was my great-great-grandfather, bid on and got a pair of hatchets, a powder gourd, two barrels of lime, a basket of sundries, a razor, a lot of old iron, a side saddle, and a pair of specktickles. He cannot have had much use of these things, for he himself died that same year.

Charles Turley was born in Henry County, Virginia, in 1786. His wife, Elizabeth Cheathem, was also a Virginian but brought up in Kentucky. In 1823, when he was approaching forty, he pulled up stakes and went north, to join his father. The route lay through rough country. Swamps and marshes had to be crossed with great exertion and fatigue, and dangerous rivers forded. They could have come in almost any kind of wagon, but it undoubtedly had a canvas cover of some sort and was drawn by oxen, with cattle and hogs being driven alongside, and a horse, and a hound dog.

Five years later they would have been part of an emigrant train, and the air would have been full of the sound of shouting, laughing, cursing, and cracking of whips, but in 1823 the Turleys were the vanguard, and probably alone. If you could have peered into the covered wagon, you'd have seen six children, the youngest a year old.

What the children saw must have been like enough to this old man's remembering (though he is not any old man I am related to): "Riding along the gently rolling prairie, now you descend into a valley and your vision is limited to a narrow circle. That herd of deer has taken fright at your coming, quits its grazing on the tender grass of the valley, and, following that old buck as leader, runs off with heads erect, horns thrown back, their white tails waving in the air, has circled around until yonder hillock is reached, when, turning towards you, they gaze with their dark bright eyes, as if inquiring why you have invaded their free pastures. As you ride along, the rattlesnake is stretched across the road, sunning itself, and the prairie wolf takes to his heels and gallops off much like a dog."

Their new home was about four miles from the village of Elkhart, in the extreme southern part of Logan County, and it was probably not very different from the one they left—a log cabin with a deerskin door, a clapboard roof, a puncheon floor, if there was a floor at all, and a stick chimney daubed with clay and straw. The children fell asleep in a room lighted with a rushlight, to the sound of the spinning wheel or the slam, crash of the loom.

Here they are walking home from school (I am quoting from the same old man): "the road was a path through the high grass and woods, and there were wolves and panthers plenty. They were frequently seen, and you can imagine how we felt when the stars began to shine. The oldest ones would form a front and rear guard, and put the smallest in the middle, and hurry them along, all scared nearly to death."

The *Logan County History* goes on to say that my Great-great-grandfather Charles Turley was a genial, generous-hearted man and had a host of warm friends; that he had his shares of the trials and hardships incident to the life of a pioneer; that he died about 1836, aged about fifty. And that in his last days he allied himself with the Christian Church.

I suppose one has a right to pick and choose among one's ancestors. In any case I have a fondness for my grand-mother's great-grandfather, William Higgins.

In 1881, at a meeting of the Old Settlers' Association, William H. Herndon, Abraham Lincoln's law partner in Springfield, delivered an address in which there were fre-quent bursts of eloquence such as this: "The wild animals that preceded the Indians are gone, the Indian treading closely on their heels. The red man has gone. The pioneer, the type of him, is gone, gone with the Indian, the bear, and the beaver, the buffalo and the deer. They all go with the same general wave, and are thrown high on the beach of the wilderness, by the deep wide sea of our civilization. He that trampled on the heels of the red man, with his wife and children, pony and dog, are gone, leaving no trace behind. . . . The trapper, bee and beaver hunter is gone—all are gone."

It is the bee hunter—that is, the hunter and trapper who always had one eye out for a bee tree, from which to gather the wild honey the frontier people used as a substitute for sugar—that I would like to consider at this point. Herndon's idea of literary style was to say everything in three different ways, and since I don't share this pleasure in pro-lixity I have cut his sentences where cutting seemed to me to do no harm to the sense. The bee hunter "is . . . a cadaverous, sallow, sunburnt, shaggy-haired man . . . his nose is . . . keen . . . his eyes . . . are sharp and in-quisitive . . . he is all bone and sinew, hardly any muscle . . . He wears a short linsey-woolsey hunting shirt . . . buckled tightly about his body. His moccasins are made of the very best heavy buck. His . . . rifle is on his shoulder or stands by his side, his chin gracefully resting on his hand, which covers the muzzle of the gun. The . . . crop-eared, shaved mane and bobtailed pony browses around, living where the hare, the deer, mule or hardy mountain goat can live. It makes no difference where night or storm overtakes him . . . He sleeps on his rifle for pillow, his right hand *awake* on the long . . . hunting knife in the girdle, carved over and over with game and deer. The will in the hand is *awake*. Such is the conscious will on the nerve and muscle of the hand, amid danger of a night, placed there to watch and ward while the general soul is asleep, that it springs to de-fense long before the mind is fully conscious of the facts. How grand and mysterious is mind! . . . This man, his trusty long rifle, his two dogs—one to fight and one to scent the trail . . . are equal to all emergencies. As for himself, his snores . . . testify to the soul's conscious security . . . he is a fatalist and says 'what is to be will be.' He never tires . . . He is swifter than the Indian, is stronger, is as long-winded, and has more brains . . . He is . . . uneasy . . . in the village where he goes twice a year to exchange his furs for whiskey, tobacco, flints, and lead. He dreads . . . our civilization. Overtake the man, catch him, and try to hold a conversation with him, if you can . . . His words are words of one syllable, sharp nouns and active verbs mostly. He scarcely ever uses adjectives, and always replies to questions asked him—'yes,' 'no,' 'I will,' 'I won't.' Ask him where he is from, and his answer is 'Blue Ridge,' 'Cumberland,' 'Bear Creek.' Ask him where he kills his game, or gets his furs, and his answer ever is—'Illinois,' 'Sangamon,' 'Salt Creek.' Ask him where he is going— 'Plains,' 'Forest,' 'Home,' is his unvarying answer. See him in the wilds, as I have seen him, strike up with his left hand's forefinger the loose rim of his old home-made hat, that hangs like a rag over his eyes, impeding his sight and perfect vision, peering keenly into the distance for fur or game, Indian or deer. See him—"

But enough is enough. The Old Settlers had nothing more on their minds that afternoon than to listen to oratory, which of necessity is packed with adjectives and seldom concise. The important thing is that the description is not taken from Fenimore Cooper but from life, and in the absence of any other, I offer it as a portrait of my great-great-great-grandfather, William Higgins. He was a Kentuckian, and forty-five years old when he settled on the south bank of the Sangamon River. The *County History* says that before he completed his cabin he crossed to the north side of the river, with his wife. "They were belated, and spent one night in the river bottom, near the mouth of Fancy Creek. A few days later, Mr. Higgins went to the north side alone, found five bee trees, and killed a panther which measured nine feet from tip to tip. He went over soon after, accompanied by his wife and two daughters, one of whom is now the wife of David England. These three are believed to have been the first white women who ever crossed to the north of the river."

Stephen England and his two sons-in-law turned up so soon after the encounter with the panther that they must have been told about it. They were the first people he could tell about it, except his wife and daughters, and it wouldn't have been human not to. I see all four men admiring the hide of this animal, and I see Stephen England fidgeting and biding his time, for he has something on his mind: He must talk to William Higgins about the Christian Church and the sufficiency of the Scriptures as a rule of faith and of life.

Apparently he did not convert him, for William Higgins's name is nowhere listed as belonging with the faithful. Like the fool in *King Lear,* he is never mentioned again by anybody, and for that reason I keep wondering about him.

When my daughter Kate was four or five years old, she dreamed that she was pursued by a snake crying "Ancestors! Ancestors!"

From the faraway past I can hear my grandmother saying "Grandpaw England," meaning David, the preacher's son. And I never heard her speak of him in such a way as to suggest that he might once have been very different from his picture, which was that of an old man in his seventies. David England was fourteen years old when he made that winter journey with his father and his sisters' husbands. When they came back with the women and children, in the heavy wagons, what he saw was not ice fields and snow but seas of grass and wildflowers.

In 1868, and again in 1869 and 1870, by which time David England was the oldest citizen of Fancy Creek Township, he addressed the annual meeting of the Old Settlers' Association. He said that he remembered seeing Indians bury their dead by putting them in troughs and suspending them in trees; also by building pens around them and leaving the bodies to decay. He once worked, reaping, three days and got three bushels of wheat in payment. When they first came to this country the price of salt was six dollars a bushel and pork was five dollars to six dollars per hundred pounds but shortly after that would not bring a fourth as much, for there was no market. The nearest mill was about four miles from St. Louis. Being a preacher's son was not the inhibiting thing it later became, because the preacher was also a farmer and hunter. Foxes, raccoons, wildcats, and great herds of deer abounded. His father was a good gunner and they had plenty to eat. Men who lived within six to ten miles were considered neighbors. If a family was sick with the ague, they were cared for. New settlers were supplied with seed corn and wheat. They had wild honey and an abundance of fresh fish for the taking.

David England was not quite twenty when his father died. That same year he married William Higgins' daughter Margaret. They had fourteen children. He was a deacon of the Christian Church, and then an elder, and he continued to live on the land his father had chosen. He could hardly have done better. Speaking of Fancy Creek Township, *The History of Sangamon County* says, "The soil is deep black loam, especially along the bank of the Sangamon River. The surface of the country is generally rolling, and timber in large quantities can be found along the banks of the streams." It was one of the best countries in the world until 1831, David England said. Prior to that time they raised plenty of cotton without cultivation—all they wanted. But after the deep snow, which all the old men remembered, there was a change in the climate and it was never the same again.

It was not merely the depth of the snow but also the defenseless condition of the land it fell on. There is a firsthand account of this disaster in *The History of Sangamon County:* "The autumn of 1830 was wet and the weather prevailingly mild until the close of December. Christmas Eve the snow began to fall. That night it fell about a foot deep. It found the earth soft, grass green, and some green peach leaves on the trees. The day was mild. The snow contributed greatly to the amusement of the boys, and called for the hilarity of all who had sleighs or sleds, or who could rig a 'jumper' with a store-box or a crate. Bells of any description, if not in the cutter, were hung on the horses by ropes or twine. . . . As the snow fell night after night, serious preparations were made by increasing the size and strength of the sleighs, and doubling teams, to break the way to mill and woods, for household bread, fuel, corn and provender. Mr. Enos, one of the wealthiest men of the place, and Receiver of the Public Moneys, turned out with a great sled and two yoke of oxen, to haul wood to the destitute. With wolf-skin cap on head, with Yankee frock, buttoned up close to the neck behind, reaching below his knees, belted over a great coat beneath, with legging protectors and ox-goad in his hand, he rolled up the bodies and limbs of trees, some of them more than fifty feet long, to the door of the writer, for which he and his family shall receive our thanks while life shall last. The same kind act he did to many others. His timber was nearest to the town. Woodmen felled the trees, rolled them on the sled, and the benevolent veteran left them at our doors.

"Snow succeeded snow, interchanged with sleet and fine hail, which glazed and hardened the surface. Nine long weeks witnessed this coming deep snow, until in all these parts its depths averaged from four to five feet. . . . The thermometer ranged close to zero; a few times it went twenty below, and the water dropped from the eaves only two days, so intense was the continuous cold. When the snow fell there was no frost in the ground; the sap of the trees had not been forced by the cold to the roots. The consequence was that the peach trees were invariably killed; apple trees and nurseries mostly shared the same fate. The summer before I had seen wagon loads of peaches in some orchards. Such a sight has never greeted our eyes since, in these parts.

"Great hardships were endured that winter by men and beasts. When the snow came it found most of the corn standing on the stalks. The fall had been so warm and wet that the farmers had better reason than common to indulge the careless habit of leaving their corn in the field, to be gathered in winter, when they wanted it. The snow became so deep, the cold so intense, the crust at times so hard, and the people were so unprepared for such an extreme season, that it became almost impossible in many parts of the country to obtain bread for family use, though amid stacks of wheat and fields of corn.

"Hundreds of hogs and fowls perished. Horses and cattle were in many instances turned out into the corn fields. Prairie chickens, whose habit is to roost on the ground, perished that winter in such number that we feared the race of this fine bird would become extinct. When their time of roost come they would light upon the snow, if the crust would bear them; or if its bosom was soft, plunge into it, and spend the night as on the earth; but if a heavy fall of snow come that night, especially as it were coated with a crust of ice, as often happened, the poor imprisoned things were locked in and thousands and thousands perished."

David England died in his sleep, in his eighty-fourth year. His oldest daughter, Louisa England, vas, as I have said, my Grandmother Maxwell's mother, and she died the year I was born, so all this is not as far away as it seems.

Charles Turley had a son Charles, and he married Louisa England, in 1842. When he was approaching forty, restlessness overtook him as it had his father and grandfather, and he moved a few miles south and settled near the brand-new village of Williamsville, which a hundred and fifteen years later is still only a cluster of houses. He was elected deacon of the Williamsville Christian Church in 1866—the year that my Grandfather Maxwell walked into his front yard, dusty and footsore, and asked for a drink of water.

I have told that story as it was told to me, but I somewhat mistrust it. What I think is that there is something missing —a detail left out because it could be taken for granted. When I was a small child and stayed overnight at my Aunt Maybel's house, I slept with my grandmother, and after I was too old for that I slept in a little room across the hall from her, watched over by enlarged sepia photographs of grim-faced, God-fearing elderly men and women—Turleys and Englands. In their youth they had looked on the earthly paradise, but this experience had been overlaid by a life of hard work, and innumerable preachers had told them to expect no ease or comfort here but to look for it in the Life Beyond. There was one old man with a grey beard and no collar or tie to detract from the importance of his collar button, and a stare so accusing that even in the dark I used to have to avert my eyes from his face in order to go to sleep.

Nobody ever said what my grandfather looked like when he walked into the farmyard, but I have an idea that he was not exactly prepossessing. After weeks and weeks under the open sky, he must have been as dark as an Indian. He would have lost a good deal of weight. Every time he got caught in a rainstorm his clothes must have shrunk a little more. He must have washed in streams, with a cake of soap that got smaller and smaller, no matter how sparingly he used it. When it was gone, he used sand from the river bottom, and beat his shirt on a stump as he had seen the women do. It was most likely in rags. Somewhere along the line he was bound to have picked up body lice and fleas.

Suppose this scarecrow had said he was a Free Will Baptist or a Cumberland Presbyterian. I would not at all put it past the fierce old man (who was only forty-four when this happened) to have asked him if he'd had all the water he wanted and let him go on his way. Instead, what I suspect happened is that my grandfather said, "Sir, I am a member of the Christian Church," and, rejoicing (for it could only be the work of Providence), my Great-grandfather Turley led the gaunt, blue-eyed young stranger, fleas and all, into his house.

6

My Grandmother Maxwell believed that there was only
the Christian Church; every other religion was a mistake,
based on total misunderstanding of the Bible and of Jesus'
intention for mankind. She had lost sight of—if she ever
knew—the fact that in the beginning the church she belonged to did not think of itself as a separate religion but a
reformation of the Presbyterian Church. The adherents at
first called themselves and were called "Reformers." Later
on, they were called "The Disciples of Christ," and that is
precisely what they thought of themselves as being. Upper-
most in their minds at all times was the intention to achieve
the impossible—to bridge the centuries and through the
purity and propriety of their religious devotion become not
merely like but spiritually indistinguishable from Simon
who was called Peter, and Andrew his brother, James the
son of Zebedee, and John his brother, Philip, and Bar-
tholomew, Thomas, and Matthew the publican, James the
son of Alpheus, Lebbeus, whose surname was Thaddeus,
and Simon the Canaanite.

That is to say, they took the New Testament literally.

The events of the Old Testament—Abraham entertaining the angels, Joseph in Egypt, Moses smiting the rock, the
wisdom and magnificence of Solomon—were at a certain
distance; what happened in the New Testament was like
something that they had heard about, and that they would
be adding to, by their own lives.

Among the people who detested them, the followers of this movement were usually referred to as Campbellites.

Thomas Campbell was a Scotch-Irish Presbyterian minister who so long as he remained in Ireland did not publicly depart in any way from orthodox belief; after six months in America he behaved with such implacable independence of spirit that informal charges were brought against him for heretical teachings, and he ended up wholly outside his own church. He was born in the North of Ireland, in County Down, in 1763. His father had been a soldier in the British Army and fought on the Plains of Abraham, and it was believed in the family that General Wolfe died in his arms. If so, he died in the arms of an eccentric and irascible man; once when Thomas Campbell was conducting family prayers at home, he prayed longer than the old man's rheumatism allowed for, and when Archibald Campbell was at last able to get up from his kneeling position, he took his cane and, to the surprise and scandal of all who were present, began to lambaste his son with it.

He had been a Roman Catholic and became an Anglican when he married. In his early youth Thomas Campbell was drawn to the Presbyterians, and attended their meetings, and this inevitably led him to feel concern for his salvation. He prayed diligently and used every means that was recommended to him in order to produce the evidence of an "effectual calling," and for this evidence he waited several years. One day, walking in a field, he "felt a divine peace suddenly diffuse itself throughout his soul."

The Scottish Presbyterian Church had not only divisions but subdivisions, and Thomas Campbell became an Old-Light, Anti-Burgher, Seceder Presbyterian—the names are enough to make your head swim until you discover that they do not represent theological distinctions but have to do with the relations of church and state.*

Most of our personal knowledge of Thomas Campbell comes from the official biography † of his son, Alexander Campbell, and Alexander Campbell's *Memoirs of Elder Thomas Campbell*. In the literature of autobiography there have been instances of a son subjecting his father's character to a cold or judicious scrutiny, but not when they were conducting a religious movement together. And the official biographer, Robert Richardson, was a pious and goodhearted man who was awed by the story he had to tell. His view of Thomas Campbell is not in all respects convincing, and because of the way Thomas Campbell's life turned out, it matters very much that one come to some sort of satisfactory

---

* By far the best history of the Christian Church is *The Disciples of Christ*, by W. E. Garrison and A. T. De Groot (1948), which I am, in general, much indebted to. And it has a concise explanation of this tangle: "The Seceder Presbyterian Church had withdrawn from the Church of Scotland in 1733 in protest against certain aspects of the connection between church and government, especially against the 'patronage' system, under which the right to appoint ministers belonged, not to parish, session or presbytery, but to the lay landlords. No question of doctrine was involved in this secession. Indeed, the Seceders were, through the latter part of the eighteenth century, stricter Calvinists than the Church of Scotland. The Seceders in Scotland soon divided into two parties, Burghers and Anti-burghers, on the issue as to whether or not the members of their communion could properly subscribe to the oath imposed by law upon any who would become burgesses. The oath was a declaration of adherence to 'the religion presently professed in this realm.' The question was whether this meant Presbyterianism in general, to which they did adhere, or specifically the established Church of Scotland, to which, although it was Presbyterian, they did *not* adhere. Burghers and Anti-burghers both sent missionaries to north Ireland . . . and gained considerable followings. . . . During the time of Thomas Campbell's ministry in Ireland each of the two parties was again divided into 'Old Lights' and 'New Lights,' on another obscure and minute point involved in church-state relations. Mr. Campbell . . . early outgrew all interest in these divisive trivialities."

† *Memoirs of Alexander Campbell* (Cincinnati, 1868).

conclusion about what kind of man he was. Richardson says that he was handsome, with a square, massive forehead, a ruddy complexion, and soft grey eyes full of intelligence. His sermons were long but livened by homely illustrations and given weight and authority by his evident earnestness. From the moment of his conversion he felt that he had been called to be a minister. He tried to talk to his father about this, and his father changed the subject. It was a well-to-do Presbyterian of the neighborhood who paid for his three years at the University of Glasgow and five annual sessions at a Scottish theological seminary. Richardson says that Thomas Campbell had an unusually sweet and sociable nature, with a ready flow of conversation, and that he was also given to introspection and self-examination. The nature of his self-examination is suggested by this passage from his diary for the year 1800—at which time he was thirty-seven years old and conducting an academy for gentlemen's sons in the town of Rich Hill, thirty miles southwest of Belfast, and preaching in a country church. "Very dull and heavy in prayer, both in secret and public. The prevalent carnality of the last week has prevailed much this day. . . . I have reason to bless God I have not felt so much concern for public approbation, nor such strong emotions of self-conceit as formerly; but alas! what weakness and timidity in publicly reproving the violation of the holy Sabbath."

Being dull and heavy in prayer is an occupational hazard of clergymen, and not difficult to understand, considering how much automatic praying is required of them. The "prevalent carnality" I take to be not his own—though, since he had seven children, it can be assumed that he was capable of sexual feelings—but that of his parishioners. And very likely what he meant was not lewdness, anyway, but unspirituality. But for a Presbyterian minister of this period to be weak and timid about publicly reproving his flock for profaning the Sabbath was not usual. What kept him from speaking out? The gentleness of his nature? An unwillingness to offend people? In years to come, gentle though he was, he offended thousands. Furthermore, he was not a timid man. He refused to join an underground organization of Catholics and Presbyterians who had taken an oath to free Ireland from British rule, and they then demanded that he speak publicly in favor of oaths and secret societies; but when he spoke, he presented his own opposing views instead, and produced such an uproar that a friend had to take him by the arm and hustle him out of the hall.

Commenting on the passage he had quoted, his son says, "Were any man, in perfect health of body, to institute a diary of his physical constitution, and proceed to feel his own pulse some three or four times per diem, and to take notes on each occasion, and, in his *memorabilia*, record the signs and symptoms of morning, noon, and evening, unless possessed of great self-command and vigor of intellect he would be sending for a physician at least once or twice a day to sit in solemn judgment upon his abnormal feelings and portentous symptoms." I have a distrust of analogy, or rather the use to which it is commonly put. But in any case, he has put his finger on it; they were abnormal feelings and portentous symptoms.

When Thomas Campbell arrived at his mid-forties he showed signs of failing health. His doctor said that if he wanted to live he must stop his unremitting mental toil, and suggested that he emigrate to America. His health would be improved by the long sea-voyage and by a change from his ordinary pursuits. Richardson says he could hardly endure the thought of leaving his school and his family, and that it was his son Alexander who persuaded him finally, by saying that he himself intended to go to the United States as soon as he was of age, and that by going now, his father would be preparing a home for them all to come to.

Perhaps that is all there is to it. But I wonder if he would have agreed to such a drastic removal if it had not coincided with an impulse from another source. I know it is questionable to insert motives into the mind of a historical figure when you do not have written facts to support you, but the winds that blow over Ireland have come straight off the Atlantic, and he did not need to board a ship to breathe fresh and invigorating air. He lived to be ninety-one, which does not suggest a frail constitution. Those signs of failing health—could they have been the flag run up by a nature that was at war with itself?

That Thomas Campbell was a saintly man I see no reason to doubt. If his saintliness had been of the kind that induces visions, it would not matter where he was or, very much, who he preached to, but he does not seem to have had more than the one supernatural experience that levered him into the Presbyterian Church. He had the Bible to sustain him, but no direct communication from Heaven. Which he must have felt as a shortcoming, as in some way his own fault.

And does it require an extremely well-educated and highly intelligent man to scold villagers for not remembering the Seventh Day to keep it holy? Couldn't any apple-cheeked country parson do as well?

His only act of any public importance had been to serve as representative of the Synod of Ireland to the General Assembly of Anti-Burghers in Glasgow, at which time he presented a petition urging the union of the two branches of the Seceder Church. The petition was adopted by the Assembly, but nothing came of it for many years.

At this time of his life he read the Bible and the Concordance and very little else. He opened the Bible and read *Blessed are ye when men shall hate you, and when they shall separate you from their company, and shall reproach you, and cast out your name as evil, for the Son of man's sake*. And nobody hated him, or separated themselves from his company, or reproached him, or cast out his name as evil, so how could his reward be great in Heaven?

He read *And a man's foes shall be they of his own household. He that loveth father or mother more than me is not worthy of me: and he that loveth son or daughter more than me is not worthy of me. And he that taketh not his cross and followeth after me is not worthy of me*, and knew that he was a family man, who loved his home, and that the men and women he preached to were like sons and daughters to him.

He read *As ye go, preach, saying the kingdom of heaven is at hand. Heal the sick, cleanse the lepers, raise the dead, cast out devils*.

Nowhere did he read *Stay ye in that pleasant comfortable place and preach to the congregation that is so used to you*.

He read *The harvest is truly plenteous, but the laborers few*, and thought, perhaps, of the Scotch-Irish immigrants in the American wilderness who had no one to preach to them.

He embarked in the spring of 1807. "Believe in the promises of the gospel," he wrote to his children, from Londonderry. When the ship landed in Philadelphia after a voyage of thirty-five days, he discovered that the Anti-Burgher Synod of North America was meeting in the city. He presented his credentials, and was kindly received, and asked to be assigned to the Presbytery of Chartiers, in western Pennsylvania, to which some of his acquaintances had already emigrated. His request was granted. To his family he wrote, "What a debtor am I to the grace of God! . . . My dear children, let me address you together: if you have any sympathy, any sincere affection for a father who cannot cease to love and pray for you so long as his heart shall beat or tongue be able to articulate, see that you follow the directions I gave you at my parting, whether by word or writing. Be a comfort to your mother; love, cherish, and pity one another. Love the Lord your God; love his Son Jesus Christ, and pray to the Lord constantly and ardently for me your poor father, who longs after you all, and who cannot rest, if the Lord will, till he has prepared a place of residence for you all, where I trust we shall spend the rest of our days together in his service."

The children so movingly addressed were Alexander, who was then nineteen, three girls of fourteen, twelve, and eight, two little boys of five and three, and a baby a little over a year old. Alexander copied the letter out in a notebook already containing numerous extracts from Young, Dr. Johnson, Buffon, Beattie, and other esteemed authors.

Thomas Campbell was allowed fifty dollars to cover the expenses of his journey over the Allegheny Mountains. His destination was Washington, Pennsylvania, a frontier community of five hundred inhabitants, situated in the midst of farms and orchards, with low wooded hills all around. The houses were mostly built of logs.

It has been suggested in a present-day book * about Thomas Campbell that it must have been exceedingly difficult for him to adjust himself readily to the rudeness and lack of culture of the American frontier. In the same way that particularly handsome men do not require beauty in the women they marry, so men of genuine cultivation are seldom put off by rudeness and lack of culture in others, and I think he was probably very happy moving among those farmers and trappers and Indian scouts. I even see him smiling benignly under a coonskin cap. How much freer life was here, and more open, must have been the thought that most often occurred to him, if for no other

* Lester G. McAllister: *Thomas Campbell, Man of the Book* (Bethany, W. Va.: Bethany Press, 1954).

reason than that it was true. And he stopped seeing religious duty as something owed by the devout to the church, and instead saw it as something the church owed to all who believed in Jesus Christ.

He went two or three days up the Allegheny River by canoe to preach to a handful of people in a backwater community, and finding that they had had no opportunity to take communion for a long time, he suggested from the pulpit that all who felt so disposed and duly prepared should, without respect to party difference, "enjoy the benefits of the communion season then providentially offered them."

He said publicly that it was not necessary to have a mystical experience to prove that you had saving faith; faith was the intelligent response of the mind to evidence.

He said all Christians ought not to be expected to have the same opinions.

He said that it was enough to be in agreement with what is expressly taught and enjoined in the New Testament, and that nothing should be made a term of communion that is not as old as the New Testament, or that is not expressly revealed and enjoined therein—and so dismissed in one sentence the Nicene and Athanasian creeds, the Augsburg Confession, the Thirty-nine Articles, the Westminster Confession, and all doctrines that spring from them.

It would be difficult to prove that saints do not enjoy the trouble they make.

There was no preacher of comparable distinction in the Presbytery of Chartiers. The Anti-Burgher Seceder Church on the frontier was even more intolerant and conscious of religious parties than it was in either Ireland or Scotland, and its ministers were small-minded men who were fanatically preoccupied with points of doctrine. A young minister who went up the river with Thomas Campbell had been shocked and when he got home spread the story around that Thomas Campbell practiced open communion. The Reverend John Anderson was appointed to assist Thomas Campbell at Buffalo and failed to appear, and gave as his excuse that Mr. Campbell had deviated from orthodoxy. At the next meeting of the Presbytery, Anderson's excuse was accepted.

What Thomas Campbell then did was not as spectacular as Oscar Wilde's bringing suit for libel against the Marquis of Queensbury, but it was the same kind of injudiciousness. He made a motion that the matter of the Reverend Anderson's excuse be reconsidered. The motion lost, and the Presbytery then inquired into Anderson's evidence for saying that Mr. Campbell had unorthodox opinions. The committee appointed to look into the matter consisted of Anderson himself and three of his former students. Thomas Campbell was not permitted to call witnesses. His appointment to preach was temporarily suspended.

A short time later, a meeting that had supposedly been adjourned was reconvened, with Anderson and two others present, for the express purpose of making the suspension permanent.

He appealed to the Anti-Burgher Synod of North America, which was again meeting in Philadelphia, and devoted a week to hearing his case. It found that the Presbytery's investigation had been irregular, and revoked the sentence of suspension. It then proceeded to conduct its own trial, which was both courteous and fair.

It found that Thomas Campbell had diverged from the standards and practices of the church, but could not bring itself to admit that his divergence was as great as it actually was, and so said that his answers were evasive, unsatisfactory, and equivocal, when they were in fact quite plain.

He was very angry, but could not yet readily imagine

breaking with the church he had devoted the whole of his adult life to. He asked to be heard before the censure was voted on, and the Synod agreed. It clearly would have liked to arrive at a decision that was acceptable to him and to the Presbytery of Chartiers. He got the Synod to accept his explanations with regard to articles 1, 2, and 3 of the charges, but not 4, which referred to his stating publicly that when Christians did not have an opportunity of hearing ministers of their own party, it was lawful in certain circumstances for them to hear ministers of another party preach the Gospel. The Synod declared this altogether unwarrantable, and he "declared his purpose to avoid giving offense on this head as much as possible."

The phrase "as much as possible" should have been a warning to them. He could have pointed out a dozen places in the Book of Matthew that expressly enjoined the opposite of what they were asking him to accept.

When the next session began, at six o'clock on the following morning, the moderator received and read a letter from him in which he wildly charged the Synod with partiality and equivocation and informed them that he could not accept their authority. He was summoned to appear immediately, and, standing before them, retracted the letter and acknowledged his rashness in bringing such charges and in declining the authority of the Synod.

He submitted to being "admonished and rebuked" for diverging from the rules of the church. And to being prayed over. At the bottom of the Synod's list of preaching appointments to the presbyteries in its care appears this notation: "Mr. Th. Campbell in Phil'a, Jun., July, then in Chartiers till next meeting." So he should have been in good standing once more. But while he was preaching in Philadelphia, the Presbytery held a meeting and the members dissented—though how they were in a position to do this I do not understand—from some of the findings of the Synod and particularly from the Synod's action in removing Thomas Campbell's suspension. He arrived in Washington and found that no arrangement had been made for him to preach anywhere. He asked why, and was told that they weren't sure he wasn't intending to stay on in Philadelphia, and anyway, he hadn't told them when he was returning. The Presbytery's copy of the minutes of the Philadelphia meeting did not agree in all particulars with the copy he himself had made—the softened verdict, in which the word "evasive" was struck out, and the final alteration of the Synod's tone had been omitted—and it was therefore a fraudulent misrepresentation both of his position and the position of the Synod.

The minutes of the Presbytery for September 13, 1808, contain the statement that on this day Thomas Campbell "in his own name and in the name of all who adhered to him, declined the authority of this Presbytery for reasons formerly given, the authority of the Associate Synod of North America and all courts subordinate thereto, and all further communications with them."

This time he didn't take it back.

During the period when things were going well for him, Thomas Campbell instructed his family to join him in America. His letter, written in January, was delivered in March, and there was a further delay when the younger children came down with smallpox.

It was the beginning of October when the family embarked, on a sailing vessel that could hardly have escaped disaster. The crew was young and inexperienced, the captain was a drunkard. The ship was blown off its course by adverse winds and ended up off the island of Islay in the Hebrides. The captain ran it into a crooked inlet and, even though he was warned that many vessels had been wrecked there, dropped anchor and waited for the wind to change, so he could return to the open sea.

On the evening of the third day, Alexander Campbell fell asleep over a book in his cabin and dreamed that the ship struck a rock and filled with water, and that he had to make the most strenuous exertions to save his family and secure their luggage. On waking, he felt the force of the dream so strongly that he said, "I will not undress tonight. I will lay my shoes within my reach, and be ready to rise at a moment's warning; and I would advise you all to be prepared for an emergency." A few hours later, the wind shifted, and the ship dragged its anchors and was dashed against a sunken rock and went clear over on its side. The sailors cut away the masts, and the ship partly righted itself, but then began to fill with water, and one has the feeling of having read the whole thing before, in Act I of Shakespeare's *The Tempest*. While the wild waters were in a roar and the sea mounting to the welkin's cheek and the passengers with whatever baggage they could rescue were crowded on the upper deck, young Alexander Campbell, having done all he could for the safety of his family, sat on the stump of a broken mast, Richardson says, and abandoned himself to reflection. "In the near prospect of death he felt, as never before, the vanity of life. The world now seemed a worthless void. . . . He thought of his father's noble life, dedicated to God and the salvation of his fellow-beings," and made up his mind to devote his life also to this elevated and most worthy calling.

The captain managed to get ashore in a rowboat, but he was so drunk nobody believed his story until daylight, when the islanders could see that a ship had run aground. They began to gather upon the beach, and by means of a rope line managed to get a boat out to the ship; the passengers were brought to shore, women and children first—but only, Richardson says, because "the more resolute, drawing their swords, stood at the gangway and threatened to cut down any man that dared to go until the weaker portion of the passengers were landed."

Wading ashore through the surf, Alexander found his mother and the children all safe, and they rejoiced together at their merciful deliverance. He then "repaired with the family to the nearest and most respectable house he saw," where they were warmly received by a widow lady with a respectable fortune and several grown-up daughters. Her husband, a clergyman, was said to have translated from the Gaelic many of the poems of Ossian. "This lady's maiden name was Campbell, and when it was discovered that her guests were of that name, she, as well as all the rest of the people, seemed to redouble her attentions, for as it now appeared, instead of going to America, they had been thrown directly among the Campbells of Argyleshire, from whom they deduced their lineage. . . . Warmed, dried and refreshed, along with many others of the passengers they proceeded to the town, which was about two miles off, where they obtained lodgings in the house of a Mr. Mc-Callister. Here they meditated with grateful hearts upon the eventful scenes through which they had just passed, and re-calling the premonition given by Alexander, were assured by him that the reality, as it occurred, was precisely what appeared to him in the forewarning. . . . He was a firm believer in special providences. . . . With him, these were simply facts, which he did not pretend to explain upon natural principles, but regarded as indications of God's watchful care and interest in the affairs of his people."

For some days afterwards he went back to the wreck, as often as the weather permitted, and recovered what books and clothing had not been washed overboard. The laird of the island, impressed by the young man's water-logged books

—chiefly works of theology—and by his good manners, invited him to his house and treated him like a relative. The schoolmaster was equally kind.

It was too late in the year to risk a second voyage and Alexander saw in their misfortune an opportunity until now denied him: They would spend the winter in Glasgow, where he could attend the university. From the islanders he obtained several letters of introduction, one of which was to the Reverend Greville Ewing, and it changed the course of his life.

In the 18th and 19th centuries there were upwards of forty small movements, none of them separate churches, that were bent on restoring in a more literal and precise way the simple patterns of early Christianity, and Ewing was at the center of a movement of this kind. As a young man he had wanted to introduce Christianity among the natives of Bengal, but the East India Company was uncooperative and the project had to be abandoned. When Alexander Campbell arrived in Glasgow, Ewing was conducting a religious seminary and preaching regularly to audiences of sometimes two thousand people, in a huge building that had originally housed a circus. He was a brilliant lecturer and a most kind and generous and openhearted man. He found better accommodations for the shipwrecked family and became Alexander's mentor and friend. At Ewing's house he met and became acquainted with other students and professors of the university, preachers of all sorts and kinds, and many persons of respectability. He had left a country village for the largest and wealthiest city in Scotland, where he found himself not only taken in but a family pet in the household of a man of importance.

He was already a member of the Seceder Church in Ireland, and he felt it his duty, while he was in Glasgow, to unite with the Scottish Seceder Church. He had no letter, and therefore had to appear before the elders and be examined. His answers were satisfactory, but he was of two minds about the step he was about to take. One cannot travel, let alone go through a shipwreck, without having one's mind opened to new ideas. At Ewing's house, Alexander Campbell heard a good deal of talk about the behavior of the clergy of established denominations—how they were consistently opposed to any attempt at reformation, and how they often resorted to unscrupulous methods to hinder the progress of propositions they did not hold with. And he came to share Ewing's belief that a religious congregation wholly independent and free from the dominating control of Synods and General Assemblies was much more in accord with the way things were in the primitive church. At the last minute, during communion service, he decided that the Seceder Church was not the Church of Christ, and he got up and walked out.

In America, Thomas Campbell continued to preach in the houses of a few loyal friends, mostly in the neighborhood of Washington. They had no intention of founding a new religion, Richardson says, but they felt themselves slowly drifting away from familiar teachings and in need of a clearer understanding of the course they ought to pursue. They met to consider the questions. "Thomas Campbell, having opened the meeting in the usual manner, and, in earnest prayer, especially invoked the Divine guidance, proceeded to rehearse the matter from the beginning, and to dwell with unusual force upon the manifold evils resulting from the divisions of religious society—divisions which, he urged, were as unnecessary as they were injurious. . . . Finally . . . he went on to announce, in the most simple and emphatic terms, the great principle or rule upon which he understood they were acting and . . . would continue to act . . . WHERE THE SCRIPTURES SPEAK, WE SPEAK: AND WHERE THE SCRIPTURES ARE SILENT, WE ARE SILENT.

"Never before had religious duty been presented to them in so simple a form. . . . It was to many of them as a new revelation . . . for ever engraven upon their hearts. Henceforth, the plain and simple teaching of the Word of God itself was to be their guide. God himself should speak to them, and they should receive and repeat his words alone."

It was quite some time before anyone presumed to break the silence. At length, Andrew Monro, who was a bookseller and postmaster at Canonsburg, said, "Mr. Campbell, if we adopt *that* as a basis, then there is an end to infant baptism." Profound sensation. "If infant baptism be not found in the Scripture," Thomas Campbell said, "we can have nothing to do with it." Thomas Acheson, greatly excited, laying his hand on his heart, exclaimed, "I hope I may never see the day when my heart will renounce that blessed saying of the Scripture, 'Suffer little children to come unto me, and forbid them not, for of such is the kingdom of heaven,' " and burst into tears. Whereupon James Foster cried, "Mr. Acheson, I would remark that in the portion of the Scriptures you have quoted *there is no reference, whatever, to infant baptism.*" Mr. Acheson left the meeting to weep alone, and the proposal was unanimously adopted.

Subsequently Thomas Campbell prepared a "Declaration and Address of the Christian Association of Washington" which, when printed in the office of the local newspaper, was a pamphlet of fifty-six closely spaced pages. It and "The Last Will and Testament of the Springfield Presbytery" are the two basic documents of the Christian Church. The "Declaration" assumes that it is possible to have a simple and evangelical Christianity derived entirely from the Scriptures; that the individual person has a right to interpret the

Bible for himself; and that when this right is recognized there will be unity among all the Christian churches. What is "expressly revealed and enjoined" in the Scriptures—such as, for example, the form of worship—does not require interpretation and should simply be obeyed.

The Address begins: "Dearly Beloved Brethren, That it is the grand design and native tendency, of our holy religion, to reconcile and unite men to God, and to each other, in truth and love, to the glory of God, and their own present and eternal good, will not, we presume, be denied, by any of the genuine subjects of Christianity;" and goes on to list thirteen propositions that have to do with building a united church and the formation of similar associations devoted to the same principles.

The Postscript contains this most admirable sentence, "Our dear brethren, of all denominations, will please to remember, that we have our educational prejudices, and peculiar customs to struggle against as well as they."

Early in October Thomas Campbell had word that his family had landed in New York, and were going by stage-coach to Philadelphia, and had made arrangements with a wagoner to convey them from there to Washington—a distance of about three hundred and fifty miles.

Sometimes walking and sometimes riding in the wagon that conveyed their luggage, Alexander and his mother and the six younger children pursued their westward way across ridge after ridge of the Allegheny Mountains. They were enchanted by the wild and romantic character of the landscape and by the colors of the autumn foliage. When they first reached the country of extensive, unbroken forest, Alexander was so excited that he went for an evening walk. "Returning to the hotel, he found that all its inmates had retired to rest, a light having been left for him upon the table. Upon attempting to fasten the door, he was surprised to find it without lock or bolt, and with nothing but a latch, as he perceived was also the case with the door of his sleeping apartment." Lying in bed, he concluded that in the New World, robbery and injustice were unknown, because here you had a purely Protestant community.

Richardson describes the inns of the period as "very spacious and comfortable buildings, and abundantly provided with all necessary comforts for the traveler. They were sometimes frame buildings, with long capacious porches in front and rear. Others were built with a species of blue limestone, which, contrasting with the white mortar between the blocks, and the white window frames and green Venetian shutters, produced a pleasing effect, and formed solid and substantial structures. On the opposite side of the road were usually placed the spacious stables, sheds, and other out-buildings required for the accommodation of teamsters; and, near at hand, was the immense wooden trough, into which poured constantly, from a hydrant, a stream of pure water, carried under the ground in wooden pipes from a spring upon the side of the neighboring hill. As the hotel stood back some distance from the road, abundant room was left, in the wide recess, thus formed for the wagons and other vehicles, from which the horses were disengaged. The interior of the hotel itself was usually plain, but commodious—a bar-room, connected with a dining room, and this with the kitchen, on one side of a wide hall; and, upon the other, the parlors for the better sort of guests. These were entirely covered with carpeting of domestic manufacture. At other times, only the middle portions were thus covered, the rest of the floor being strewed with white sand, arranged in curving lines and forming various patterns, according to the taste of the tidy hostess. In some cases, the white sand was used as an entire substitute for carpeting, and gritted unpleasantly beneath the feet. Above stairs were usually the comfortable sleeping apartments. At this period hotels of this character could be found every ten or twenty miles . . ."

When they were about three days' journey from Washington, Thomas Campbell's family stopped for the night at just such an inn. He himself slept at another, to the west of them. Early in the morning he started on and met his family a short while after he left the inn. He "kissed and embraced them all with the utmost tenderness. When Jane was presented to him, so much changed in appearance by the effect of the small-pox that he would not have recognized her, he said, as he took her into his arms, 'And is this my little white-head?' a phrase of endearment amongst the Irish, and kissing her affectionately, gave thanks to God for her recovery."

All that day, and the next, and the next, they talked. He told them about the wilderness they were coming to, and they told him about their voyages, and about Glasgow, and Mr. Ewing's kindness to them, and the last news they had had from home. At some point he got around to telling Alexander about the Declaration and Address, but he could not do this without also explaining the circumstances in which they had been written. Leaving out as much as possible of the animosity he had met with—for he wanted his family to like their new home—he presented rather fully the background of his withdrawal from the Seceder Church. As he did this, he was aware that Alexander kept opening his mouth as if there was something he wanted to say.

7

Thomas Campbell sent a copy of the Declaration and Address to ministers of all denominations, and in an accompanying letter assured them he would thankfully receive written objections but that he did not want to enter into verbal controversy. There was no response whatever. No one was moved by or even interested in his plan for uniting the Christian churches with the Bible as the one broad basis for belief. However, the minister of the regular Presbyterian Church in Upper Buffalo encouraged the Christian Association of Washington to think that the Synod of Pittsburgh would accept them into that branch of the Presbyterian Church on the principles they advocated. It was a good deal to hope for, but Thomas Campbell did not want to start a new church when there were already so many, so he tried to believe that it was possible. Their application was curtly rejected, and they constituted themselves a separate denomination consisting of one small country church at Brush Run, Pennsylvania, with thirty members. Thomas Campbell was chosen elder, there were four deacons, and Alexander was licensed to preach.

He preached his first sermon from a stand in a grove of maple trees on a farm eight miles from Washington. His audience was sitting on rough planks or on the grass. "He was now in his twenty-second year," Richardson says, "still preserving the freshness of complexion and bloom of the cheeks with which he had left Ireland," but he had grown taller, and his frame had filled out; it wasn't a boy who was speaking to them. In the beginning he betrayed a certain nervousness, but it soon left him and his clear ringing voice resounded through the grove as he recounted—not as if he were speaking of a parable from the New Testament but as if it were a fact—how the wise man built his house upon a rock but the foolish man built his house on the sands.

"Afterward the young gazed upon the youth with wondering eyes, and the older members said to one another in subdued tones, 'Why, this is a better preacher than his father!' " This opinion probably ought to be taken as the expression of excessive amiability and enthusiasm. In time he was a better preacher than his father.

During the next twelve months he preached on a hundred and six occasions. He was trained by his father in the form that must be followed. There must be no violation of the rules of logic and rhetoric. The precepts should be truly those of the text, and there should be no distortion of it through failure to consider the verses that came before and after. There should be no fanciful interpretations or farfetched applications, and the sermon itself must not go beyond the range of the ideas in the text. When I think of them sitting side by side at a rude table in the backwoods of Pennsylvania, with the Bible and the Concordance open before them, and pen and ink and paper, I think of another scene that is superficially quite different but in essence identical: In Venice, in the Piazza San Marco, I saw a waiter showing his fifteen-year-old son—with the utmost professional seriousness and also with so much love that I felt obliged to look somewhere else—how the knife and fork should be placed and the only proper way to fold a napkin.

Working together over those first sermons, father and son must have come rather soon to a realization that their minds were different in certain fundamental ways. If Thomas Campbell was called upon to admire the view, he would politely express his admiration and the next moment be talk-

ing eloquently about the goodness of God and the salvation
of mankind. When somebody pointed out a flower to him,
he was likely to ask whether it had medicinal properties.
Richardson says that Alexander had an appreciation of the
beautiful, and especially of the grand, in both nature and
art; and he took great pleasure in sacred music, and was
visibly affected by it, though he was not very good at carrying a tune. He read and also wrote poetry:

> *When darkness o'er the deep extended lay,*
> *And night still reigned, unbounded yet by day;*
> *When awful stillness filled the boundless space,*
> *And wild confusion sat on Nature's face* . . .

For fiction, Richardson says, he had no taste whatever, and
in later years would "express his wonder that anyone could
take an interest in works of mere invention, such as ro-
mances, when they knew, perfectly well, that not one of the
things related had ever happened."

In Buffalo Valley lived a man named John Brown, who was
a carpenter and had a gristmill and a sawmill and a very fine
farm, and on it a comfortable two-story frame house where
Thomas Campbell was often made to feel welcome. Though
a Presbyterian, Mr. Brown had an independent and inquiring mind. He also had a childlike confidence in people he
trusted. Thomas Campbell sent some books to him by
Alexander, who had never been in that valley before, and
Mr. Brown took an immediate liking to him, and Alexander
was drawn not only to the carpenter but to his hazel-eyed
daughter, and eventually proposed to her. At morning
prayers, on the day after the wedding, Alexander's sister
Jane, who was then eleven years old, recited the last twenty-
two verses from the concluding chapter of the book of Pro-
verbs, which are a description of a model wife. Such the

bride turned out to be. The young couple lived with her father, and Alexander, who had had some experience of farming in his boyhood, threw himself into the work of spring plowing and planting. He had determined never to accept pay for his preaching, and was at this time without any means of support. But soon afterward the Christian Association of Washington, discouraged by the fact that they had failed to make any impression on the community, and somewhat infected, Richardson says, with the prevailing spirit of migration, considered removing to a place near Zanesville, Ohio. They didn't, largely because Alexander Campbell's father-in-law, not wanting his daughter to go so far away from him, deeded the farm to Alexander and so provided him with a home and a livelihood for the rest of his life.

After he put up a hundred panels of rail fence with his own hands in one day, the neighbors did not look down on him for being a scholar and a preacher. "No one could be more observant of the duties of social life," Richardson says "or more careful to maintain the most agreeable relation with all his neighbors, than Mr. Campbell. . . . Full of the vivacity and wit belonging to the Irish character, and ever cheerful as the morning light, his presence diffused an agreeable charm over the social life of the neighborhood." Even the religious prejudices of the Methodists and the Presbyterians "melted away under the influence of personal acquaintance."

Of Alexander Campbell's vivacity and wit, some written examples have survived. When he first came to America he wrote, and published in a weekly newspaper, a series of ten essays, using the pen name of "Clarinda." In the second, after describing a moment of general silence such as in my childhood always produced the remark, "It must be twenty minutes of or twenty minutes after," he goes on to say, "when one of those chasms occurs in conversation, when invention is on the rack, you will observe that the person who speaks begins by telling you (as if you did not know) something about the weather. You will also observe that when one has broken silençe in this way, there arises a general chatter among the rest, as when one goose of a flock chatters all the rest begin. When I am a spectator at these gabbling matches, the Turkish maxim comes into my mind, namely, that 'women have no souls,' and although this sentiment shocks me and causes me to search my own breast, yet frequently I must confess, if I were to judge from the frivolity of the conversation and the levity of the sentiment at these parties, I must conclude that female minds are not capacious." And six sentences farther on, there is a smell of smoke and brimstone. "Will it be comfortable for you to say when you are bidding an eternal adieu to the world, I have spent many a *precious evening* in a genteel party, many an hour in giddy dissipation, in thoughtless mirth, in needless festivity? At some distant, far distant point in eternity, will you remember with joy or with sorrow that you spent an evening once a week, or once a month, for, it may be, then, twenty, or thirty years, in one of these parties which you now so much like? Ah, my female friends, did you but consider the value and dignity of your nature" and so on.

The opinions and prose style of a young man of twenty-one ought not, I suppose, be held against him. Thirty-nine years later, when asked whether people who attend dances, theaters, the Thespian Society, or who indulge in chess, backgammon, or draughts should be allowed to stay in the church, he replied, in the *Millennial Harbinger*, that these were the works of the Devil and all who delighted in such amusements were not fit for the Kingdom of God.

The whole history of the Christian Church hangs on a conversation the young Alexander Campbell had with a rather

disagreeable Presbyterian minister. They had met accidentally, and it was probably Alexander and not the minister
who brought up the matter of the Declaration and Address.
They found themselves discussing article 3, which states
that nothing should be required either as an article of faith
or as a term of communion but what is expressly taught and
enjoined in the Word of God.

"Sir," the minister said, "these words, however plausible
in appearance, are not sound. For if you follow them out,
you must become a Baptist."

"'Why, sir," Alexander replied, "is there in the Scriptures no express precept or precedent for infant baptism?'"

"Not one, sir," said the minister.

When Alexander found that he could not refute this statement, he asked Alexander Munro the bookseller to furnish
him with all the books he had that dealt favorably with
infant baptism. He went through them and was disgusted
by their fallacious reasoning. Turning to the Greek New
Testament he found no support there either.

He spoke to his father about the matter and his father
said, as always, that whatever was not found in the Bible
they must of course abandon. Alexander was not ready to let
the question drop. He could not bear uncertainty. He would
have liked to believe in the claims of infant baptism, but the
more he read, the more convinced he became that it was a
human invention. His father said, "For those who are already members of the church and participants of the Lord's
Supper, I can see no propriety, even if the scriptural evidence for infant baptism be found deficient, in their un-
churching themselves, or in putting off Christ, merely for the
sake of making a new profession; thus going out of the
church merely for the sake of coming in again."

Infant baptism had already on one occasion made Thomas
Campbell lose his temper. Riding along beside James Foster,
one of his deacons, he remarked that though there was no

mention of paedobaptism in the New Testament, it was a concession that, for the sake of Christian union, he was willing to make. Turning to him, James Foster said, "Father Campbell, how could you, in the absence of any authority in the word of God, baptize a child in the name of the Father, and of the Son, and of the Holy Spirit?" Whereupon Thomas Campbell grew red in the face and said, "Sir, you are the most intractable man I ever met!"

With respect to the proper form of baptism, Thomas Campbell was of the opinion that there was no question but that immersion was the action meant. "Water is water," he said, "and earth is earth. We certainly could not call a person buried in earth if only a little dust were sprinkled on him." But that did not mean that a person who had been sprinkled should consider himself a pagan. And he recommended that, since it had nothing to do with essential faith and therefore was not a doctrine of the first importance, it be left a matter of forbearance.

When three members of his following who had never been baptized asked him to immerse them he consented. Standing on a root that projected out over a deep pool, he said, "In the name of the Father," etc., and pushed their heads under. James Foster was present and didn't approve either of the manner of the baptism or of the fact that someone who had not himself been immersed should undertake to immerse others.

Out of respect for his father's feelings, Alexander Campbell agreed to let the question of infant baptism alone. But when his first child was born, he was no longer content to abide by mere expediency: There was the child's soul to consider. His wife and father-in-law were both members of the Presbyterian Church, whose position it was that a child who dies unbaptized is eternally damned. He applied himself to the Scriptures once more, and came to the conclusion that "the sprinkling of infants does not constitute baptism"

because the word *baptism* in Greek could only mean immersion, and furthermore only those who believed in Jesus
Christ as the Son of God was it proper to baptize. So his own
baptism in infancy was the application of an unauthorized
form to an incompetent subject.

Richardson does not say what conclusion Mrs. Campbell
came to with regard to the baptism of their child.

Dorothea Campbell confided to her brother that she was
greatly troubled about her own baptism, which had occurred in infancy, and had taken the form of sprinkling,
and she begged him to speak to their father on her behalf.
He did. But first he arranged with a Baptist minister who
lived nearby to come and baptize him and his wife and sister,
and only then did he reveal to his father that he had come to
the conclusion that the form of baptism *was* a matter of the
first importance, and that he was about to be immersed. To
his surprise, his father had very little to say. Thomas Campbell stated his own position once more, and then said, "I
have no more to add. You must please yourself." But in view
of the position they occupied in the movement it was only
right, he said, that Alexander should make a public announcement and that the baptism should take place in the
presence of the people they preached to.

The next day, when the minister arrived, Thomas Campbell remarked that his wife was bringing a change of clothing
for herself and him, and that was the first anybody knew that
he had changed his mind and was going to be immersed with
the others.

On the riverbank, before a large gathering, he reviewed
his past and present opinions about baptism at length, and
when he sat down Alexander stood up. Together, they spoke
for seven hours. Very likely the Baptist minister had something to say also. In the end they all went into the water,
and the movement was in trouble from then on.

·   ·   ·

In 1836, Alexander Campbell, "though of the opinion that the science of phrenology is but in progress and not yet perfected," allowed his head to be studied. In the scale of numbers, 20 represents the highest possible development.

"Skull, thin; frontal sinuses rather full; temperament, nervo-sanguinous. Amativeness, 16; Philoprogenitiveness, 18; Concentrativeness, 18; Constructiveness, 14; Destructiveness, 17; Combativeness, 16; Secretiveness, 15; Firmness, 19; Self-esteem, 15; Love of Approbation, 14; Cautiousness, 16; Conscientiousness, 20; Hope, 12; Veneration, 13; Wonder, 10; Adhesiveness, 13; Acquisitiveness, 16; Ideality, 18; Causality, 17; Comparison, 20; Mirthfulness, 15; Tune, 11; Time, 12; Locality, 20; First Individuality, 18; Second Individuality, 14; Form, 16; Color, 12; Size, 17; Weight, 18; Method, 20; Language, 18; Eventuality, 14; Imitation, 17; Benevolence, 19."

This reading is on the whole, I should think, quite accurate.

By insisting that immersion was the only form of baptism sanctioned by the Scriptures (a belief shared only by the Baptists), Alexander Campbell narrowed the field to a point where there was no one the new movement *could* join but the Baptists. After many discussions, the Brush Run church managed to get itself accepted into an association of Baptist churches ("provided always that we should be allowed to teach and preach whatever we learned from the Holy Scripture, regardless of any human creed"—in short they were willing to join the Baptists but did not intend to be indistinguishable from them) and this connection lasted seventeen years.

They got on badly.

I don't mean to slight in any way the combativeness and self-esteem of the Baptists, but it was largely Alexander's doing. He accused the Protestant clergy in general of being proud, pretentious, covetous, interested in advancing their own personal ends, given to affectations of piety and professional mannerisms of speech and dress, to setting themselves above their brethren. "Amongst the Baptists," he wrote, "it is to be hoped there are but few *clergy*, and would to God there were none!"

He attacked Bible societies, all ecclesiastical structures, synods, presbyteries, conferences, and assemblies. He denounced all creeds—and the Redstone Baptist Association, which the Brush Run church had just joined, subscribed to the Westminster Confession. He said there were no missionary societies in the first century, there could be no missionary societies now. Organs were not used in public worship in the churches of Jerusalem and Corinth. They were "founded on the Jewish pattern of things" and in the same general category as the sprinkling of infants. The unimmersed must not be admitted to communion.

He had begun to publish a small magazine, the *Christian Baptist*, which all the denominations found annoying, but the Baptists most of all, for they were being criticized from within. He said, referring to the poor Baptists, "I intend to continue in connection with this people so long as they permit me to say what I believe, to teach what I am assured of, and to censure what is amiss in their views and practises." He described the unity of the early Christians in their simple obedience to and faith in Christ, and then went on to quote Jeremiah 1:10—"See, I have this day set thee over the nations, to root out, and to pull down, and to destroy, and to throw down, to build, to plant."

Among the laity his preaching was very popular. His sermons were clear, and his approach to all religious questions was essentially rational and practical. His audience felt that they were on solid ground, even when with the greatest frankness he was cutting the ground out from under their feet—which he did regularly.

He didn't stick to his own churches but made preaching trips twice a year among the Baptist churches, from which he couldn't be excluded because he was a member in good standing of the Redstone Baptist Association. He raised a thousand dollars and built a Reformer church in what was considered Baptist territory. He brought out a new translation of the Bible.

The committee in charge of the annual meeting of the Redstone Association tried to keep him off the program, but there was a vacancy at the last minute and they gave way to pressure and had to sit and listen to him hacking away at the Ten Commandments.

He was a more aggressive and disputatious preacher than any the Baptists had, and his position on baptism was sound, so when a Presbyterian minister of Mount Pleasant, Ohio, issued a general challenge to debate on this subject, the Baptists invited Alexander Campbell to represent them, and, putting aside his "natural aversion to controversy," he did. Unfortunately he would not stick to the subject. Or rather, he enlarged the area of reference so as to include his views on the degree to which, and in what ways, and on whom the laws of the Old and the New Testament were binding. The laws of the Old Testament applied only to the Jews, he said, and had failed; with the coming of Christ, God made a new covenant that was radically different in principle and content and that applied to the whole human race. This was not what the Baptists had in mind when they invited him to represent them, and neither did they agree with what he said. To imply that the Mosaic Law was obsolete was surely antinomianism. But it was generally agreed that he had triumphed gloriously over his opponent.

Though he took part in only five debates, in each instance he used the occasion to clarify his position on important matters of faith and doctrine, and so the Walker debate, the Maccala debate, the Purcell debate, and the rest, were constantly referred to by his followers and stand like so many signposts indicating where the church was going. The debate that achieved the most notoriety was with the reformer and philanthropist, Robert Owen, and took place in Cincinnati, in the spring of 1829, in a Methodist meetinghouse, before an audience of a thousand persons. Mrs. Trollope was present. Around the pulpit, she says, there was a small stage, large enough to accommodate Owen and Alexander Campbell and two stenographers. "The pulpit was occupied by the aged father of Mr. Campbell, whose flowing white hair, and venerable countenance, constantly expressive of the deepest attention . . . made him a very striking figure of the group." On another platform—Mrs. Trollope doesn't say where—sat the seven moderators.

Her traveling companion, Auguste Hervieu, made a drawing of the interior of the meetinghouse that is reproduced in her book. In the foreground there is a row of large-brimmed bonnets trimmed with ribbon and ostrich feathers. Owen is on his feet, speaking, and looks rather like a member of the Pickwick Club. Alexander Campbell, with a book in his hand, is listening intently to his opponent's argument, and Thomas Campbell's head is seen over the top of the pulpit, faintly drawn, and unearthly.

The debate lasted through fifteen sittings, and Mrs. Trollope was struck with the fact that neither Alexander Campbell nor Owen ever appeared to lose their tempers. "I was told that they were much in each other's company, constantly dining together. . . . All this I think could only have happened in America."

Owen undertook to prove that religions are founded on ignorance and fear, that they are in conflict with unchanging natural laws, and that the entire history of Christianity was a fraud. An excited speaker saying the same things might have been tarred and feathered, but Owen's tone of voice was so gentle, his manner so candid and mild, he showed such affectionate concern for "the whole human family" and his smile was so genuinely kind that the audience simply listened.

When a half hour had passed, the moderators looked meaningly at their watches, and Owen then looked at his, smiled, said "A moment's patience," and continued speaking for another half hour.

Mrs. Trollope found Alexander Campbell's person, voice, and manner all greatly in his favor. His watch, she said, was "the only one which reminded us that we had listened to him for half an hour; and having continued speaking a few minutes after he had looked at it, he sat down, with, I should think, the universal admiration of his auditory."

Owen read a two-hundred-page manuscript largely devoted to what he called the twelve fundamental "facts" or laws of human nature. To Mrs. Trollope they appeared "twelve truisms that no man in his senses would think of contradicting; . . . how he can have dreamed that they could be twisted into a refutation of the Christian religion, is a mystery which I never expect to understand."

Owen entrenched himself behind his twelve laws, which Alexander Campbell said applied equally well to a goat, and he in turn confined himself to quoting one theological authority after another as evidence of the truth of revealed religion. Neither one ever seriously attempted to answer the arguments of the other. As soon as Owen had finished reading his manuscript he conceded to his opponent the privilege of speaking uninterruptedly, and Alexander Campbell completed the course of his argument in a speech that went on—with adjournments—for twelve hours. Four or five sentences are perhaps enough to suggest what his manner of speaking was like when he closed his books and trusted to himself: "Whatever comes from religion comes from God. The greatest joys derivable to mortal man come from this source. I cannot speak of all who wear the Christian name, but for myself, I must say that worlds piled on worlds, to fill the universal scope of my imagination, would be a miserable per contra against the annihilation of the idea of God the Supreme. And the paradox of paradoxes, the miracle of miracles and the mystery of mysteries with me, was, is now, and evermore shall be, *how any good man could wish there were no God!* . . . Everything within us and everything without, from the nails upon the ends of our fingers to the sun, moon, and stars, confirm the idea of his existence and adorable excellences."

In following Alexander on the arguable question of immersion, Thomas Campbell, in effect, handed the leadership of the movement over to his son. He himself was approaching fifty, with a large family to support, and his heart was not in creating a new church but in uniting all the existing ones, which more and more appeared to be an impossibility. So he kept drifting away—to Cambridge, Ohio, ninety miles to the west, and then to Pittsburgh, where he opened a school, and eventually to Kentucky, where he started another. It was ten years before he came back to the neighborhood where the movement originated. Not very much had happened in the meantime. The ideas of the Brush Run church had been accepted by four other small congregations, two in Brooke County, Virginia, one in Harrison County, Ohio, and one in Guernsey County, also in Ohio. At every annual meeting of the Redstone Association, charges of heresy were brought against Alexander Campbell and voted down. And when at last his opponents believed they had mustered enough votes to bring about his removal, they discovered that they couldn't get at him: He had taken the five Reformer congregations out of the Baptist association, and they weren't a part of any other.

His fame as a preacher had spread throughout the countryside, but all told there were no more than two hundred members in the five congregations. Then there was a great change, which came about through the ideas and efforts of a young man named Walter Scott. The son of a music teacher with ten children, Scott attended the University of Edinburgh. His name is so common in Scotland that it has not been possible to discover whether he received a degree. When he was twenty-one years old, he came to America at the suggestion of an uncle in the New York Customs office. A year later, he and a friend walked to Pittsburgh, admiring the scenery and, very often, in a state of extreme merriment at what they saw along the way. On arriving at Pittsburgh, Scott took himself to task for behavior incompatible with the gravity and solemnity of a Presbyterian, and there is no record that he was ever funny again.

He became an instructor in a school conducted by a fellow countryman who was a Kissing Baptist, and he ended up running the school and preaching. He was something of an oddity, with many of the attributes of a poet—timid, diffident, delighting in comparisons. Through his reading Scott had arrived at a position so near that of Alexander Campbell that when they met they were immediately congenial. The congeniality seems to have been enforced rather than inhibited by temperamental differences. Scott wrote a number of articles for the *Christian Baptist,* and when he moved to Steubenville, Ohio, the two men were, in a manner of speaking, neighbors. By this time the five Reformer congregations had been accepted into the Mahoning Baptist Association. As a roving evangelist for this group of churches, Scott worked out an entirely new approach to religious conversion. There were three things, he said, for man to do: "He must believe, upon the evidence, that Jesus is the Messiah, the Son of God; he must repent of his personal sins with godly sorrow and resolve to sin no more; and he must be baptised." After which God would, according to His promises, deliver man from the guilt, power, and penalty of his repented sins; bestow the gift of the Holy Spirit; and grant eternal life.

The response to this blending of rationality and authority was spectacular. "Mr. Scott," Richardson says, "fully conscious of the momentous nature of the issues he had evoked, but confident in the power of the gospel and all aflame with zeal, passed rapidly, like a meteor, throughout the Western Reserve, startling the people by the abruptness and directness of his appeals, but exciting many to enquiry and obedience."

The year before his appointment there had been thirty-four baptisms, thirteen additions otherwise, and thirteen brethren had been excommunicated. During the next twelve months, Scott baptized over a thousand people, and the number of churches in the association doubled. It was, of course, what they wanted, but it was also much more than they had had any expectation of, and at first they were doubtful. Rumors and misrepresentations spread, and Thomas Campbell, fearing that Scott's precipitate nature had betrayed him into indiscretions which might be prejudicial to the cause, came to examine for himself how things were, and could only admire what he saw. The Baptists did not admire what they saw, and threw the Reformers out—the phrase is perhaps too strong to describe an event that occurred over a period of years and resulted from actions by both sides—that is, it was both a withdrawing and a rejecting. But anyway, this separation did not hurt the cause of the Reformers. A minor religious movement had become a major one, and nothing could stop it.

The debates and the *Christian Baptist* had made Alexander Campbell's ideas known in Kentucky, and in 1823 he came there himself to debate with a Presbyterian minister on the subject of infant baptism. The debate stirred up so much excitement that Campbell returned the following year for a three-month speaking tour. Barton Stone went again and again to hear him and concluded that the Reformers were, in all but three or four rather minor points, in exact agreement with the Christian Church. In his autobiography, after knowing Alexander Campbell for roughly fifteen years, he wrote: "I will not say there are no faults in brother Campbell; but there are fewer, perhaps, in him, than in any man I know on earth; and over these few my love would throw a veil, and hide them forever."

Disconcertingly, the all but faultless man published a pamphlet entitled "Strictures on 'Two Letters' of B. W. Stone on Atonement," in which he accused Stone of denying the Lord that made him, of being an apostate, of uniting with errorists and deists of every age, to destroy the sheet anchor of the Christian's hope.

Stone was used to being called names, and he reconsidered his position on the Atonement and moved closer to Alexander Campbell's, and forgave the harsh words, which were part of the usual rhetoric of pamphleteering.

For eight years Alexander Campbell continually made overtures to the Christians and to Stone, and the two movements slowly moved together.

Among the things they differed over was the Reformers' insistence that immersion should be a condition of membership in the church. Barton Stone said, "As well might we forbid unimmersed persons to pray, to praise, to teach, as to forbid them to commune. . . . What authority have we for inviting or debarring any pious, holy believer from the Lord's table." Richardson says, "Mr. Campbell had formerly expressed sentiments precisely similar, but a fuller comprehension of the relations of baptism to the regeneration and the remission of sins had latterly inclined him to stricter views. He dreaded even the appearance of setting aside any divine institution, or of assuming to judge of men by their supposed *sincerity* rather than by their actual *obedience* to the word of God."

Though the Christians could not bring themselves to exclude the unimmersed from communion, they stopped going out of their way to invite them and instead let every person examine himself regarding his fitness, and this seems to have satisfied the Reformers.

Ministers of both movements met for four days in Georgetown, Kentucky, and a week later, at Lexington, on New Year's Day, 1832, where Stone spoke in favor of the merger. Since there was no hierarchical structure in either movement, they could not unite by a single decision. What happened was that competing congregations of Disciples and Christians in a given community would agree to merge and make common cause, and, as they took in new members through their evangelistic efforts, the division was more and more lost sight of.

In 1834, Stone moved to Jacksonville, Illinois, where he found a Christian church and a Disciple church, and he refused to join either until they united. Only a small number of Christian churches failed to unite with the Reformers. They ended up as the Christian Denomination.

Thomas Campbell and Stone preferred that the united movement be called the Christian Church, and Alexander admitted that the name was proper and appropriate and only wished that all were worthy of it, but preferred "disciple" as more humble and more often used in the New Testament.

Both names are in use to this day. My grandmother always said the Christian Church, and so that name seems more natural to me. Under one name or the other the new religion spread rapidly. From Kentucky the pioneers streamed out into other states—into Ohio, Indiana, Illinois, Missouri, and Iowa—taking the new church with them. By 1842 it had reached Texas, and the following year it arrived in Oregon, in a wagon train from Missouri, causing an angry churchman to exclaim, "The Campbellites and the fern are taking the Willamette Valley!"

8

The only history of the Christian Church in Illinois is not
the work of a professional historian but of a minister who
was assigned the task by a committee appointed by the State
Board of the Illinois Christian Missionary Society. It was
written between 1912 and 1914, by which time nearly all
the pioneers were dead and the records of many of the older
congregations had disappeared, but the main hindrance, the
author says, was "the lack of appreciation by very many of
such a volume and their consequent indifference to its
preparation." Each congregation has anywhere from two
sentences to two or three pages devoted to it, and there is
no effort at literary style, but it has, nevertheless, a tone I
recognize from my childhood—the pleasure that comes
from allowing oneself to correct other people's mistakes.

"In this work," the author says, "preachers are not called
'elders' but ministers. Some ministers are elders but all cannot be; hence, as a general designation, it is wrong. . . . A
true preacher is a servant of Christ, and this relation and its
consequent obligations are Scripturally expressed by the
word 'minister.' If an abbreviation is needed, 'Min.' is
easily written and is so used herein. Nor are preachers
termed 'clergymen,' since the Spirit calls the Lord's 'flock'
his clergy or inheritance. The title 'Reverend' and its con-
traction 'Rev.' are also avoided. By the mouth of David the
Lord says 'his name is holy and reverend,' and it is not be-
fitting that we so denote ourselves. If this title, which has
become in recent years so glibly prevalent among the Dis-

ciples of Christ, is to be used and recognized, then why not 'Very Reverend' and 'Most Reverend,' and so on up the scale to the climax of wicked assumption?"

Barton Stone died in 1844, Thomas Campbell in 1854, Scott in 1861, and Alexander Campbell in 1866. The second and third generations of ministers in the Christian Church were not university men like the founders and did not have anything like as much knowledge, scriptural or otherwise, to impart. What they did have was fervor.

The name of Hughes Bowles turns up more frequently than any other in the sparse records of the early period of the church in Illinois. He came from Kentucky in 1830, married twice, and was the father of twelve children. "He was a kind and sympathetic man, but very positive. . . . He was well versed in the Scriptures and could almost quote the New Testament from beginning to end. Members of his family maintained the farm of two hundred acres while the father gave his time to preaching the gospel. His trips were made on horseback and reached from ten to fifty miles. The storms of the winters, the miry sloughs and swollen streams of the springs and early summers frequently challenged the faith and courage of the itinerant preachers. But Mr. Bowles seldom missed an appointment." The largest sum of money he ever received at one time was ten dollars, for his services at a protracted meeting that lasted two weeks, and this he gave to a poor widow, who had been thrown from her horse and injured while on her way to the meeting.

And here is his son, Watt Bowles, who was a friend of Abraham Lincoln: "In plowing time he would work in his fields Saturdays till 11 o'clock a.m., then come to his house. Then he would whet his razor on his boot-leg, hone it on the palm of his left hand, and shave his face clean and smooth without the aid of a mirror; then grease his boots, wash up and redress; after eating his dinner, he would saddle his horse and gallop away ten to thirty miles and preach Saturday night and Sunday in a residence or schoolhouse to fifteen or more people. For this work he received not a dollar. His reward was the sweet consciousness of duty well done and that God was pleased."

Hughes Bowles and his son Watt were simple-hearted, self-educated men who had passionately embraced the idea that God has revealed to each of us his whole duty, in plain unmistakable terms, and that the Bible contains rules sufficient for every good work. But it was becoming much less easy to adhere to the patterns of primitive Christianity in a period that was so rapidly leaving behind the virtues and vices of—and in fact all resemblance to—a primitive society (that is to say, a society where people live by the labor of their hands). More and more the Disciples of Christ found themselves faced with situations a careful reading of the Bible did not throw any light on whatever.

Within the body of the church, one group (in the end, the prevailing one) tended to be open-minded and reasonable, and to tolerate a variety of opinion. The other group viewed any change as an innovation and was fanatically opposed to it.

What is the point of tolerating a variety of opinions if only one is true and all the others are errors? "An unimmersed person may be eminently good and pious," a church quarterly for the year 1865 states, "but he is not a Christian; God may esteem him very highly, much more so than many of the immersed, and even very certainly save him, but he is not a Christian."

And another quarterly says, "Let us agree to commune with the sprinkled sects around us and soon we shall come to recognize them as Christians, and immersion, with its deep significance, is buried in the grave of our folly. Then in not one whit will we be better than the others. Let us countenance political charlatans as preachers, and we at once become corrupt as the loathsome nest on which Beecher sets to hatch the things he calls Christians. . . . Let us agree to admit organs, and soon the pious, the meek, the peace-loving, will abandon us, and our churches will become gay worldly things, literal Noah's arks, full of clean and unclean beasts. To all this to us let add, by way of dessert, and as a sort of spice to the dish, a few volumes of inner-light speculations, and a cargo or two of reverend dandies dubbed pastors, and we may congratulate ourselves on having completed the trip in a wonderfully short time. We can now take rooms in Rome, and chuckle over the fact that we are as orthodox as the rankest heretic in the land."

At the point at which I began to have a general working knowledge of persons, places, and things—that is to say, about 1912—Lincoln was a modestly flourishing county seat that seemed to have been there forever. It was not even very old, though it did have the air of being deeper in the shadow of the past than many of the towns around it. Nothing of any historical importance had ever happened there, or has to this day.

There was an older village named Postville, which the town of Lincoln absorbed. It was laid out in the eighteen-thirties by a Baltimore adventurer. He was caught in the financial panic of 1837, and the buildings and lots went at a forced sale for a tenth of their expected value. When the county was organized, two years later, Postville, with a population of about a hundred persons, became the first county seat. It also became a regular stopping place for stages on the direct road from St. Louis to Chicago when Chicago was still a village. It was a lively place, with a post office, a jail, an inn, and stores, all built around the courthouse square.

Nearby there was a sizable pond for watering stock and for skating on in winter.

When I was thirteen I had a newspaper route that consisted of thirteen houses in this shabby part of town. Riding along on my bicycle, I used to send a folded copy of the Lincoln *Evening Courier* sailing in the general direction of the front door of an unpainted two-story frame building that I knew had once been used as a courthouse. A Negro family lived in it, which seemed only proper since The Great Emancipator had practiced law there. But still, it wasn't as interesting as it ought to have been. What was missing was this (I am quoting from *The History of Sangamon County*): "we sauntered into the courthouse. The court was in session, and a case was then in progress. . . . Upon the bench was seated the judge, with his chair tilted back and his heel as high as his head, and in his mouth a veritable corn cob pipe; his hair standing nine ways for Sunday, while his clothing was more like that worn by a woodchopper than anybody else. There was a railing that divided the audience outside, of which smoking and spitting and chewing of tobacco seemed to be the principle employment." Which is not to say that there was no such thing as good manners. The fourth governor of the State of Illinois was a man named John Reynolds, who for a time was judge of the circuit court of his county. He was not polished, but he was very polite. When he had to pronounce a sentence of death on a man found guilty of murder, he said to him, "Mr. Green, the jury in their verdict say you are guilty of murder, and the law says you are to be hung. Now, I want you and your friends down on Indian Creek to know that it is not I, but the jury and the law who condemn you. When would you like to be hung?"

Of all this, only the courthouse was left in my childhood. Postville had the misfortune to be a mile from the railroad. Because Abraham Lincoln practiced law in the old courthouse, Henry Ford bought it in 1929, for $10,000, and carried it off to his museum in Ft. Dearborn. Where it stood there is now a replica, built by the town fathers.

After the farmers came and spoiled the land for the trappers and hunters by staking out homesteads everywhere, as far as the eye could see, there was a new general wave of men, brought up in towns and looking for a situation that—if they were patient and sufficiently farsighted—would put money in their pockets.

In 1839, two Pennsylvania land speculators, Isaac and Joseph Loose, acquired title from the Federal Government to a quarter section of land in central Illinois in what had just become Logan County. They paid $200 for it, without ever seeing it, and eventually one of them sold his share to the other. Until the coming of the railroads, the settlements were nearly always on the streams, in the shelter of the timber, and this quarter section was marshy, unbroken ground. The great-grandfather of a boy I went to school with, riding over it some time in the 1830's, roused a herd of forty deer.

During the summer of 1852, the Chicago and Mississippi Railroad was being extended north from Springfield to Bloomington, and the survey ran diagonally through Logan County. Abraham Lincoln was the railroad attorney; after a term in the House of Representatives, he was again practicing law in Springfield. One of the directors, Virgil Hickox, a friend of Stephen A. Douglas and for twenty years the head of the Democratic party in Illinois, had the job of securing the right of way. It was mostly done by condemnation proceedings, which the sheriff had to carry out. The sheriff of Logan County at this time was a young man named Robert B. Latham, who owned a great deal of land in the county and was also speculating in it with a partner whose name was John D. Gillett. A not negligible part of the whole arrangement was the chief engineer's promise that Latham would have the choosing of a station, for the railroad needed a watering and fuel stop halfway between Springfield and Bloomington. Knowing that the quarter township owned by Isaac Loose lay along the right of way, Latham went to Pennsylvania in February, 1853, and bought it from him for $1,350. He then gave a two-thirds interest in it to Hickox and Gillett in exchange for their financial backing. Abraham Lincoln drew up the documents establishing the joint ownership of the land and, when it had been surveyed, contracts for the sale of lots. The townsite was named after him, though somewhat against his advice. What he said was that he never knew anything named Lincoln that amounted to much. The streets of the new town were laid out parallel to the railroad instead of according to the cardinal points, and the proceeds of the sale of lots amounted to $6,000. During the sale, Lincoln walked around inspecting the lots, and remarked that they were cheap and desirable but that he couldn't afford to buy. Four years later he ended up owning one, even so. He went on somebody's note, as people were always doing in those days, and when the note came due the borrower couldn't pay off the loan and Lincoln had to. He was given the lot in compensation.

According to the *History of the Disciples of Christ in Illinois,* John England, the brother of my great-great-grandfather, David England, and the son of the pioneer preacher, Stephen England, "preached the gospel in various parts of Logan County in the forties and early fifties." He was born in Kentucky in 1811, and grew up in Illinois before there were any schoolhouses, so he was a man of limited education. He became a blacksmith, then a wagon maker, then a farmer, and finally a preacher, like his father. And while preaching he farmed a hundred and forty acres in Logan County. He had conscientious scruples about taking money for preaching, and was always afraid in his business deals that he would get the better of the other person. His son said of him, "If, in the evening, the topic of conversation would run upon anything of a financial character, in five to ten minutes he would be sleeping; but if there would be anything said pertaining to the Scriptures and the life beyond, he would be standing on his feet talking. He never seemed to be the least tired or skeptical about his hope for the future world."

At one time there were seven Christian churches here and there in the county. A series of revival meetings on a farm near Lincoln resulted in the forming of a church, which at first met in a warehouse and other places, all in town. In 1854 the congregation of about thirty people built a chapel, and for years struggled to pay for it. When the courthouse burned down, the Circuit Court was held in this building. The church I went to with my Grandmother Maxwell was built during 1903–4. It had 605 members, the *History* says, and the value of the church property, including the parsonage, was $29,000. Toward the end of the account, which takes up a little more than a page, I was pleased to come upon this elegiac sentence: "Among those who did much for the church were John A. Simpson, R. C. Maxwell, H. O. Merry, and L. P. Hanger; they merit remembrance."

My Grandfather Maxwell taught school for the first six years after he married. During the next five he farmed. My Great-grandfather Turley had nine children who survived to maturity, and he gave each of them eighty acres of land. The farm he gave my grandmother was three miles from Lincoln. After working in the fields all day, my grandfather saddled the poor horse and rode into town and read law in the office of the most eminent member of the local bar, a man who made a practice of taking on certain odd cases that his confreres shied away from. A farmer accused of having carnal knowledge of his daughter or of buggering his animals would be defended by him, cleared, and relieved of his farm by way of legal payment. My grandfather also had a year of law school; there was a brand-new university in Lincoln—one not very large Victorian brick building is what it amounted to physically— and he went there. He was admitted to the bar in the spring of 1877, and then spent a year in the office of my maternal grandfather. As a child I used to think how nice it would have been if my two grandfathers had been law partners, but this was not a very sensible idea. They were both ardent Republicans, and honest men, and so far as I know, much esteemed by all who knew them, but my Grandfather Blinn was a member of the Buttercup Hunting and Fishing Club, he kept whiskey in the sideboard of the dining room, and it is quite possible he was a Unitarian. As partners, he and my Grandfather Maxwell could only have got on one another's nerves. But they were joined, after a fashion, in my older brother, who was given the first name of one and the middle name of the other,* and from an early age felt obliged to become a lawyer because his two grandfathers were.

In 1878, the year that my Grandfather Maxwell hung out his shingle, the town of Lincoln had roughly six thousand inhabitants, and it was already well-supplied with

* He was almost never called by either name. When he was a baby someone started calling him "Happy"—my Aunt Bert said she named him after Happy Hooligan in the funny papers; my Aunt Annette, my mother's younger sister, says it was because he had such a happy disposition. When two family stories do not agree, I tend to believe both of them. In any case, the name stuck.

lawyers, but what with one thing and another he managed. He was elected city attorney during the first year of his practice. At various times he was elected or appointed to the offices of public administrator of Logan County, township collector, township clerk, and justice of the peace. I have been told by an elderly member of the profession that he was a very competent office lawyer—that is, he examined abstracts, wrote wills, and was engaged in the probate practice.

They lived in a little one-story house on Pekin Street, directly behind the jail.

Though Alexander Campbell looked with disfavor on secret and fraternal orders, believing that the church was intended to do every good thing these societies could possibly do, my grandfather belonged to Glendower Lodge No. 45 of the Knights of Pythias, Lincoln Chapter No. 147, Lincoln Council No. 83, Constantine Commandery No. 51 —all in Lincoln. He was also a member of the Mohammed Temple Ancient Arabic Order Noble Mystic Shriners, and a thirty-third degree Mason, and member of the Oriental Consistory at Peoria, which was sixty miles away—in those days a considerable train ride from Lincoln. Though the number of lodges seems excessive now, it probably wasn't considered so then.

When my grandfather stopped farming and moved into town, he also moved into the middle class, taking his family with him. What this meant was that to their other concerns a new one was added—the concern for respectability—which I do not suppose was of much interest to those men and women who walked six or seven miles to hear somebody preach, and found their way home by the light of a piece of burning hickory bark. On Sunday morning, my grandmother kept my grandfather waiting while she ran a couple of long hatpins through her hat and adjusted her veil and buttoned her gloves. And then, with the church bells ringing, they walked a block and a half to the Christian church. Sitting in her pew, my grandmother did not give her attention so completely to the sermon that she didn't notice what Mrs. Spitley and Mrs. Holton were wearing. Certain things were necessary or she couldn't hold her head up.

In a place where everybody's life was an open book, my grandfather was counted among the respectable. He paid his bills as promptly as he was able, his four children were properly fed and clothed and educated, and there was some but apparently not very much money left over at the end of the week to put in the bank or the collection plate. The older children were born on that eighty-acre farm. My father was born in town.

In my grandfather's upright nature there was a vein of rigidity—of harshness even—that was no doubt inherited from his Scottish forebears. When my father was a little boy, he longed for a pair of copper-toed boots, such as he had seen other boys wear at school. My grandfather tried to discourage him, but my father kept on talking about those boots until he got them. They proved to be extremely uncomfortable, just as my grandfather had said, and after two or three days he hated the sight of them, but my grandfather made him wear them out. It is not something my father would have done to me.

For twenty years, my grandfather was an elder of the Christian church in Lincoln, and I have no doubt that the controversies that the Disciples of Christ were expending so much heat and energy on during this period were all thrashed out at the family dinner table, especially when some visiting preacher was bedded down on the couch in the parlor. It is questionable whether my Aunt Bert, with her delight in ribbons and bows, heard a word of what was said, but my father could not withdraw his attention so easily, and what he heard created a lasting impatience. His bent was toward whatever is practical, and he was neither persuaded by nor interested in the argument that because the church in Corinth in St. Paul's time did not have an organ, it could not be used in the Christian church in Lincoln. My grandmother, having no mind to speak of, bypassed all questions of doctrine and went right to the heart of the religion. She never stopped talking about immersion, or thinking about it. She kept track of who was and who wasn't. She had the makings of an evangelist.

My grandmother did not like being stuck away in that little one-story house behind the jail, and she nagged at my grandfather to sell the farm her father had given her and use the money to build a house in town. My grandfather did not think very much of this idea, but my grandmother was a mulish woman, though dear, and very little ever came of arguing with her. The land, after all, was hers. In the end, he did what she wanted.

All Middle Western houses of that period were dark and gloomy, and I have no reason to think that the house my grandparents built on Kickapoo Street was an exception. I used to ride past it sometimes on my bicycle, but I was never in it. It was large, for that time and that place, with a round tower on one corner and spiderwebs of carpenter's lace all around and even under the various porches. From an old photograph, it appears that the carpenter's lace and the lace curtains in the bay window were almost identical. Driving past the house when he was an old man, my father shook his head and remarked sadly, "That fretwork cost eighty acres of the finest land in Logan County!"

Without the income from the farm, and with four children to educate, my grandparents found they were living beyond their means. My father, lying in bed upstairs, heard his father and mother quarreling over money. It was the barbaric custom for dry goods stores, and no doubt other stores as well, to bill their customers *annually*. Night

after night, all through the month of January, my Grandfather Maxwell walked the floor with the shocking and
interminable statement from A. C. Boyd in his hand. "This
item of five yards dress material," he would begin, as if he
had my grandmother on the witness stand. "What *kind* of
dress material?" My grandmother didn't remember what
dress material she had charged on the twelfth of April of
the year before. My grandfather didn't see why she
wouldn't remember. "On the twenty-second you charged
seven spools of cotton thread. And ten days later there's
another charge for ten more. And seven yards of silk
braid . . . Does it ever occur to you when you are charging
all these things that a day will come when they have to be
paid for?" Though there were several possible answers to
this question, my grandmother was not the woman to give
voice to them. Instead she burst into tears, and perhaps
wished they were back in that little house behind the jail.
The next night it would begin all over again.

The house on Kickapoo Street passed out of the family
before I was born, but my Aunt Annette spent a night there
when she was a young woman and was outraged by an
electric bell that rang loudly all through the upstairs when
it was time to get up, and again when it was time to come
hurrying to the table, where, to her surprise, they had
steak for breakfast. Her mother—my Grandmother Blinn
—was a Kentuckian, and though she believed in the Life
Hereafter, she did everything in her power to make life on
this earth agreeable to her family and herself. When her
daughters married and started raising a family, all it meant,
really, was adding more leaves to the dining room table.
And people were never hurried to it; they came when they
were ready. It has occurred to me that the electric bell may
have served a purpose my Aunt Annette was not aware of
—that it was a piece of ritual magic, intended to keep

disaster away from the house. Other men may think, if they choose, that man is not born unto trouble as the sparks fly upward; orphans know better.

In his old age my father enchanted the Rotary Club with a speech which he titled "Memories of Lincoln Way Back When." Being rather proud of this success, he presented me with a carbon copy of the notes he spoke from.

He began by describing the town in his boyhood in the 1880's—the, for the most part, unpaved streets, the original courthouse and the hitching posts all around the courthouse square, the horse fountains, the volunteer fire department, the coal-oil lamps in the houses, and the outside privies. At this time the town of Lincoln was less than forty years old. Up and down the streets of the happy past my father went, locating defunct hotels and dancing academies, banks that had changed their names or failed, dry goods stores, livery stables, boarding houses, barber shops (colored and white), saloons, meat markets, jewelers, gents' furnishings, greenhouses, ice houses, brickyards and coal mines, the collar factory and the shooting gallery. He mentioned long-dead doctors and dentists, lawyers and judges, bankers and newspaper editors, the main Negro families of the town, the major social events of the years, the sports and the sporting characters. But not one church did he name, and not one preacher.

9

Nothing as splendid as the World's Columbian Exposition ever had happened in the Middle West before or has since. "For the first time cosmopolitanism visited the western world," Louis B. Fuller wrote; "for the first time woman publicly came into her own, for the first time on a grand scale, art was made vitally manifest to the American consciousness." And Theodore Dreiser wrote: "All at once and out of nothing, in this dingy city of six or seven hundred thousand which but a few years before had been a wilderness of wet grass and mud flats, and by this lake which but a hundred years before was but a lone silent waste, had now been reared this vast and harmonious collection of perfectly constructed and showy buildings, containing in their delightful interiors, the artistic, mechanical and scientific achievements of the world."

If only these showy buildings had been made of white marble—but they were made of staff, a material that looked like marble and was, unfortunately, impermanent. One building, the Palace of Fine Arts, was rebuilt afterwards in marble and still stands, in Jackson Park. Everything else is gone without a trace. The huge exhibition buildings, the thousands of statues proved to be no more substantial than the jets of the fountains and the shafts of colored light. But for a whole generation of Americans who had been trying to make up their minds between Victorian Gothic and Romanesque, an image was set, and they went about reproducing on a smaller scale in every town and city of the country the neo-classical style of those white buildings.

At some point in the summer of 1893 my Grandfather Maxwell took his family to Chicago. My father was fifteen, my Aunt Bert was seventeen, my Aunt Maybel nineteen, and my Uncle Charlie twenty-one. Putting various old photographs together, I see them moving in the immense crowd, clutching at each other's hand or coatsleeve, lest they be separated—one eye out for purse-snatchers and pick-pockets and the other for the artistic, mechanical, and scientific achievements of the world—and now and then, to their infinite amazement, coming face to face with somebody from home.

Later my grandparents went again. In my grandmother's scrapbook there is a postcard of the Electrical Building, in color. It is impossible to tell who the card is addressed to, my grandmother's flour-and-water paste having absorbed the writing on the other side. The message is on the front, in pencil, in my grandfather's even hand:

Mecca Hotel. Chicago, Illinois, 9.22.93
We are at the Mecca and having a nice time. Uncle Will and Aunt Etta Uncle Joe and Aunt Mary and Mr. Matthewson and Mrs. Matthewson are here. We go to the fair in day time and eat breakfast and supper and spend the evening together very pleasantly. We will leave here Sunday night for home. Weather cool. Hope you will watch after the house closely.

Your father,
Robt C. Maxwell

My guess is that it was addressed to my Uncle Charlie, who had just graduated from college with high honors and was reading law in his father's office.

· · ·

*With me, education and the formation of moral character
are identical expressions.* The words are Alexander Campbell's. The Disciples founded many schools here and there
around the country, and my Grandfather Maxwell was a
trustee of Eureka College, which took its ridiculous name
from the small town where it was located. He sent all four
of his children there. My father always spoke slightingly
of it; he would have preferred to go to the University of
Illinois. From my Aunt Maybel's references to it you
would have thought that Eureka College was the only
institution of higher learning. Her mind expressed itself
most naturally in mythological terms, and there was usually
just one of everything. While she was a student at Eureka
College she was the victim of an injustice that still rankled,
and that she would tell about every time the subject of Eureka College came up. If my father and my Aunt Bert were
present, they would join in, because the story was common
property. When my Uncle Charlie was a freshman, one of
his professors mispronounced a word in class and my Uncle
Charlie set him straight on it. Professor Hieronymous didn't
forgive him for this, nor did he forgive my Aunt Maybel,
when she came along two years later; nor my Aunt Bert, two
years after that; nor my father. He flunked all four of them
because my Uncle Charlie corrected him on the pronunci-
ation of a word. Judging by the photographs of my father
taken in college, he did not let this blight his life.

There are three of them in my grandmother's scrapbook:
My father with a black derby on the back of his head and a
huge football-game chrysanthemum in his buttonhole. My
father and three friends, in four-button suits, with their hats
tipped back and their hands on each other's shoulders and
their teeth clamped on half-smoked cigars, which are tilted
at a not quite convincing angle. My father with a girl. She is
wearing a shirtwaist and a boater, and is posed selfconsci-
ously, with one elbow on a property garden gate that has

climbing daisies on it. There is, naturally, no garden. My father is on the other side of the gate and holds a furled umbrella rakishly over his right shoulder. I never saw him hold an umbrella in that way. It must have been the photographer's idea. My father's other hand is in the pocket of his white flannel trousers. His leather belt is three inches wide, and he is wearing a white bow tie. The girl is gazing at my father with a look of unfocused mistrust. And he, with his easy, off-balance stance, his strong arms and wrists, his good shoulders and thick hair, his mysterious half-smile, is a creature of physical perfection.

He was not always like that. The earliest picture of him I know was taken when he was somewhere between seven and nine years old. I recognize the shape of the head and the large ears and the mouth, and am baffled by the clear blue eyes, which are full of light but have no expression whatever in them. Was it again the photographer? Or was it those frightful attacks of asthma in which he more than once thought he was going to suffocate?

After a little experimental fingering he could play any instrument he got his hands on. I don't know how old he was when he began to take violin lessons, but at the age of twelve or thirteen he performed in Gillett's Opera House, which appears to have been a large hall over a clothing store on the courthouse square. Again I see them all—on the front row, and clutching their programs this time, and measuring their applause so that it will not seem exaggerated and foolish, even though they have a right to feel proud. He also played in the church orchestra. His violin teacher, who was a member of the Christian church, suffered from the unchristian emotion of jealousy—or so it was said in the family—and when my father composed a schottische for orchestra, he failed to tell him that the score for certain instruments had to be half a tone higher or lower for harmony. There was no rehearsal. The violins and clarinets were allowed to play what my father innocently put down on ruled music paper. His shame was so great that he never composed another piece of music. I don't for one minute think that the world was thereby done out of a second Mozart, but still I wish it hadn't happened.

He helped pay his way through college by organizing a mandolin club and giving lessons to the members. A woman on the music faculty at Eureka College thought that he was talented and said that she would teach him to play the piano if he would give up ragtime in favor of Bach and Czerny. My father extricated himself from this kind offer and went right on reading the treble and faking the chords in the bass. His plans were made: When he finished college he was going to study medicine at the University of Illinois, and perhaps he would have if things had gone differently at home. That maddening electric bell didn't do the trick. Before the year was out, my Aunt Bert had made a disastrous marriage and my Uncle Charlie was dead.

My Aunt Bert announced that she was going to marry him after she had known him exactly two weeks. My grandfather got on the train and went to Waukesha, Wisconsin, the place where Louis Fuller was born and brought up, and asked the cashier of the bank about him, and was told that he came of a good family. Why the cashier did not feel free to tell my grandfather that he was the black sheep of that family I don't know, any more than I know why my grandfather felt he could not address his questions to Louis Fuller's family.

Although it is a scene I find hard to imagine, I don't think my father was speaking metaphorically when he said, "Father begged Bert on his knees not to marry Fuller. She wouldn't listen to him." My grandfather was up against the same streak of mulishness in his daughter that he had to deal with in his wife. Or she may have been so in love that she didn't care what anybody said. My grandmother's scrapbook contains an engraved announcement of my Aunt Maybel's marriage to David Paul Coffman, but not of my Aunt Bert's marriage to Louis E. Fuller. They didn't run off, but were married in the parlor of the house on Kickapoo Street, by the minister of the Christian church, on April 2, 1898. On the back of the wedding license the groom's occupation is given as "journalist."

When my father and mother went out for the evening they took me with them and put me on a sofa in the next room, or sometimes the same room, and I woke up in the morning in my own bed without knowing how I got there. Falling asleep I heard a good many things that were not intended for my ears or that it was assumed I would not understand. In time I discovered that if I kept my eyes closed and didn't move and was careful to breathe regularly, the conversation often became more interesting. Ordinarily it was mostly about crops and recipes; now and then it widened to include disappointment and heartache. I soon had a very good idea not only of what husbands were inconsiderate of their wives' feelings but also of what they said or did that was so intolerable and that would have provided adequate grounds for divorce if only the wife could bring herself to take action. My Aunt Bert's difficulties with her second husband were sometimes referred to, but her first marriage and divorce were never mentioned— I now think because the only persons who knew the facts did not choose to discuss them. I decided that whatever the trouble was, it was so far in the past as to be of no interest to anybody any longer. This was not true.

My aunt appeared in court, in Lincoln, on May 19, 1902, with my grandfather acting as her attorney, and was granted a divorce and the custody of her child. The details remained safely buried in the County Clerk's office for more than half a century. They are (the deletions being in every case simple legal longwindedness) as follows:

"Oratrix . . . represents that the said Louis E. Fuller . . . on or about the 9th day of January A.D. 1900 . . . absented himself . . . without any reasonable cause, for the space of two years and upwards, and has persisted in such desertion.

". . . that the said Louis E. Fuller . . . had been guilty of extreme and repeated cruelty toward your Oratrix, that he is a man of great austerity of temper, and frequently, during the time your Oratrix lived . . . with him, he indulged in violent sallies of passion and used toward your Oratrix very obscene and abusive language without any provocation whatever . . ."

("Bertha's tongue," my father used to say, and shake his head. But no doubt she thought there had been no provocation.)

". . . when your Oratrix was confined in childbirth at Springfield, Ill., the said Louis E. Fuller cruelly and heartlessly absented himself from their Boarding House . . . and your Oratrix had to solicit the aid of strangers for care and assistance of herself and newborn child until help could reach her from her parents . . .

". . . that on or about the third day of January A.D. 1900, the said Louis E. Fuller, at their home in Dubuque, Iowa, struck your Oratrix a violent blow in the face . . .

". . . that the said Louis E. Fuller, in contracting marriage with your Oratrix, was guilty of defrauding your Oratrix in that he claimed to be an honorable man, and that he had at no time committed any crime against the laws of any state in which he had lived whereas . . . in fact the said Louis E. Fuller . . . was confined . . . in the States prison at Stillwater, Minnesota, from the 23rd day of January A.D. 1894, to the seventh day of May, 1895 . . .

". . . that the said Oratrix was dragged from place to

place, through the states of Illinois, Indiana, and Iowa, in numerous places, by the said defendant, leaving unpaid Board-bills, and being harassed for the payment of same, until in the said month of January A.D. 1900, she was compelled to accept the charity of strangers and return in shame and beggary to her father's home.

". . . that the said defendant threatens by force to take from the custody . . . of your Oratrix their child and place him in the custody of entire strangers . . ."

Poor giddy, frightened creature! And what a coming of age. But it is still true that education and the formation of moral character are identical expressions. My aunt was twenty-six when she returned in shame and beggary to her father's house, and it is too much to hope that nobody said I told you so.

My father's older brother had a beautiful tenor voice and my Grandmother Maxwell's guileless blue eyes. The description in the *Logan County History* of Charles Turley, who led his descendants safely into the ark of the Christian Church—"He was a genial, generous-hearted man whom everybody loved"—instantly made me think of my Uncle Charlie. Perhaps he was a throwback. He was born, as I have said, on that farm three miles from Lincoln that my grandmother was so determined to sell, and he was five years old when they moved to town.

While my grandfather was walking the floor with the bill from the dry goods store in his hand, my uncle was out earning money by whatever jobs were open to schoolboys— among other things, he was a newspaper carrier, and he posted and circulated bills. He must have gone at this with a good deal of energy for he was elected treasurer of the Illinois Bill Posters' Association. A year after he graduated from college, and while he was reading for the bar examination, he married the daughter of a judge in Petersburg, Illinois. He and his wife lived with my grandparents in the house on Kickapoo Street. In 1895, all in the space of a few months, he had a son and was admitted to the bar, and the name on the frosted glass door of my grandfather's law office was changed to Maxwell & Maxwell.

My uncle was everything that people in those days admired in a young man, and for the most part still do. He was hard-working, intelligent, and ambitious, and his ambitions were of a kind that could easily be understood: to provide for his family, to do well in business, to be well thought of. If he met with a setback, he cheerfully doubled his efforts and usually overcame it. He was of an open, honorable nature, and at the same time he was a natural diplomat. He was everybody's friend and darling. But when it came to seeking out legal advice they consulted, as always, older and wiser heads. Instead of sitting despondently in his office, he began to write life and fire insurance on the side, and did so well that one of the fire insurance companies sent him on the road as a part-time special agent. He traveled around the state inspecting risks and settling claims and cultivating the friendship of local agents, and was so successful that if he had lived it is quite possible his career would have been in that field and not in law.

Like my father, he was musical. He composed military marches, several of which were published, and he was the leader and director of the Methodist church choir. I assume that he was merely earning money. If he had gone over to the Methodists, he would not have been living at home; it would have been too uncomfortable for him. He was the assistant manager of Gillett's Hall, and he conducted a series of theatrical entertainments in the Broadway Theater. There appears to have been no limit to his capacity for driving himself. In one photograph, taken when he was about twenty, his eyes are abnormally large and he has a full mouth and a seraphic expression. In a later photograph, the angel has departed, leaving a young man in a dress suit who has already begun to be encased in fat.

He was twenty-six when he drank contaminated well water in some small town in southern Illinois, and contracted typhoid fever. The first symptom was a severe chill, on the evening of the 4th of July. The next day, a Monday, he went on a business trip, and he came home on Wednesday evening not feeling any better. He went to see the family doctor, who gave him something to take but must not have diagnosed the disease properly, for that evening my uncle was still on his feet being installed as chancellor commander of Glendower Lodge Number 45 of the Knights of Pythias. He made one more business trip, to Petersburg, and came home on Saturday morning with a raging fever and took to his bed.

The obituary notice that appeared in the paper two weeks later begins: " 'Charlie Maxwell is dead.' Such was the word passed from lip to lip Saturday morning. . ." Knowing the place, I see it happen.

They did not at first believe that he was in mortal danger. The family doctor laid great stress on the fact that my uncle was young and strong. But as his temperature continued to rise and he grew weaker and weaker, they went on being hopeful because hope was all there was to cling to. He didn't always recognize the people standing around his bed. His speech was disordered and at times he had to be forcibly restrained. The family spoke with lowered voices in parts of the house that were remote from his bedroom, when they could have shouted in his ear and he wouldn't have heard them. My grandfather and my father followed the doctors around, waiting for the tactful moment to ask questions the doctors could not answer. Any remark the nurses made was considered to be of the utmost significance. Aften ten days the fever went down suddenly, and he left his bed for a short time. Then it shot up again. At noon on Friday, he had a brief period of lucidity and recognized his father-in-law. Toward the end, in his delirium, he directed the Methodist church choir and sang with them. My Aunt Bert and her husband arrived from Springfield a few hours before he died. Three ministers spoke at his funeral.

The obituary notice in the other evening paper says: "The death of Charles C. Maxwell removes from Lincoln one of its most promising young men, one widely admired by all who knew him. Full of energy, pluck, and stick-to-it-iveness, he had begun a foundation that was, even in early life, a marvel in itself. He experienced the rough sides of practical life, but, undiscouraged, worked diligently, ever striving to attain some practical end. He was just beginning to realize that man is the chief architect of his own success, that through the channel of personal effort will flow the tide that brings happiness."

The tide can be interfered with.

My father went back to college in the fall, and after a few weeks my grandfather wrote him that he would have to come home and take over Charlie's insurance agency. Sitting at a desk in my grandfather's law office, he began to write insurance. After he had persuaded somebody to take out a policy, he then had to take it to my grandfather to be signed, because he wasn't of age and his signature wouldn't have been legally binding. The insurance company tried him out in my uncle's job. All he had to do, it seems, was give up wearing quite such interesting neckties. The rest came easily and quickly to him.

My father always regretted the fact that he was not able to follow his first inclination, and he would, I think, have made an excellent doctor. But on the other hand he made an excellent businessman. He was sober and responsible—

those jazzy photographs were just manifestations of a stage he was passing through—and would have done well at almost anything he set his hand to, so long as it was of a practical nature. Imaginative effort he had no gift for, which is perhaps why he was not very tactful. He wasn't everybody's friend; those friends he had were all admirable but rather complicated men, who were drawn to him by his bluntness and by the fact that they could see right to the bottom of his character.

One of them, Dean Hill, became my friend during the last years of his life. A more enchanting man I have never known. He and my father and another friend used to go fishing together when they were in their seventies. Dean Hill had a bad heart and wasn't allowed to row the boat, my father was more than half blind, and the third man was deaf as a post. They took a humorous pleasure in compensating for one another's physical deficiencies. When my father had a bite but couldn't see that his cork was bobbing wildly, the other two would cry, "Bill, you've got something on your line!" And when this crisis was passed, out would come the pint of whiskey. Sooner or later, the conversation always got around to a subject that both Dean Hill and my father loved to talk about—the Gillett family lawsuit. Dean Hill's mother was an interested party, and my Grandfather Maxwell figured prominently in the trial, as counsel for Miss Jessie Gillett, who was Mrs. Hill's sister. The facts could be depended on never quite to fit together, and that it all took place long ago in their youth probably added to their pleasure.

In my Grandfather Maxwell's day, the most common litigation was over the ownership of land, and what every lawyer waited for was a lawsuit that would go on and on and on, with the ownership of *a great deal* of land at stake, and the lawyers' fees reflecting the amount of time and labor they had spent on the case and the value of the prop-

erty under dispute. One morning my grandfather was informed that Miss Gillett was in the outer office. His chance
had come, and it was all anybody could ask for. The background of the case is contained in a biographical sketch of
John D. Gillett in the *Logan County History:* "When he
first came to Illinois nearly one-half the land was in the
market at government prices, and availing himself of the
opportunity he entered at different times about 12,000
acres, selling lots or sections as he found purchasers. In
1852 he with R. B. Latham entered about 7,000 acres. He
is one of the most extensive farmers of Illinois, his home
farm containing 9,000 acres.* In addition to farming he has
paid considerable attention to cattle dealing and real estate,
and his vast accumulations are due to his good judgment,
industry and strict attention to business. He raises the finest
blooded stock cattle in the United States, as his exhibits at
various stock shows demonstrate, he invariably receiving
first premiums. He is now engaged extensively in shipping
fine stock to European markets. In 1873 he was one of the
incorporators of the First National Bank of Lincoln and has
since been its president. In politics he is a Republican, but
gives no attention to public affairs. May 31, 1842 he was
married to Miss Lemira Parke, whom he met in 1840,
while crossing the Sangamon River, now at Clingman's
Ferry, she being on her way to spend Christmas with friends
at Springfield. Her father, Elisha Parke, settled in that part
of Sangamon County now included in Logan County, in
1837, and built the first jail in Logan County. Mr. and
Mrs. Gillett have eight children—Emma (wife of Hon.
R. J. Oglesby, Governor of Illinois), Grace (wife of D. T.
Littler, of Springfield), Nina, Amy, Kate (wife of James
Hill, of Chester, Illinois), Jessie, John, and Charlotte. The

---

* How vast the holdings of John D. Gillett were the historian apparently
felt it would be in poor taste to say.

family are members of the Episcopal church at Springfield."

I have seen a photograph of John D. Gillett, taken when
he was well along in years. He has a white beard shaped like
the cow-catcher of a steam locomotive, a flower in his buttonhole, and the look of a bouncy man. His death gave rise
to a Balzacian novel. Part I has to do with his will. In devis-
ing his land to his children he gave his only son, John Parke
Gillett, a double portion and so set the plot of the novel in
motion. He also left his widow a lifetime interest in 3800
acres of land and personal property worth $100,000. In Part
II she died and her children could not come to an agreement
as to how her share of the estate should be divided, so it was
owned by the heirs in common. In Part III one of the sisters
died and willed her share to her brother. With what was
eventually going to come to him from his mother, he ended
up owning seven-sixteenths of the original estate. In Part IV
he made a will in which he left the bulk of his property to
Miss Jessie Gillett, my Grandfather Maxwell's client. In
Part V he added a codicil in which the same property was left
to Mrs. Oglesby and a nephew. In Part VI he died and the
sisters, waiting to be informed of the time and place of the
reading of the will, were informed, instead, that the will
could not be found.

I remember sitting on the floor in the living room at home,
playing with some beat-up lead soldiers, and hearing my
father's voice rise as he said, " 'Would a hundred and fifty
acres of land refresh your memory?' And the will was in
_____'s office at nine o'clock the next morning." But who
made that offer? And who took him up on it? I can't remember. It could even—though I don't really think it was—have
been some other will my father was talking about. It was a
very long time ago.

The will, or a will, of John Parke Gillett must have
turned up, because in Part VII certain of the sisters tried to

have it set aside on the ground that their brother was insane. In Part VIII the plot becomes dizzying. Two of the sisters would combine forces against the others and then they would have a falling out and there would be new combinations. What was being fought over was, at a rough estimate of its present-day value, five or six million dollars.

I still don't know anything like the full details of this immensely complicated story; the broad outlines I got partly from a newspaper clipping in my grandmother's scrapbook and partly from a Lincoln lawyer, a man of my father's generation. He was a schoolboy when all this happened and was present at the trial.

"Practically every lawyer in the county was involved in the case," he wrote me, when I asked him about it. "Your Grandfather Blinn was one of the battery of lawyers representing Mrs. Oglesby, and apparently by questionable means he had got hold of some highly useful letters. He would get one of the girls on the witness stand and would ask her a question about certain happenings. After she had answered he would say with great delight, 'I will see if I can refresh your recollection,' and then he would produce a letter she had written which contradicted her testimony in some one or more details. It was a great show and it lasted all summer. The jury found that John Gillett was of sound mind when he made his will, but it was not the easiest thing in the world to determine because he was drunk most of the time."

My Grandfather Blinn won the case, who didn't need to win it. My Grandfather Maxwell, as I have said, was on the opposite side. My father used to say that it was the first case my Grandfather Maxwell ever had where the fee was substantial, that the part he took in the trial considerably enhanced his reputation, and that if he had continued to be Miss Jessie Gillett's legal advisor he would no longer have worried about the bill from Boyd's Dry Goods Store.

Instead, his health broke down. Other lawyers attended

to Miss Gillett's legal affairs, and my grandfather spent the remaining year or two of his life in and out of bed.

Because of my grandfather's failing health—so intricately are the strands of human life woven together—Professor Hieronymous met with his comeuppance. Given though the Disciples were to arguing among themselves, there was one principle that was held by all Campbellite preachers and teachers to be self-evident and never disputed—namely, that they should never put up at a hotel if there was anywhere else that would take them in. One evening a year or so after my father had withdrawn from college, Professor Hieronymous turned up, at dinner time. He was fed and stayed on, waiting to be asked to spend the night. My grandfather was upstairs in bed, ill. My grandmother and my Aunt Maybel could not invite the professor to stay because it was my father's place, as acting head of the family, to do this. At nine o'clock they excused themselves and retired, while my father sat up with the guest. Professor Hieronymous talked on and on pleasantly, and my father listened. At eleven o'clock, thinking to force my father's hand, he stood up and said, "I guess I'd better go to a hotel," and my father said, "I think so too." The satisfaction of this moment stayed with him, undiluted, for sixty years.

When my father came home from work he went straight up to my grandfather's bedroom and had his supper there, while he poured out all that had happened to him during the day. And during one of the periods when my grandfather was not confined to his bed, he allowed my father to persuade him to enter a saloon and, with his foot on the brass rail, drink a glass of beer. It is hard to see how love could go any farther.

·   ·   ·

"Father never saw me until Charlie died," my father remarked once, without bitterness, merely as a statement of
fact. But I wonder if it was a fact. What seems more likely
is that my grandfather saw him quite plainly, and didn't
approve of what he saw. He could not have failed to see
that my father was never going to be a faithful tiller in the
Lord's Vineyard. What he actually was—an upright man
—may not at that point have been quite so apparent.

My father was promised a good violin if he didn't smoke
until he was eighteen—I assume in the belief that he would
then be old enough to see the folly of nicotine and abstain
from all forms of tobacco. No sooner was the instrument
put in his hands, on his eighteenth birthday, than he took up
smoking. Cigars and cigarettes and a pipe. My grandmother
never got over this disappointment, and felt—quite unfairly
—that my father had not kept his end of the bargain. But in
any case they had lost him. And must in all likelihood have
refused to recognize this at first, until a sufficient number of
family arguments made it clear that my father was going to
go his own way, smoke, drink, play cards, and do whatever
he pleased on Sunday. He delighted in the company of
women. He was not a skirt chaser, any more than he was a
gambler, but how was my grandfather to know that? He had
not been able to prevent his favorite daughter from throwing her life away by a bad marriage. He may have been expecting my father to do something equally damaging to his
future, and, as they all set out for Sunday morning worship,
have viewed with a sinking heart the angle of that derby hat
and the dandified cut of my father's clothes.

What he should have noticed (and I dare say he did)
was my father's attitude toward money. My father used to
tell me solemnly how my grandfather said to him, "If you'll
just put aside a little money whenever you can until you've
saved up a thousand dollars, you'll never be without money
the rest of your life." Then my father would add, "And I

did manage to save a thousand dollars, and I've never been without money since."

At what point, I have often asked myself, did money—that is to say, money in the bank, money invested in stocks and bonds, for they never thought in terms of extravagant living—become so real to them all? And why? And was it true of other Middle Western families as well? Was it the period? Or was it the inevitable consequence of my grand-parents' moving to town? I think of John England, who fell asleep the minute people began to talk about money. To him it was an object of no value. You couldn't plant it. The rain didn't rain on it. You couldn't harvest it or watch it ripen. It was a dead thing and what interested him was life. Eternal life. I find it a terribly strange—and terrible—fact that the only words of my grandfather which my father ever quoted to me—his testament, so to speak—were not about faith or honor or truthfulness or compassion for other human beings but about saving money.

10

"All the Maxwells die young," my grandmother used to say. She could have said, with just as much reason, "All the Maxwells live to a great age." They did one or the other.

My Grandfather Maxwell was taken ill in Galveston, Texas, where he had gone on business. He wired my father to come immediately. There was a train that night, but it was evening when the telegram was delivered, the banks and stores were closed, and in those days nobody kept a hundred dollars in the house. My father went downtown, to Tim Hardin's saloon, and showed him the wire, and Tim Hardin, knowing what the Christian church and my Grandfather Maxwell thought of saloonkeepers, nevertheless gave my father the money he needed to get my grandfather home.

In this final stage of his illness, my grandfather suffered excruciating pain whenever he put his feet to the floor and tried to stand. I have been told that it is a classical symptom of a nervous breakdown. My Aunt Maybel was married and living in Omaha, but during the last three months of my grandfather's life she was at home helping my grandmother care for him. He was fifty-four years old when he died, on the third of January, 1904.

The obituary notices of the period were both more emotional and more graphic than anything we are accustomed to, and grammar and syntax here and there gave way under the strain. My grandfather's obituary tells exactly how he died. "Although Mr. Maxwell had been a constant sufferer from a complication of troubles for more than one year past, and although up to a few weeks ago his condition was such as to alarm his family and friends, he showed a decided change for the better and had been in fairly good condition until the last few days, when he was seized with an attack of the grip. He had improved to such an extent recently that all arrangements were completed for he and Mrs. Maxwell to go south with the hope of a complete recovery. On last Sunday he was feeling badly the largest part of the day, and seemed to want his wife close to him. In the evening he was taken with a violent spell of coughing and called to his wife to lie down on the bed beside him. He arose with nausea in his stomach, and after vomiting he fell into his wife's arms, who at first thought he had simply fainted, but the bursting of the blood vessel resulted in instant and painless death."

Underneath the clipping, in my grandmother's scrapbook, is pasted this five-line notice: "The public schools will be dismissed Wednesday afternoon that the teachers may attend the funeral of the late Hon. R. C. Maxwell, a worthy member of the Board of Education."

Every human life is a story, and my grandfather's story, as his wife and children understood it, was that he was taken ill just as he was about to make a killing. They didn't use this vulgar modern expression, but nevertheless it was what they meant. He hadn't been as successful as he deserved to be. And to the end of their lives, whenever they spoke of him, their voices were tinged with an unfading regret.

My grandfather's will was brief and in only one or two instances interesting. The third item reads: "I direct that the share of my Grandson, Robert Blane Maxwell be charged with the sum of $500 heretofore advanced by me to his father Charles C. Maxwell"—which strikes me as rather rigid and Scottish, considering that the heir in question was a minor and somebody was going to have to provide for his care and education. It was perhaps a way of not admitting that my Uncle Charlie was in any way different from my father and my aunts—that is, of not admitting that he was dead.

Item four reads: "If at the time of my decease my said daughter Bertha L. Fuller should then be the wife of Louis E. Fuller, I direct that her entire share of my said estate be paid to her in cash the amount thereof to be estimated by the County Court in which my estate is settled." The will was dated March 31, 1902, and my Aunt Bert was granted a divorce six weeks later.

My father was the executor of my grandfather's estate. The payments to my grandfather's creditors are duly listed in the final report. He had also borrowed money from various people, including $700 from his brother-in-law, James Turley, and $333.83 from my Aunt Maybel, which suggests that his financial circumstances during the last years of his life were verging on the desperate. Nevertheless, having saved that magical thousand dollars, he was not without any money. At the time of his death he had $486.70 in cash.

The family residence at 503 North Kickapoo Street, built with the money that my Great-grandfather Turley gave my grandmother for a wedding present, is listed among my *grandfather's* assets. So are the household goods, appraised at $144.72. The claims against the estate amounted to $6700. The net assets amounted to $18,858.52. My grandmother's share (with the widow's allowance of $800 and one-half of the money from the sale of 325 acres of land in Kansas and $1310 more than the other heirs of the sum derived from the disposal of personal property) came to $7190.64. My two aunts and my father each got $2791.97, and my Cousin Blane the same amount less that

$500 his father had borrowed from his grandfather.

My Grandmother Maxwell could not go on living all by herself in that big house on Kickapoo Street. My Uncle Paul Coffman was starting out in the fire insurance business like my father, but in Nebraska. My father found a better job for his brother-in-law, traveling in southern Illinois, and gave my Aunt Maybel his share of my grandfather's estate, with the understanding that she would make a home for my grandmother for the rest of her life.*

My Aunt Maybel and my Grandmother Maxwell and my Uncle Paul ended up in a box-like white house on Union Street, which my Aunt Maybel built with the money from my grandfather's estate.

A church quarterly for the year 1864 says, "Let every preacher resolve never to enter a meeting house of our brethren in which an organ stands. Let no one who takes a letter from one church ever unite with another using an organ. *Rather let him live out of a church than go into such a den.* Let all who oppose the organ withdraw from the church if one is brought in."

In this series of statements I recognize the intellectual climate of my Aunt Maybel's house on Union Street. It undoubtedly was brought there, along with the horsehair couch, and the picture of Caerlaverock Castle, and a great many other items of furniture, when my grandmother gave

* I remember his telling me that's what he had done. My Aunt Annette says that my Grandfather Blinn advised him to take as his portion of the estate some shares in the Central Illinois Telephone and Telegraph Company, at that time worthless but, in my Grandfather Blinn's opinion, likely to be worth a great deal someday. And my father did, and they were. This does not jibe, of course, with what my father told me, but I know he owned stock in the telephone company, and whoever said things had to jibe?

up her own house and went to live with her older daughter. It was probably also the climate of the little house behind the jail, and perhaps even of the farmhouse near Williamsville where my grandfather stopped to ask for a drink of water.

The house on Union Street knew the Bible backwards and forwards, and could quote chapter and verse to prove that dancing was wrong, in itself and because of what it led to. So was playing cards for money. And swearing. And drinking anything stronger than grape juice or lemonade. And spending Sunday in any other way than going to church and coming home and eating a big dinner afterward.

Though my Aunt Maybel's house was only three blocks away, it was as different from our house as Jerusalem in the time of Herod was different from ancient Athens. It sat on a high foundation, with a porch across the front, and very little yard and no flowers or shrubs. There was a fern basket hanging from the porch ceiling and I suppose that did them. The two upstairs front windows were so placed and of such a size and shape as to suggest a self-righteous expression. There was also a barn in back. To my astonishment, when I passed the house recently, the barn was still there, a half century after all the other barns in Lincoln were torn down and replaced by garages.

It is abundantly clear that the carpenter who built the house was quite positive he didn't need any help from an architect. Pigheadedly proceeding, he solved his problems as he went, making the foundation too high, cutting off a corner here and skimping there, and scratching his head when he found that he hadn't allowed enough room for the stairs. Not being old enough to understand the part money plays in human affairs, I assumed it was entirely from choice that my aunt and uncle lived where they did, and, actually, I never heard them express any discontent with their house, which was very like them. But probably if they had been given a choice they would have preferred to go on living in the house on Kickapoo Street, if only because from the front windows you could see the Christian church. It stood back to back with the stores and office buildings on the courthouse square, and looked out on a little park with a bandstand in the center of it. All the churches in Lincoln were inclined to be ugly at that period, and the Christian church was no exception. On the platform, alongside the minister's chair and lectern, there was a baptismal tank. There was also a mortgage. This word turned up quite often in the conversation of my elders. I understood both what it meant and that it was not a desirable thing to have. And I concluded that the congregation of the Christian church must be made up of poor people.

When I was six years old, my father started to teach me the value of money. He gave me an allowance of ten cents a week, and impressed it on me that I must not go into debt to buy the things I wanted but wait until I had the money. If the Christian church didn't wait, it could only be because they knew they weren't ever going to have the money to do what they wanted.

I rather think the congregation of the Christian church *was* made up of poor people, for the most part, but there were other churches in Lincoln that this could also be said of, and so it wasn't really a distinguishing characteristic.

The baptismal tank was, of course, an innovation. Alexander Campbell and his wife and father and mother were baptized in running water, as their Savior was. The early baptisms in Illinois were always out of doors. In the *History of the Disciples of Christ in Illinois,* there is a moving account of a baptizing that took place a few miles from Lincoln in 1889. Sugar Creek was too scant of water, and three ministers, one of them in his seventy-sixth year, walked out into the country and found a little lake where, a few days later, the baptizing took place. "The lake was surrounded by sugar maples and the leaves were like gold. It was a beautiful afternoon and the great crowd of people gathered there was quiet and reverent. The sloping ground gave all an opportunity to see and hear. I gave an invitation at the water's edge. A young lady came forward. Her mother approached and whispered to me, 'My daughter is deaf and dumb. She is educated and I think she understands the step she desires to take.' This was the first experience I had ever had in introducing a deaf mute into the kingdom. I took a blank book and pencil from my side pocket and wrote, 'Do you believe with all your heart that Jesus is the Christ, the Son of God?' In response she took the pencil and wrote, 'I do.' And I baptized her."

Until I was old enough to go to school, it was customary for me to spend Friday with my grandmother. In winter the front door was enclosed in a small wooden vestibule, removed when warm weather came. The front hall smelled of hot-air registers. Like most old people, my grandmother had very little heat in her body, and my aunt saw to it that the thermometer in the dining room registered an even eighty all winter long. If it was summertime and I continued straight on through the dining room, I would find my aunt in the kitchen at the stove, uncorseted, in a Mother Hubbard, with the sweat running down her face and neck, putting up tomatoes or sweet corn or string beans or pickled peaches.

"Well, how is my Bill Bump?" she would exclaim, and give me a steamy kiss. I wasn't her Bill Bump, I belonged lock, stock, and barrel to my mother, and my Aunt Maybel knew it.

The exact number of the jars that were waiting for sealing wax and their metal screw-tops would be announced to me proudly, and then my aunt would say, "Your grand-

mother is expecting you. Mind the stairs. I say, your grandmother is expecting you."

The stairs were in the front hall, and treacherous, the
treads being an inch or two narrower than usual and so
thickly varnished they were like glass. At home I sometimes
slipped and went flumpety-bump bump bump, but here the
danger was so obvious I never did. My grandmother and I
would start down together like voyageurs shooting the
rapids of some uncharted river in the wilderness. Clinging
to each other and the bannister, we would arrive at the oil
painting of the Castle of Chillon on the landing, turn and
start down again, and finally arrive at the cuckoo clock at
the foot of the stairs. Once more we had made it.

The woodwork all over the house was dark and highly
varnished. The shades were drawn in the parlor all the way
to the sill, to keep the blue Chinese rug from fading. In the
other rooms, upstairs and down, they were always exactly
at half-mast, and net curtains kept out much of the remaining light. If you have light, the first thing you know you
have joy, for which there is some but not very much warrant in the Scriptures, and what there is can be interpreted
figuratively. The light in my aunt's house was that of a
perpetual grey day.

My aunt did not think that people who are sitting down
should be still; they should rock gently back and forth in a
rocking chair. In the parlor there were two of them. Gigantic
they were, of Grand Rapids mahogany, with arms that hit
you in the wrong place, and knife-like edges, and proportions
that had no relation to the human body. There was also a
matching divan that everybody always avoided because it
was even more uncomfortable, and an upright piano that was
never tuned or played on, and two large oil paintings, the
work of my Great-aunt Mandy, who was my grandmother's
sister. The paintings were both of a winter sunset—I think
she never painted anything else—with an orange sky, a

brook with ice on it, and one or two antlered deer in the middle distance. Salt had been sprinkled liberally on the white paint to make it glisten.

My great-aunt lived in Williamsville, and used to come and visit my grandmother sometimes. Nothing about her suggested that she had ever held a paintbrush in her hand, or that she'd been married. Her husband had a grocery store. She was a little dried-up old woman, who sat and rocked and kept an eye out for young girls whose skirts were too short.

The parlor was never used except when my father came, and as my aunt went about raising the shades and finding an ashtray for him, I would be reminded of the fact that, even though she was older, she considered him the head of the family. She spoke of my grandfather as if he were larger than life-sized. If she had been as respectful toward her husband as she was toward her father and her brother, she would have been totally boxed in.

The sitting room was directly beyond the parlor and could be shut off from it and from the dining room by sliding doors. High up over the open doorways two painted plaster heads looked down on the sitting room in such a way as to suggest that though the heads could not hear they could certainly see what went on. Nothing much did. One of the heads was black and the other white, and I wonder if they represented Europe and Africa. Above the desk there was a row of Max Fuller in his petticoat. The horsehair couch was, like all horsehair furniture, scratchy. The rest of the furniture was golden oak, and quite as uncomfortable as the furniture in the parlor, though not so massive. In glass-fronted bookcases all along one wall were kept my grandfather's books, specimens of minerals, pieces of coral, several starfish, a seahorse, and a neat pile of parrot eggs, regarded with great affection by my aunt and my grandmother. The parrot that laid them was thought for nineteen years to be a male. One night they heard a frightful screeching and squawking, and when they came down in the morning—I would have had to get up and see what was going on, but people are either curious or they are not—they found these nineteen eggs and Polly dead on the floor of the cage.

I never succeeded in getting my hands on any of the objects in the bookcases, or even the books, except one. My grandfather's copy of Dante's *Inferno,* with the Doré illustrations, was presented to me by my Aunt Maybel when I graduated from college, with the stipulation that if I was ever obliged to put my things in storage, I was to return it to her for safekeeping. This was not really a feasible plan, because she died nine years later. The book is still safe, though it shows its age, and in some of the plates somebody (who could it have been? my older brother? Max? my Cousin Blane Maxwell?) has traced the sexual parts in pencil.

Over the bookcase, in the darkest corner of the sitting room, there was a sepia photograph of my Grandfather Maxwell in his open coffin, surrounded by floral tributes from the various lodges he had belonged to.

Breakfast and lunch were eaten in the kitchen, and the evening meal in the dining room. The telephone was attached to the dining room wall. Above the swinging door to the kitchen, or on the dado, or along the high shelf under the dining room windows, were still more interesting objects: ruby-red cups with "Souvenir of" this or that World's Fair etched on the glass; a highly ornamental and of course never used Bavarian beer stein; a picture of an English bulldog looking out menacingly between the apertures of a real picket fence—that is to say, the fence was *outside* the glass; a dusty peacock feather. My aunt didn't know, and I don't suppose anybody else in Lincoln did either, that peacock feathers bring bad luck.

At the head of the stairs was a watercolor rendering of the Maxwell coat of arms (did Miss Jessie Gillett bring this also from Scotland?) and two framed diplomas proving that my aunt and uncle had graduated from Eureka College. To the right, down the hall, were my grandmother's bedroom and two much smaller rooms—the bathroom, which smelled of glycerin soap and had a Rube Goldberg contraption for heating bathwater on the spot, and my uncle's office. This room was furnished with a desk and a typewriter, two chairs, and a narrow bed I sometimes slept in, watched over not only by my ancestors but also the special agents of the New York Underwriters Insurance Company.

To the left, down the same hall, was the bedroom of my aunt and uncle, and then the spare room, as it was always called. Children have no sense of history. It has to be drummed into them. And until this process is completed, the past always takes place in the surroundings and circumstances of the present. I knew that my Uncle Charlie, in his delirium, as he lay dying, sang "Nearer, my God, to Thee," and where could he have done this except in the big brass double bed in the spare room?

It looked as if nothing had happened there since. Things did happen in that house, though—mostly scenes, of an appalling nature, which I heard about from my father when I was older. He remained on the outside, but was called in when things got out of hand. I myself was once called upon to adjudicate an argument between my Aunt Maybel and my Aunt Bert—about whether the Oberammergau Passion Play was in Switzerland or the Holy Land —and so I have an idea of what heat they brought to bear on matters of real emotional substance.

II

My father was walking to the train one morning, carrying
his heavy grip, when two girls went by in a pony cart. He
saw that the girl who was driving had black hair and large
brown eyes, and that she was looking at him. In that instant
both their lives were rearranged. Living in so small a place,
they couldn't possibly have failed to see each other before
this, and in fact my Aunt Annette, who was four years
younger than my mother, remembers watching with her a
lawn party they were too young to be invited to. There was
a dance platform under the trees, and Chinese lanterns—I
see it as a Middle Western small-town version of Renoir's
Dancing at the Moulin de la Galette—and my mother was
staring at one particular couple. "I would give anything in
the world to be that girl," she said, "and wearing that blue
dress, and dancing with that man." The young man in question was my father. As she, later on, had premonitions of
her death, so this was a premonition of love. But if she hadn't
been driving a friend to the same train my father was taking,
would they—It's an idle question. They saw each other at
the same moment and, as if they were exchanging favors at
a cotillion, gave up their hearts.

When my father came back from that business trip he
telephoned my mother and asked if he could see her. From
that time, Annette says, my mother never went out with
anybody else. One of my mother's beaux managed to get the
assembly changed from Friday to the middle of the week,

when my father would be out of town, and my mother refused to go to it.

The rules about courting were strict in my Grandfather Blinn's house: If there was a party, the guests left at midnight; at other times, the young men said good night at ten o'clock and left or my grandfather asked them to leave. That was the rule, but he didn't always know when they lingered. My mother was afraid that if my grandfather asked my father to leave he would never come back, and so she got her younger sister to keep watch for her, through minute after minute of sweet foolishness. My mother was even so indiscreet as to have dinner with my father in a hotel. There would have been hell to pay if my grandfather had found out.

My mother was married at home, in the parlor, in June, 1903. My father was twenty-four, she was three years younger. Annette was the matron of honor. The bridal book, with the signatures of the minister and the wedding guests, has ended up in my possession, so I know that the service was performed by the Reverend W. H. Cannon, minister of the Christian church in Lincoln, and that my Grandfather Maxwell was well enough to be present. Max Fuller signed his own name. He was only four, and it doesn't look as if somebody guided the pen. There were more than a hundred wedding guests. How they got into that house (let alone how they sat down to a full wedding supper, which my Aunt Annette says they did) I cannot begin to imagine. Somebody sneaked into the summer kitchen and made off with a drum of ice cream and the coat of one of the waiters. The waiter remarked in my Grandfather Blinn's hearing that he was not going to profit very much from this day's work, and my grandfather gave him the money to buy a new coat. The ice cream was in molds.

When I asked Annette where my father and mother went on their honeymoon, she couldn't at first remember.

"Mackinac Island?"

"No."

"French Lick?"

"Yes. That's where they went." A huge frame hotel with long verandahs lined with rocking chairs. "I can see your mother's face when they came home. How her eyes shone. It wasn't a very long stay, but your father had done it handsomely."

During the first year of their married life, my mother and father lived at my Grandfather Blinn's. My grandfather did not think my mother ought to be alone when my father was on the road. My father greatly admired his father-in-law, and from the beginning he was more comfortable with my mother's family than with his own. The warm soft wind from Kentucky. They took him in, and made over him—made him feel that it was his true self that was wanted—and nearly everything was an innovation. Probably the greatest innovation of all was that religion was not viewed from a fixed position.

My Grandfather Blinn was a New Englander from Vermont. I have not been able to discover what faith he was brought up in—only that it was very rigid. The family were at church all day on Sunday, the congregation brought their food along and ate together, and my grandfather, being a shy boy, held back. Often when the faithful had satisfied their hunger there wasn't anything left for him to eat. He knew, without my father's having to tell him, what my father's upbringing had been like and how he felt at being released from so confining a view of human life.

Also, pleasures that my father had looked longingly at from a distance were now suddenly open to him. In the will that caused such prolonged litigation, John P. Gillett left his widow a large farm with the story-book name of Grace-

lands, and when she remarried and moved east she asked my
Grandfather Blinn to manage it for her. He managed it as
carefully and with as much satisfaction as if it had been his
own. I was nearly grown before I discovered it wasn't. On
Saturday mornings my grandfather would invite my father
to go there with him, on the electric line that connected
Peoria, Lincoln, and Springfield. And on Sunday the rest
of the family would join them for a picnic. The house was
old and had been much added onto, and stood in a grove of
trees, surrounded by cornfields. The barns were full of
blooded stock, to be soberly considered, and there were
beautiful walking horses. On horseback, as they walked
through the fields, as they wound their fishing reels and
with a precise flick of the wrist sent the fly sailing out over
the quiet part of some bend in the creek, the two men
revealed themselves to each other. My father intended to
own a farm himself some day, and everything my grandfather said about the management of Gracelands was of interest to him. But he was also alert to the ideas that were
offered for his consideration by my grandfather's wide-
ranging mind, and would not be so mentally alert again until
he was an old man reliving his life in the clear cold light of
how things had turned out.

My older brother was born in my grandfather's house.
With his arrival the time had come to spread out, and my
father bought a modest two-story frame house on Eighth
Street, a block from my Grandfather Blinn's. Annette* says
that it had eight rooms, but that they were small. My
father wasn't going to make the mistake his father had of
living in a house that was grander than he could afford.
They knocked out a partition between two of the downstairs

* Though it was not customary then for children to call adult relatives by
their Christian name, my brother and I called Annette by hers; the alliter-
ative "Aunt" was awkward to say, and leaving it off we indicated how close
to her we felt.

rooms and put in a fireplace, and the house was very pleasant and homelike. It was painted a dirty shade of yellow when I was a little boy, and we no longer lived there, and compared to the house we were living in it didn't look very permanent to me. Walking past it I used to worry that it would not be there when the time came to put up the plaque. I think I expected to be President of the United States.

Annette used to stay there sometimes when my father was away. "One night," she said, "a young man came calling on me and stayed too late. Your mother was furious and said, 'Annette, how can you do that, when Will isn't home and people will see a man leaving my house at eleven o'clock!' " Remembering all the times she had stood watch for my mother when she was saying good night to my father, my aunt was deeply hurt.

My mother's temper flared up as suddenly as a brush fire, but she didn't nourish her anger and it was all over in a matter of seconds. I can only remember three times in my whole childhood when I encountered it head on.

Annette did not marry the lively, penniless young lawyer everyone expected her to marry but someone else. My Uncle Will Bates had graduated from Yale. This distinguished him from every other young man in town very much as having one brown eye and one blue eye would have. His father owned a great deal of land, and nothing I have ever heard about Erastus Bates was unprejudiced, but he appears not to have been very amiable. Annette and her husband went to Europe on their wedding journey, along about the year 1907, and brought back a collection of bibelots and a glass-and-gilded-wood cabinet to hold them, some colored prints of famous masterpieces by Raphael and Michelangelo, a photograph of the Bridge of Sighs, and an even larger view of the Colosseum in Rome. These hung in my aunt's front hall and living room for the next half century. In those days, when people drove a nail in the wall and put up a picture, it was for life.

My Grandfather Blinn took my father and Annette's husband to Gracelands, intending some fishing, and my Uncle Will put soap in the minnow bucket. It was his idea of a joke.

On the outskirts of town there was a state hospital for feebleminded children, and while my Aunt Edith was working there she met a young doctor named William Young, whom she married. He left the hospital and started to practice in Bloomington. I don't know when this happened. Sometime in the years just before I was born. He was over six feet and very broad in the shoulder, with a long head and dark skin and the beaked nose of a Indian. He was so secure in his own physical dignity that he could afford to speak of it with comic appreciation. I have a photograph of him sitting on a beautiful black horse, in a cap and plus fours, smiling as if at a joke with sixteen sides. One of them was should a man that big be sitting on a horse in the first place. As for learning to dance . . . With my Cousin Peg sitting on one of his size twelve shoes and me on the other he walked back and forth talking to my mother as if nothing whatever was going on down around his shins. Or sometimes he would act as though he had no choice, as if we made him walk around with us sitting on his shoes. And he was such a huge man that we were beside ourselves with our own power to do this to him. But then suddenly we couldn't manage him. We were somewhere (I have no idea where it was) and Peg said, "That isn't water down there, is it, Uncle Doc?" and I said, "That is too water down there, isn't it, Uncle Doc?" and he drove us frantic by agreeing with both of us, even when we explained to him that it couldn't be water down there and not be water down there.

He was brought up on a farm outside Bloomington and had put himself through medical school, and his ideas about life were neither countrified nor platitudinous. He smelled faintly of disinfectant, and his hands were mottled with some brown discoloration which I took to be from his work— he ended up being the anesthetist for all the surgeons in Bloomington. The fact that he took his time about everything probably had something to do with this. He thought it excruciatingly funny that my father would get himself and everybody else at the station an hour before the train was due. He always arrived in time to pull himself up onto the steps of the last car just as the wheels were beginning to turn.

You never could tell what was going to come out of his mouth. Once at the breakfast table he remarked cheerfully, "I used to take cream in my coffee and then your Aunt E got me to drink it black, and now I don't like it either way." And when the country was well into the Depression, he surprised me by saying, "You know, Little Bill, your Aunt E and I thought of sending you to Oxford and I'm very glad we had the idea while we could afford it."

I was in college when I discovered that my Aunt Edith had married someone else before she married Uncle Doc. She took me with her when she went calling on a friend, and at the last moment, when we were leaving her house, I had pulled a book out of the bookcase as a prop against possible boredom and had taken it with me. Noticing the name on the flyleaf, I interrupted the conversation to ask, "Aunt E, who is Edith Cosby?" and narrowly escaped being turned into stone. Small-town people manage to endure the inexorable proximity of their lives only by deceiving themselves into thinking that nobody knows what they couldn't not know. I am in favor of this. But all in the world I know about my Aunt Edith's first husband to this day is his last name, and that he worked in a bank in Lincoln, and they lived on Ninth Street for a while, and the temptation to help himself to the money that passed through his hands was too much for him, with the result that my aunt found herself a single woman again, living at home, and with something to live down.

Annette and her husband were not willing, like most married people of that period, to take turns rocking the boat but went at it together. Then she would rush home to her mother, or to my mother, or to my Aunt Edith, with the newest developments. My Aunt Edith retained a kind of diplomatic frigidity with my uncle for half a century. She was never rude, but also never not disapproving. My mother and father stopped speaking to him. If my mother saw my uncle anywhere in public she came home in an excited state, and whoever was there had to hear about his extraordinary behavior. Annette's father-in-law was drawn into it, and my uncle's two sisters, and even a brother-in-law. When Annette's name figured in those conversations I overheard lying in the next room, my mother would draw up a bill of indictment that included, among other things, nagging, being insanely jealous, and being ungenerous about money. My father would tell the story of the minnow bucket. The word "divorce," the words "separate maintenance" floated around in my sleepy brain.

I was fifty before I fitted the pieces of that marriage together, and saw that it was not what people said it was, or even what my aunt said it was. For she was young and excitable, and when she quarreled with her husband she couldn't help drawing everybody in the family into it. The truth is that, in his own way, he loved her. My uncle was a romantic; the Brontës would have understood him better than the women of my mother's and Annette's bridge club did.

When the building his office was located in burned down, the firemen could not restrain him from rushing up a flight of rickety wooden stairs, through the smoke and flames, to rescue the only existing print of a photograph of my aunt as she was when he married her. And she confessed to me once that it was only after he died, at the age of eighty, that she knew what it was to pull a comforter up over herself in the night; he always did it.

My father and mother had become intimate friends with a somewhat older couple who lived next door to them on Eighth Street. Dr. Donald was a veterinary, and had a livery stable on the courthouse square. He also bought and sold purebred horses. He was born in Scotland, and all his life spoke with a strong burr. His wife was from a small town near Lincoln, and when I knew them had an endless list of complaints against him which she drew upon in conversation, always as if she were telling a joke on him, and it made everybody uncomfortable. She was the only person in town who didn't admire him. Perhaps the trouble was that when it was his turn to rock the boat he wouldn't do it. Or it may have been something quite different. Neither of them ever confided to anybody what it was that had come between them. Whatever it was, I think it happened after they moved to Ninth Street. When my father and mother first knew them she was not the bitter-tongued woman she later turned into. And as evening came on, my mother, waiting for my father to finish his traveling and come home to her, was aware of the lights in the house next door, and less lonely because she knew that the Donalds were also aware of the lights in her house.

Aunty Donald never tired of telling me that when I was a baby she carried me on a pillow, and that I looked more like a baby bird than anything human. I weighed four and a half pounds when I was born, and somewhat less at six weeks. My mother's milk did not agree with me nor did anything else, until the family doctor suggested goat's milk. The minister of the African Methodist church kept a goat, and my father made an arrangement with him. When I was a little boy, I used to encounter the Reverend Mr. Fuqua occasionally on his bicycle and we would exchange polite salutations. I knew I had a great deal to thank him for, and so did he. By the time I was six or seven the friendship between my mother and Aunty Donald had cooled, though the two women continued to see each other. My mother's fondness for Dr. Donald continued unchanged.

When Judge Hoblit went bankrupt and the Hoblit house on Ninth Street came on the market, my father bought it. It was almost directly across the street from my Grandfather Blinn's, and much larger and more comfortable than the house we were living in. By that time, my father had bought the farm he had his heart set on owning and put aside enough money so that he didn't need to go into debt, but even so the house did not rest lightly on him. No old house would have; he liked things to be new and without a scratch. Soon after, Dr. Donald bought the Kings' house, next door: Eighth Street was too far away. I was two years old when all this happened, my brother six or seven.

The house on Ninth Street was steeped in family life. All the Hoblit children had grown up there, and somebody had lived in it before the Hoblits. At one time Mr. Hoblit was my Grandfather Blinn's law partner. Judging by the only picture of him I have ever seen, the word handsome hardly does him justice. Annette says that Mrs. Hoblit believed anything her children told her, no matter how improbable. And as the house had ample occasion to observe, they lived beyond their means. I think they also must have been very happy. On top of a shed in the back yard there was a playhouse, long since gone when we lived there, that was the rendezvous of all the children in the neighborhood. My father as a young man used to stand plinking his mandolin under Claire Hoblit's window. His intentions were not serious. They merely liked each other. She was a sultry-looking girl, and mischievous, and for idle amusement made trouble between couples who were courting, and the girls did not like her. In addition to her other failings she was witty. When a younger brother who was as diminutive as a wren married a girl who matched him perfectly, she remarked that they were a sample copy of a marriage. She fell in love with a singer—a Mexican whose skin was a darker shade than was acceptable in Lincoln—and her father said, "You can't marry this man." She said, "I *will* marry him," and did, in the living room of the house I grew up in. After which nobody saw her for a long long time. She lived all over the world, and did not come home until her husband died. This time she was at some pains not to offend the women who were her contemporaries, and they let bygones be bygones. Because I was my father's son, she was particularly nice to me. I remember her saying she'd had a lovely life. Annette says she didn't. Lovely or not, she sat looking as quietly pleased with herself as a cat with its tail curled around its forepaws, and I used to wonder what would happen if she were to ask me to run off with her.

With the freedom children have to go where curiosity takes them, my mother must have been familiar with every nook and corner of the Hoblit house before she moved into it. She couldn't bear dark varnished woodwork, and had it painted white upstairs and down. In the dining room the walls were dark green and the molding was black, requiring coat after coat after coat of white enamel. It was the only resistance the house put up. After that it was hers. The ceilings were high, the rooms good-sized, and the big windows let in light and air and sunshine, which big mirrors studiously duplicated. My mother was as hospitable as my Grandmother Blinn, and the house didn't mind how many people she asked to stay and have hot biscuits and whatever she could find to make Sunday night supper out of. The more she filled the rooms with flowers and people, the more the living room and the dining room and the library and the kitchen seemed full of her. I didn't distinguish between the house and her, any more than I would have distinguished between her and her clothes or the sound of her voice or the way she did her hair.

The charm that old houses seem to accumulate around themselves effortlessly, this one also had. The big yard was enclosed by a low iron picket fence. The trees were full-grown but did not crowd each other or us. The wide comfortable porch went clear around to the side of the house, with a swing suspended by chains from the porch ceiling, and deep wicker chairs that, when you made the slightest move, added their creak to the late summer chorus of locusts and katydids. Under the bay window in the living room there was a bed of lilies of the valley. By the dining room window a huge white lilac bush. And farther still by the back steps, a trumpet vine and a grape arbor. Things you cannot go and buy. Time has to bring them about. During the years we lived there, there was a continuous anthropomorphic exchange of feeling and perception that was partly my responding to the house and partly the house's responding to me. When I was separated from it permanently, the sense of deprivation was of the kind that exiles know. I rather think it was the same for my older brother.

The house was a world in itself, set in the larger world of Ninth Street, which must have been about the same age. "Ninth Street" has for me a most beautiful sound. If you put it beside "Life, like a dome of many-colored glass . . ." or "Absent thee from felicity a while . . ." I would not perceive any incongruity. During the whole of my childhood I never thought it or said it or heard it without my heart responding, and fifty years later it still does— so much so that it is hard for me to realize that for other people what the name suggests is probably something quite ordinary. A quiet, tree-lined street in a small town shortly before the outbreak of the First World War is, in any event, what it was. And on hot summer evenings when my father hitched the horse up to the high English cart he was so proud of and we went out driving, I saw where we were in relation to everything else.

The courthouse square and the business district that had grown up around it were on one side of the railroad tracks, and most of the residential section of Lincoln was on the other. The streets were paved and lighted, except on the outskirts of town. There was nothing that we would now consider a factory, but what with the usual banks and small business enterprises, two coal mines, and the asylum, it was generally possible to make a living. This is not to say that no woman ever had to take in some other woman's washing, or that the shacks the Negro families lived in and the unpainted houses provided by the coal companies for the miners had a porte-cochère and half a block of lawn around them, but you could count on the fingers of one hand the houses that did. Lincoln was not a typical small town, because there is no such thing, any more than there is a typical human being. Every person was exceptional in some way. When I think of the Rimmerman girls, three middle-aged and unmarried sisters who never stopped talking, and of old Mrs. Hunter in her rusty black hat, and the plumber's wife who stopped my brother on the street and said, "I dreamt about you last night, Edward, wasn't that habitual?" and the Presbyterian minister's son who had ears like a faun and induced a kind of sexual delirium in girls without even having to get off his bicycle, and the discontented dentist's wife who was straight out of Ibsen, I wonder that so small a place could hold so much character. In the same way, every street was exceptional. You could not possibly mistake Fifth Street for Eighth Street (even when I dream about them I know which street I am on) or Broadway for Pulaski Street, and no two houses were exactly alike, either. Some of them were so original that they always seemed to have something they wanted to say as you walked past: perhaps no more than this, that the people who lived in them did not wish they lived in Paris or Rome or even Peoria. What would be the point of living somewhere where you did not know everybody?

If you wanted to walk downtown you could. If you were beyond walking distance you were outside of town, in the cornfields. But there was the streetcar if you didn't feel like walking. And in the summer they were open, and you arrived home refreshed and cool from the ride.

When the streetcars left the business district they kept to their course down Broadway, rocking and teetering and giving off overhead sparks. Across the tracks of the Chicago and Alton Railroad, and then past the Opera House, past the high school. At the corner where the grade school was, the two streetcar lines diverged. One went off, at a slight angle, down Eighth Street, depositing passengers in front of their houses, or at the asylum, or the cemeteries, or, in July and August, the Chautauqua grounds. The other line turned right and went down Union Street, past the beginning of Ninth Street, and Tremont Street, past my Aunt Maybel's house, and on out to Woodlawn, which was newer than the rest of town, and so far out that people tended to forget it existed.

The population of Lincoln stayed between ten and eleven thousand, and with very few exceptions they were all in bed by ten o'clock.

The people I knew as a child had the quality of seeming slightly larger than life size. This was, of course, partly because I was a child; but it is also true that the person with plenty of air and space around him takes on an individuality that is felt as stature.

You could be eccentric and still not be socially ostracized. You could even be dishonest. But you could not be openly immoral. The mistakes people made were not forgotten, but if you were in trouble somebody very soon found out about it and was there answering the telephone and feeding the children. Men and women alike appeared to accept with equanimity the circumstances (on the whole, commonplace and unchanging) of their lives in a way that no one seems able to do now anywhere. This is how I remember it. I am aware that Sherwood Anderson writing about a similar though smaller place saw it quite differently. I believe in Winesburg, Ohio, but I also believe in what I remember.

The glory of the town—its high-arching elms—is gone now. The elm blight did away with them in one short heartbreaking season, and Lincoln is once more exposed to the summer sun the way it was when my Grandfather Maxwell was a young man. It may yet go one step further and revert to prairie. In my childhood Lincoln was entirely canopied with elm, silver maple, box elder, linden, and cottonwood trees. Their branches frequently met over the brick pavement, and here and there, above this green roof, steeples and bell towers protruded: the Methodist, the Baptist, the Cumberland Presbyterian, the German Catholic and the Evangelical Lutheran, the Christian, the Irish Catholic, the Presbyterian, the Congregational, the African Methodist, the Universalist, the Episcopalian. On Sunday morning the air was full of the pleasant sound of church bells.

In later years, when my father spoke of the house on Ninth Street, what he remembered was the size of the coal bill, for it was not well insulated and his annual salary as state agent for the Hanover Fire Insurance Company was

$3,000. So he stood on the window seat in the library and stuffed little wads of toilet paper in the cracks where the windows did not fit snugly. I don't mean to suggest that he had no feeling for the house. He loved it, but in spite of himself, the way you love someone you don't approve of.

Since I didn't have to worry about the coal bill, what I remember is the violets; and sitting on the back steps making orange gloves for my fingers out of the blossoms of the trumpet vine; and the place, between two trees, where you could climb up onto the roof of the summer kitchen and from there get to any part of the roof you wanted; and the barn; and the flower garden; and the cities I built in my sandpile; and the shaded rustic table and chairs where we ate lunch in the hot weather; and the fact that, indoors, the rooms rested as lightly on me as a thought.

Annette says that the house was always reassuring, even when my mother wasn't there. When you walked in from outdoors, there were traces everywhere of human occupation: the remains of a teaparty on the wicker teacart in the moss-green and white living room, building blocks or lead soldiers in the middle of the library floor, a book lying face down on the window seat, an unfinished game of solitaire, a piece of cross-stitching with a threaded needle stuck in it, a paintbox and beside it a drinking glass full of cloudy water, flowers in cut-glass vases, fires in both fireplaces in the wintertime, lights left burning in empty rooms because somebody meant to come right back. Traces of being warm, being comfortable, being cozy together. Traces of us. No wonder people liked to come there.

The house was the outward reflection of a very happy marriage. Children are not always reliable witnesses in this area but I think I have it right. My parents were quite different in temperament, but they had many pleasures in common. I can't remember my mother's asking my father to do anything he didn't want to do, or to be anything he wasn't. And he betrayed his feeling for her every time he said her name. Her life had its share of sadness, some of it unbearable and still having to be borne. And if migraines have a psychological cause, what caused hers? I have no way of knowing, any more than, probably, she did. But across the felicity of her marriage to my father only one shadow stretched: She could not keep him always across the dinner table from her. Like a character in a fairy tale he was required to leave at set intervals. Every Tuesday morning he kissed her good-by and picked up the heavy grip that she hated so and went off to the railway station. He came home on the late Friday afternoon train, to be greeted on the front steps by her and my older brother and me and an old hound dog that nosed his way in between us until he got to the object of love.

If my father and mother quarreled, I never heard them at it. Or any tension in their voices when they spoke to each other. Her name was Blossom, and he called her Blos. After her death he did not like to talk about her. "That's water over the dam," he said once, when I asked him to tell me about his life with my mother. But in his old age, when five o'clock came, he liked to have a glass of Scotch at his elbow, and company, and conversation, and sometimes he would be reminded of something in the past. Once when I was home on a visit he said, "While your mother was carrying Happy we went to a wedding." He paused, and I did not encourage him to go on, though I was interested. He either said the thing you were waiting to hear or he didn't; there was never any dragging it out of him. He also, I'm sure, knew what sort of thing interested me and what didn't. And perhaps being a fisherman he liked to let out a little line and then reel me in. "It was out of town," he said finally. "The girl and I were very good friends. I'd even thought of marrying her . . . Your mother had morning sickness, and she would be sick the first thing, and then she'd get all dressed up and do whatever was expected of us. And in church I looked from one to the other of them. And I was so proud of your mother—of the way she looked and all that she was—and I broke out in a sweat at the thought of how close I'd come to marrying another woman."

12

To continue the tour of my Aunt Maybel's funereal and really very ugly house on Union Street: At the threshold of my grandmother's room, the strangeness and the oppressiveness suddenly ended. The striped wallpaper had cheerful pink roses on it, and the curtains were pinned back to make more light for sewing. The room was furnished with a heavy mahogany sleigh bed, an armoire, a dresser, and a small desk, also of mahogany, and a sewing table that could be folded up and put away but seldom was. There was a corner fireplace, but like the one downstairs in the sitting room all it amounted to was an ornamental brass shield, with no flue or hearth behind it. In this room the musty odor of the rest of the house gave way to a potpourri in which the smell of camphor and horehound drops was agreeably mixed with that of 4711 soap and lavender sachet.

When my grandmother had greeted me, she took me by the hand and led me to the attic stairs, behind what looked like a closet door in the room my uncle did not die in. Though I came to see her once a week, my toys were kept in the attic, in an egg basket. Along with its other attributes, the house on Union Street was very neat. So was the attic. They were both ready at a moment's notice for whatever would be required of them at the Last Judgment. My Cousin Blane Maxwell, my Uncle Charlie's only child, was by this time almost old enough to vote, but as my grandmother and I went down the aisle of boxes and discarded furniture, we had to pass an orderly collection of his toys,

and another of Max Fuller's, and still another that belonged to my older brother, which seemed almost to give
me a legal right to play with them. I never did.

My grandmother let me have anything I needed or
wanted, with one exception; I could not use her best sewing
scissors to cut paper with. It was my aunt who stood between
me and these marvelous playthings. The one time I dis-
obeyed her and touched a key of the little white and gold
piano on my way past, a voice spoke through the floor:
"That's your Cousin Maxwell's piano, Billie, and you are
not to play with it."

I understood that this was not unkindness but custodianship. Years hence, when Max came to her and said, "Where
is my little white and gold piano with the angels painted on
it?" she could say proudly, "In the attic, where you left it."
The same with the toys in my egg basket.

These toys—a swan sleigh that ran on concealed wooden
spools contributed by my grandmother from her sewing
basket, the furniture for Goldilocks and the three bears cut
out of the *Ladies' Home Journal*, and so on—were made by
me, with my trusty scissors and flour-and-water paste. My
grandmother's occupation was sufficiently similar that I
could follow what she was doing and appreciate her satisfaction in it. She designed and made appliquéd quilts. The
pattern was usually taken from nature—the wild rose, the
morning glory. What I cut I pasted. What she cut she pinned
or sewed. We got on perfectly.

She had yellowish-white hair, which she wore in a flat
pompadour. Her skin was soft, and her touch gentle. Her
voice I cannot convey; words do not always do what you ask
of them. It was related to hymn singing but not lugubrious.
All sorts of mysterious sounds and hesitations went on in it,
as they do in the ticking of an old clock. In her clothes she
was partial to lilac and lavender shades. She seldom moved
from her low rocking chair, and when she did it was to

search in a leisurely fashion for something she or I needed. I think it must be a common dislike of hurry that makes very young children and elderly people so congenial.

Over the big dresser in my grandmother's bedroom there was a constellation of family heads in black oval frames— my two grandparents facing each other at the apex, and two young men and two young women forming the base. These pictures must have been taken about 1897. My Aunt Bert, with her hair done up on top of her head except for one long curl (see the pictures of Ethel Barrymore in *Captain Jinks of the Horse Marines*), had not made a single disastrous marriage; my father was still intending to practice medicine; my Aunt Maybel, though not a beauty, had not yet acquired the tight-lipped expression that the front of her house had and that it undoubtedly copied from her; my Uncle Charlie looked forward to a long and happy life; my grandfather, with a splendid iron-grey mustache and those remarkable blue eyes, had no inkling that the day was going to come when he could not put his feet to the floor; and my grandmother had her husband and her children where she could watch over them and keep them from harm. I was too young and too uninformed to draw ironic conclusions. All I saw was that the people in the photographs were safe behind a layer of glass and I was not. It didn't take very much to make me feel threatened. One impatient remark could change the whole quality of the day. My grandmother's bifocals usually reflected the window or the door or the chandelier or objects in the room or a gentle consideration of what I was telling her, and if by chance they did express disapproval, it was of the Methodists or the Baptists or Woodrow Wilson, never of me.

"Come here and let me nurse you," she would say, meaning come sit on her lap and be rocked and held. When I put my arms around her I encountered a familiar obstruction, her corset, which was as rigid as her ideas about religion.

The old mahogany clock on the mantelpiece was never pressed for time, and I could feel it slowly drawing the light from the sky and the long afternoon to a peaceful close.

Sometimes I spent the night. Going to bed was a leisurely process that began with taking the pillows out of the hard round hollow bolster, and ended with the ceremony of putting my grandmother's false teeth in a glass of water. After which she opened the window the merest crack—the night air was bad for people—and turned out the light and we knelt down in the dark beside the big double bed and said our prayers.

I assumed it was in this very room (but of course it was in her bedroom in the house on Kickapoo Street) that, being up with my grandfather in the night, she heard a sound outside, and discovered that a burglar had put a ladder against the side of the house and was about to send a little boy up it to her window. She loved to tell this Dickensian incident as we were undressing for bed, and it may have had something to do with my kicking so much in my sleep that we had to have a pillow between us.

It would have been better, of course, if my grandfather had held out against her a little longer, at least until their children were educated, before they built that big house the burglar was trying to get into.

Annette once remarked, "Your Grandfather Maxwell said the kind of things to your grandmother that women like to hear, and that husbands do not always remember to say. Father and Mother were staying at Hot Springs at the same time that he was, and when they were leaving, Father asked if there was some message he could take back to Lincoln. 'You can phone my wife,' he said, 'and tell her that I haven't seen anybody as beautiful as she is since I've been gone.'"

Their deep affection for one another was not seriously affected by the annual fracas about how much money she needed to dress herself and her two daughters. But neither did they reach an understanding in the matter. He just stopped questioning her along about the first of February. Somehow he always found the money to pay Mr. Boyd, and my grandmother went on helplessly charging cotton thread and dress material and silk braid and ribbons and gloves, which sooner or later she knew she was going to be called to account for. How peaceful her last years must have seemed, in that upstairs room of the house on Union Street, with the clock that was never in a hurry, and me.

My Aunt Bert teased my grandmother affectionately, out of high spirits, as she teased everybody. My father teased my grandmother because he liked to get a rise out of her; not quite the same thing. "Your addiction to drinking warmed-over coffee is no different from my liking for whiskey," he would say. And then he would smile indulgently at the fluster and indignation this statement produced. I could not understand why he did it. She was too innocent to defend herself, and had her feelings hurt.

Once I went with her to a meeting of the Eastern Star, the ladies' auxiliary of the Masonic Lodge. My grandmother and an old man who lived next door to her were being honored—she was a charter member; what he was being honored for I don't now remember. They were presented with a decorated cake to cut, on a little table in the center of a large hall, with everybody watching. Old Mr. Stokes and everybody else in the room, including me, soon perceived that there was something wrong with that cake, but my grandmother went on trying to cut it until the cardboard cake was taken away and a real cake substituted for it. She did not see the need of jokes, and they usually had to be explained to her.

If I sneezed three times running, my grandmother gave me butter and sugar mixed in a spoon. She had absolute faith in flannel waist bands, goose grease and onions, spring tonics, and camomile tea. She used to tell that when she was a little girl and ran a high fever, they put a fly poultice on her. "I saw the eyes," she said—at which point, of course, so did I.

Some of the things that had happened to her struck me, even though I was a child, as archaic. She had been talked into having all her teeth pulled before she was forty. And she or perhaps some member of her family had been fleeced by somebody practicing the Spanish con game: She firmly believed that she was one of the rightful heirs to the land Trinity church now stands on, and that when the missing deed was located she would come into immense wealth. I knew she wouldn't, but I never argued with her—not because I was afraid of her but because I knew that about most things she couldn't change her opinion even if she had wanted to, which she mostly didn't. And her opinions had nothing to do with why I loved her.

She read the Bible, and the Lincoln *Evening Star,* and a quilting magazine that had published several of her designs. Whatever made an impression on her innocent mind she cut out and pasted in the scrapbook I have so often referred to. The greater part of the printed matter consists of yellowed clippings about the First World War. Also pages and pages of stale accounts of the life of Abraham Lincoln, and contemporary newspaper clippings about the assassinations and funerals of Garfield and McKinley. Garfield was the only preacher and the only member of the Christian Church to become President of the United States, and my grandmother thought highly of him.

What a mishmash that scrapbook is! Theodore Roosevelt and his wife and children. Woodrow Wilson's daughters. Lady Duff Gordon's eyewitness account of the sinking of the *Titanic.* Dante and Beatrice. The Longfellow house. The birthplace of Benjamin Franklin's father. Christmas and New Year's cards, business cards, letters, family photographs that I have never seen anywhere else, wedding an-

nouncements, George Washington and Buffalo Bill, Richard
Mansfield, Useful Things to Send a Soldier, a mock wedding at the Christian Church, conundrums, recipes, instructions for making quilts, the greatest snow in fifty years,
photographs of the Chautauqua grounds, receipts for the
payment of membership dues for the Order of the Eastern
Star, a cat holding a fiddle (which a note in her handwriting
says I cut out and colored), a Mother's Day telegram from
my Cousin Blane Maxwell for his dead father, the Maxwell
plaid, the program for the commencement exercises when
Max graduated from the University of Cincinnati, Mark
Twain standing in the doorway of his old home in Hannibal,
Missouri, an automobile that went over an embankment, a
twelve-year-old boy who fell into the line shaft of an
electric generator and got a thorough spinning, the buildings of Eureka College, and so on. She also set certain pages
aside for information that she felt worth preserving—facts
about my Grandfather Maxwell's family and her own, the
directions for making the crocheted table mats that she distributed so liberally through the family at Christmas time,
the occupations of her husband, her six brothers, and her
three brothers-in-law, the marriages of her children, the date
of the death of her husband and her son, the miracles of
Jesus, and the following account of the Civil War:

1860   "CIVIL WAR"
Commencement of War between North and South
1860, 1,2,3,4,

During the campaign between Lincoln and Douglas, who
were Bosomed friends at time and until death, I was a little
girl but went to Lincolns political meetings sing for him on
big floats. 25, or more Girls Sang his songs yelled untill we
were hoarse, (I was leading singer). an honor so always had
the high seat those were hot times, and full of excitement
but we all did our duty. Indians and Cowboys or Scouts,

*Ladies riding horseback, not astride he would have been
shocked. O how I wanted to ride. only a little Girl. Was
not to be thought of.*

*Lincoln became President and if he had lived everything
would have planed out right, but fate was against such a
wonderful man.*

*He called out his soldiers My father did not have to go,
sent a substitute Later on my Brother Sanford Turley Ran
away, about fifteen, a robust boy. went to St. Louis, Mo En-
listed, in 11th Mo. Regiment He stayed, over four years,
never wounded in all hard Battles, heart-rendering, to hear
him tell his hardships. Soldiers loose their health. we lived
at Williamsville about twelve miles from Springfield I shook
his big old hand.*

*His body was brought to Springfield. So his friends could
view his remains. I went to Springfield Stopped at a Demo-
crat house, and the man of house was so mad because they
made him drape his house. He got on a terrible tare. A
Rebel. every house stores and dwelling Houses were draped
thirty days*

*Procession went by the house where I stayed. His old
Horse old run down Boots across the Saddle bag and several
other things Out to Oak Ridge Cemetery. His last resting
place they put Douglas and Lincoln Suits they wore in
campaign in Museum in Chicago. Suppose they are there yet.*

Such education as my grandmother had was in a one-room
country schoolhouse, and it enabled her to spend her life
reading the Bible, so it was sufficient, until she came to writing. She used quotation marks when she began a new line,
and didn't distinguish between a comma and a period. Her
spelling is sometimes by ear ("valubel" for "valuable")
and sometimes distracted ("bosomed friends") and sometimes it is even correct. But she invariably left off the "e"
at the end of her brother Meade's name, and in listing her
children in the scrapbook she—this I really don't understand

—spelled my Aunt Bert's middle name "Louweze." I mean you'd think she would know how to spell the name of her own daughter; she must have been thinking about something else.

My father considered the scrapbook an object of genuine historical value and asked my grandmother to leave it to him in her will, but she had made it for Max Fuller, because he was interested in family history, and Max got it.

Turning the pages, I came on a letter to her from my father that casts a rather different light on his teasing. When he wrote it he was twenty-eight years old and had been married two and a half years.

Lincoln, Ill   12/18/1906

My Dear "Mammy"

I was greatly disappointed when I learned you would not be with me Christmas, as far as I can remember I cannot re-call that we were ever separated before. I do not say this to cause you any regret as I fully believe you and Aunt Etta * will enjoy Xmas day together. We have a fine tree planned for Edward and do wish so much that you could see him as usual. We have such a lovely present for you but it is impossible to send it to Parsons so will have to await your return.

Have been greatly upset since last week Mother as Higley and Hubbard have quit the Hanover and organized another Company and I cannot say as to the new management whether it will be congenial to me. If I had lost my own job I could not have been more crushed and stunned but I will not feel that another streak of bad luck has overtaken me† and I will fight for my rights and win out in the end.

---

* The widow of my Grandfather Maxwell's brother Will (the one who turned up in the hotel lobby) lived in Parsons, Kansas.

† What were the others? All gone. Never mentioned in my hearing and probably forgotten by the time I came along, but the explanation, perhaps, for his habitual caution.

Well Mammy Dear this does not seem much like Xmas times. I am able to grasp the fact however after wading through a Xmas list of fifty but "Shaw Mamm" let's try and get a little out of life while here as we are a long time dead.

You mustn't get lonesome now and cry on Xmas as we will all think about you and have your presents waiting for you on your return.

Better try and get to St. Louis before the first of the year so that your passes will not expire on you. Happy is sending you a little remembrance and we all hope you will make this Xmas a happy one and not give way to lonesomeness.

Lovingly
Will

Fred Hubbard and Charlie Higley, the two men my father worked under, did not in the end leave the company; the storm blew over, and his life went on as before; but the letter is for me like coming upon a door to a closet I didn't even know was there. I had no idea that my father was ever so unconfident or so vulnerable. Or that he was so deeply attached to my grandmother.

It is also true that children prefer not to inquire too closely into the natures of their parents. In a storeroom off the kitchen of the house I lived in as a child there was a grocery carton full of letters that my father wrote to my mother from the road. I had no curiosity whatever about them.

All my grandmother's brothers were interesting to her, but the one who turned up the most frequently was Uncle Sanford, the drummer boy. He was the oldest, and she was next and I suspect followed him around when they were little. He lived in Kansas, and according to a note in my grandmother's scrapbook, he combined farming and the music business—that is, he sold sheet music and upright pianos and band instruments. But it is an unlikely combination and I can only think he must have had help. Her other brothers, Dave, James, Marshall, and Meade, all at one time or another farmed land that their father had given them. Uncle Meade's full name was General Meade Turley, after the Union general who won the greatest battle of the Civil War, at Gettysburg, and then didn't follow it up. My grandmother also had an uncle who was named Commodore Perry Turley. Uncle Marshall had a button factory.

Judging by another letter I found in the scrapbook, dated April 13, 1917, he was a joker.

> . . . *By this time you have heard that I was in your part of the country and as it was fully my intention to come and see you regardless of the rain I finally located the telephone in the city of Williamsville and upon two attempts they failed to reach you and upon the assistance of your neighbors the information I got that you had gone to war But the recruiting officer had turned you down for the same reason that my wife was when she tried to enter in my absence, that they was only one place they could use you and that was the trenches and it would be too much to dig the ditch for your size but later if they decided to dig the trenches bigger they would send you word. Now I did not get to see you when I was over but we are coming over in June and we will make you tired then your brother Marsh.*

The only one of my grandmother's brothers who lived in Lincoln was my Great-uncle Dave. The paragraph about him in the county history is really about his wife—her maiden name (Elva L. Stolz); her parents (Solomon and Maria Stolz); her father's death when she was four, and her mother's second marriage and removal to California; her elder sister's marriage in New York State to a Mr.

Lynde. From which I deduce that when the historian came
to the door, *she* talked to him. At the time the history was
published my great-uncle was farming. Later he moved to
town and opened a shoe store, which failed. Two children
died in infancy. It would seem that sadness followed him
around like a dog.

One winter day my grandmother and I walked down
Union Street to his house. For some reason I remember
walking there through the snow with extraordinary clarity.
And afterward, sitting on the floor of the parlor, with my
head on a line with the isinglass windows of the potbellied
parlor stove. I have been given a marvelous page of the
Sunday paper to cut out: the cat fiddling (when put together
with brads, the arms and legs are movable) and the cow
jumping over the moon. The conversation of my grandmother and her sister-in-law, whom she didn't much like,
is carried on peacefully above my head. As I cut and fold on
the dotted line, I learn (but without any emotion) that my
grandmother's brother, in an upstairs room, is dying of
cancer.

Her sisters my grandmother simply accepted, the way she
accepted the fact that the week has seven days. Sue married
a doctor and lived out her life in or around Williamsville.
Mandy's husband had a grocery store, as I have said, and
Ina married a plantation owner and lived in Mississippi.

She was seventeen years younger than my grandmother,
and came to Lincoln only once during my childhood. She
brought her whole family—her husband (who was born on
a farm near Williamsville but had long since acquired a full
set of Mississippi vowels), her two nearly grown sons, her
daughter and son-in-law and their little girl. Some of them
stayed at our house, since my Aunt Maybel's house wouldn't
begin to hold them all.

They were the first Southerners my brother and I had
ever encountered, and we tried to manage so they were

never out of our sight. If one of the boys went down the hall to take a bath, I didn't let the closed bathroom door deprive me of the pleasure of his conversation. Even when they sat and didn't open their mouths, they were fascinating, the way animals are—beautiful animals who arch their back or lick their hind leg and you are in the presence of the Creation. But they were encouraged to talk, and felt a solemn obligation to be entertaining. Someone would make a commonplace remark and Aunt Ina, fanning herself with one of my grandmother's palm-leaf fans, would smile appreciatively and turn to her husband and say, "Doesn't that put you in the mind of Old Bess and her blind billy goat?" and they'd be off, creating characters and scenes out of the air. What seemed like effortless charm must have been a performance of considerable virtuosity, but I don't think it was something they did particularly or exclusively for our benefit. If somebody had actively disliked them, I don't know that they could have stood it—No, that isn't true, people are never as vulnerable as they seem. But anyway, nobody in Lincoln disliked them. Or even came near to it. So I have no way of knowing how they would have reacted if someone had.

In spite of the date on her wall calendar, my Grandmother Maxwell's life was deep inside the 19th century. The Civil War was no farther away in her memory than the beginning of the First World War now is in mine. And the historical names—Gettysburg, Missionary Ridge, Chattanooga and Chickamauga, Bull Run—often figured in her conversation.

At some point she and my grandfather spent a winter in Tennessee for the sake of his health. They lived in a cabin on the side of Lookout Mountain, and the Negroes who lived nearby used to come and visit them in the evening. "We got along very well," she would remark complacently —the complacency of the Northerner over the Southerners, who *lost*.

"If the Southerners had only been nice to the darkies, and

called them Mr. and Mrs., there wouldn't have been any Civil War."

My Grandfather Maxwell had been a Republican so my grandmother was too, in principle; and in the end, thanks to a Democratic president, she had the right to vote. No doubt she exercised it, but she wasn't given to intellectual complexities. What interested her was not the broad political issues of the day but the rumor that the first Mrs. Woodrow Wilson died of a broken heart, because of her husband's infidelities, and that when the second Mrs. Wilson accompanied him to the Peace Conference in Paris, her clothes closet was lined with satin. How indignant my grandmother was with that clothes closet!

I assumed that my mother loved my grandmother because I did, but they were cut out of very different cloth, and Annette says that my mother found my grandmother trying. She *would* give me horehound drops and other dubious things to eat that upset my stomach. And once when she stayed with my brother and me so that my father and mother could go on a trip together, she went through every drawer in the house, tidying and straightening and putting things away in new places, according to a system that, over the years, she had settled on. She must have known that my mother wouldn't like it, because no woman would, but the temptation was too much for her. She even went into my mother's dressing table. It was months before my mother found everything.

I also assumed that my grandmother loved my mother, and nobody has ever said that she didn't. But she may have loved my mother and been glad that my father had a wife who made him happy, and at the same time been jealous of my mother, too. You cannot go to the cemetery and ask to be enlightened on matters of this kind, though it would ease my mind considerably if you could.

·   ·   ·

The cemetery in Lincoln is situated in a grove of oak trees on a bluff looking out over the rich farmland—a serene and timeless frame for lives concluded and beyond grieving over. My mother took me with her when she went there to tend the family graves. From the winding cinder drive I read the names on the tombstones. The cemetery was a replica in a few wooded acres of the town, for the names that constantly occurred in the conversation of my elders were all here: Gilchrist, Foley, Buehler, Crain, Ewing, Maltby, Randolph, Frorer, Cadwaller, Keys, Bates, Humphrey, Hill—the smaller, weathered headstones marking the individual resting places, and obelisks of marble and granite establishing the family territory. The graves were not neglected, and the dead were not forgotten but only a little removed from the heart of things.

My mother picked off the dry blooms from the geraniums and threw away the withered flowers and rancid water in the tin vases that were sunk in the ground, and stood contemplating the headstones: "Edward Blinn, 1844–1913" and "Annette L. Blinn, 1848–1914." She let me fill the vases with fresh water from the nearest faucet, and as she arranged the flowers she had brought from the garden at home she would talk to me in a voice pitched a little lower than ordinary, making me feel the presence of the people all around us in their graves. Sometimes she would find fresh flowers in the vases, indicating that someone had been here before us, someone not the family who continued to remember my grandparents with love after they were dead—and she would wonder aloud who it was. Then we would get in the carriage and follow the winding cinder drive until we came to my Grandfather Maxwell's grave. Throughout the cemetery there were flags, some bright, some faded, in star-shaped metal standards, marking the graves of those who had fought in the Spanish-American or the Civil War. I loved all flags. Here and there among the graves were family mausoleums, hardly bigger than a child's playhouse but made of white marble and with no windows and an iron grating across the door. What if somebody wanted to get out? But this applied also to people buried in the ground, and I tried not to think about it. And did think about it, even so. What was to prevent people from opening their eyes and seeing what had happened to them?

"Do you remember your grandfather?"

The sadness I hear in my mother's voice makes me search around in the back of my mind for something that turns out not to be there. I feel that she will be distressed if I say I don't remember him, and so I manage to conjure up a shadowy figure (as in six or seven years' time I would be calling on recollection for what she looked like). "I remember him coming up the street," I say. I am aware that the image is perhaps invented, and I expect she was too.

When I study his picture—the fine forehead, the line of the jaw, the mouth half concealed under a drooping mustache, and the eyes, particularly the eyes, which I know so well because I have known them all my life, they are just like Annette's and they have looked past me so often with just that expression, as of someone staring at life itself—I regret deeply that I cannot remember him. It is the picture of a man of intelligence and feeling, with a vein of sadness running through his nature, and a commitment to various abstractions, including honor.

My grandfather was born in St. Johnsbury, Vermont. His last name was originally spelled Blynn, and his father, writing in the family Bible, changed the *y* to an *i*. Annette says that the family is descended from one of two brothers who came over on the *Mayflower*. I looked up the passenger list and was relieved to find no Blynns, and no brothers who fit the description my aunt has given of them. My Great-grandfather Blinn and his brother were both cattle farmers, one in Vermont, the other in Canada. My Grandfather Blinn's mother, Leefee Harrington, was descended from Jonathan Harrington, the first man killed in the American Revolution. His house still stands on Lexington Common. He was wounded in that historic volley of Pitcairn's redcoats, and crawled across the green and died in his wife's arms, on the morning of April 19, 1775. Shortly after this, his son James took all his worldly possessions and tied them up in a bandanna and with the bundle slung from a cane resting on his shoulder, walked to Vermont. The cane came down through the family and only in the last fifteen years disappeared, accidentally, during a housecleaning. That is to say, it was left on the lawn, along with the rest of the contents of the front hall closet at my Aunt Annette's, when she was in Florida, and somebody walking past stole it. Leefee Harrington was James Harrington's granddaughter. Her sister Candace married my great-grandfather, Charles Blinn, had two children by him, and died. Leefee Harrington was engaged to a man named Edward Dunallen, whom she deeply loved, but my great-grandfather persuaded her that it was her duty to marry him instead, and look after her sister's children. She named her first-born child, my grandfather, after the man she loved, and, though she later had a daughter, gave him the whole of her heart.

My great-grandfather wanted my Grandfather Blinn to go into the cattle business with him and was very angry when my grandfather told him he wanted to be a lawyer, instead. My grandfather left home at the age of eighteen, and got a job as a bookkeeper in a pump factory in Cincinnati. The *Logan County History* says that two years after he came there he began to read law in the office of Kebler & Whitman, and in 1866 was admitted to the bar. That would mean he was twenty-two. Annette says that he was admitted to the bar before he was twenty-one, and that when he was asked how this happened he said, "I worked awfully hard, and didn't have much to eat, and I looked older than I was, so they didn't ask me how old I was and I didn't tell them."

I don't know what the connection was that brought him to Lincoln, in the fall of 1866. He started in the office of one of the two leading lawyers, and two years later went into partnership with the other. This statement is perhaps misleading in that it suggests that everything fell into his lap when actually there wasn't a great deal to fall into anybody's lap. The *Logan County History* says, "In the early days of the courts of this county most of the business was done by lawyers from other places. Logan County was regarded as an outpost of Springfield and Bloomington lawyers, who claimed it as a part of their bailiwick and gobbled up all the paying practise; but a time came when the lawyers here were not only able to sustain themselves and hold their practise at home against all comers but were able to retaliate upon the enemy by carrying the war into their own camps and foraging upon them. For many years past, all the business in the courts, at least all of any importance and having any pay in it, has been done by the members of the local bar." That my Grandfather Blinn had something to do with this reversal, I see no reason to doubt.

Speaking at my grandfather's funeral, one of the lawyers of his generation said, "I have practised law with Mr. Blinn and against Mr. Blinn for over forty years, and I learned early, very early, in my practise that if Mr. Blinn was on the other side of a lawsuit I had to thoroughly understand every feature of the case, for if you made a blunder, you were out of the Court House. If he was on your side of the lawsuit he was a constant inspiration and strength, by reason of his wonderful grasp of all the minutiae of the facts, as well as the law in the case under consideration. And whether he was on the same side of a case with you or against you, he commanded not only your respect but your admiration by reason of his wonderful, wonderful intellectuality.

He was perhaps the best all round advocate and lawyer combined that I ever had the pleasure of knowing or ever had the pleasure of hearing, and that is saying a great deal."

The schoolboy who followed the Gillett trial with such a precocious interest became a lawyer when he grew up, and he once said "In matters pertaining to the law, your Grandfather Blinn was highly intelligent, a lawyer's lawyer, and during the years when he sat on the bench, an impartial judge. When he was trying a case before the jury and it suited his purposes, he could act the fire-eater." Since this doesn't appear to fit very well with the statement that he was a lawyer's lawyer, I assume it must be true; opinions that are all of a kind have usually been tampered with.

I do not think my grandfather discussed his cases at home, and his children tended to think of the courtroom as a kind of empyrean quite beyond their understanding. Annette says that my grandfather had a license to practice in the District of Columbia (from which I infer that he argued cases that were being tried before the Supreme Court) and that some of his opinions made law. But she doesn't know what this statement means; it is only something she heard said.

While my grandfather practiced law with one partner or another he also dabbled in politics. In the 1870's, at which time he was a young man in his early thirties, he ran for Congress and was defeated. Later, when the nomination would have been equivalent to election, he refused it. He had found that he preferred practicing law. Perhaps also he preferred being behind the scenes. In 1880 he was a delegate to the Republican National Convention at Chicago, and in 1884 he was one of the Presidential electors for the State of Illinois. From 1888–92 he was a member of the Court of Claims, from which he resigned when John P. Altgeld was elected governor. Apparently he was too much of a radical for my grandfather to serve under. Altgeld was a

German immigrant. He wrote a book* contending that American judicial methods were weighted against the poor, which nobody in his right mind would deny now, but a great many people refused to believe then. As governor, Altgeld was the champion of labor, reform, and liberal thought, and I wish that my Grandfather Blinn had been among those who fought at his side, but you have to take your ancestors as you find them.

My grandfather's obituary notice says that he was "modest in all his actions, never seeming to recognize his own greatness," that he often asked advice from other lawyers, even the most lowly in the profession; that he headed the bar of Logan County; and that he died "with a legal fame extending to other states and with a standing for probity and honor so high that it was never tarnished by idle report or by the jealousy of his opponents or his competitors in whatever walk of life he choosed to walk." I have never heard anything that would cast doubt on the truth of these statements, and small-town people like nothing better than whittling somebody down to size.

* *Our Penal Machinery and Its Victims* (1884).

13

The paragraph on my grandfather in the *Logan County History* concludes: "January 1, 1869, Mr. Blinn was married at Cold Spring, Kentucky, to Nettie L., daughter of John C. Youtsey, a prominent citizen of that place."

You don't begin by being a prominent citizen, you arrive there in the fullness of time, after quite a lot of agricultural or commercial activity. The first Youtsey I know anything about floated down the Ohio River on a flatboat loaded with whiskey and molasses, shortly after the year 1800. His name was John, he was my great-great-great-grandfather, and Annette says he started from Knight's Ferry, Virginia, which I have yet to find on any map. According to a statement by an unnamed person born about 1820 and probably a second cousin of my Grandmother Youtsey, John Youtsey first settled in Maryland, then moved on to Pennsylvania, and "made some money there and bought a little flatboat, and floated down the river to Cincinnati. Didn't have a brick house in it—so I have been told. Old Dick Southgate was a young lawyer at that time, and he noticed my grandfather's little boat lying there at the water's edge, and it was called the *Pennsylvania German*."

For a moment the telescope is in perfect focus.

My mother's cousin Hugh Davis said that Nicholas Longworth, the grandfather of the Speaker of the House of Representatives, was with him. Nicholas Longworth was the third son of a well-to-do Tory family in Newark, New Jersey, who, because of fines and confiscations, were in reduced circumstances. I have been slow to accept this connection, but on the other hand it seems rather an odd thing to invent. It is a fact that Nicholas Longworth came west on a flatboat at this time. He was nineteen years old. He had a leather chest with him, and history has preserved an inventory of its contents: "Six coats, black and blue; one dozen plain and fancy waistcoats; four pairs of silk and eight of woolen breeches; six dozen plain and ruffled shirts; a like number of hose and handkerchiefs, with cravats and other et ceteras." In short his mother sent him forth prepared for every social emergency. I somehow doubt if John Youtsey had much more than the clothes on his back.

If Nicholas Longworth was an amiable young man, and probably he was, he invited my great-great-great-grand-father to sit on the trunk with him, and together they came floating down the Ohio all the way from Pittsburgh, between two solid walls of timber.

This suggests Jim and Huckleberry Finn on the raft, though it was the Ohio, not the Mississippi, and the flatboat no doubt was considerably bigger. But they were subject to the same alternation of blue sky, white clouds, grey clouds, stormy weather. Sun burning through the fog. The sound of waves lapping on the shore of an island. A hawk wheeling, herons wading. The sad colors of daybreak. The excitement of smoke rising from the trees. Voices coming across the water. The Big Dipper and the Little Dipper, the Pleiades, and Cassiopeia's Chair.

There is a legend in the family—my family, I mean—that John Youtsey was offered the land Cincinnati now stands on in exchange for his whiskey and molasses, and turned it down, on the grounds that it was a hog wallow, and went up the Licking River and raised strawberries. Something like that happened, if not exactly that. Nicholas Longworth settled in Cincinnati, and became a lawyer. Unlike other men of that profession he was willing to take land in settlement of fees, and, since Cincinnati was rapidly changing from a village into a city, it wasn't long before he was immensely wealthy. He also became a horticulturist of some importance. One of his discoveries was that in order to raise strawberries profitably the farmer had to use both male and female plants. So perhaps he was a friend of my great-great-great-grandfather and really did come down the Ohio with him on a flatboat, only my great-great-great-grandfather must have waited quite some time, until Nicholas Longworth made that discovery, before he started raising strawberries for the market in Cincinnati.

In 1844, his grandson, John C. Youtsey, bought a farm of 106 acres, at Cold Spring, in Campbell County. And at some point he took his family and went north into Illinois, in a covered wagon. He arrived in Postville on a Saturday night, and was so appalled by the drunkenness and the fistfights that he started back to Kentucky early the next morning. In 1855, still living on the farm at Cold Spring, he started to build a new house, of brick fired on the place. It was not finished when the war broke out.

My great-grandfather would not own slaves, Annette said, but his brother did, and went bankrupt because of this. At different times, both Union and Confederate troops camped in the grove in front of my great-grandfather's house. He was a United States marshal, and my grandmother's sister remembered their father being shot at twice, from ambush. Once when they were expecting a detachment of Southern forces, somebody sent a Negro servant out to bury the family silver. He didn't return, and the silver was never found, though they dug and searched the place over, with a singular lack of suspicion, for years.

John C. Youtsey had four sons and three daughters. Three of the boys fought in the war, on the side of the North. Among the letters that have come down in the family is one from my grandmother's brother John, written in a fine copperplate hand, on lined notepaper.

Dear Father:

Again we are on the eve of another grand movement. Our Command has orders to be in readiness to march by day after tomorrow (17) The probability is that we shall strike South Carolina, this time. Sherman will make Savannah his base, for the present and as his Army moves toward Charleston he will keep Communication opened through the Charleston and Savannah Railroad. Our Cavalry will cover his left flank, making raids into the interior meantime. Consequently you will not be apt to hear from me for some time after we leave this place. . . .

Though she never saw him, my Aunt Annette remembers her mother's saying that he was very handsome, with dark, reddish hair and a mustache.

He was the last of the brothers to get home, and when he walked up the drive in the middle of the night, the house was dark. A dog that had been a puppy when he left was now full grown and a fierce watchdog. It knew him and didn't make a sound. He shinnied up a post and got into his room by way of the porch roof. But he had arrived in the midst of spring housecleaning, and his mother had emptied an upstairs bookcase and dumped the books on his bed. So when he started to get in between the covers, a pile of books he didn't know was there fell on the floor and woke the entire household.

John C. Youtsey's mother lived with them. She was Scottish—"a small but mighty person." The same thing was said of John C. Youtsey's wife, my great-grandmother. She was also a great reader. "Grandfather and the man would come in from the fields," Annette said, "and she'd be sitting with a book and the stove would be cold. When Mother was fourteen she took over the cooking, and her father never came in to a cold stove after that time. She was so beautiful that, when she took the ferry, the men who had just crossed over would cross again with her so they could look at her. She had black hair and big brown eyes, like your mother. When she looked at you with those eyes, you'd do anything in the world she asked."

As bookkeeper of the pump factory, my grandfather made routine visits to the bank, and there he struck up an acquaintance with one of my grandmother's brothers, who was a teller. He invited my grandfather home for the weekend, and after that, he came often. My Great-grandfather Youtsey was very strict in his observance of the Sabbath. The horses were turned out to pasture and the family walked to church. What they ate on Sunday was all cooked the day before. One Saturday, my great-uncle and my grandfather wolfed every scrap of food that had been prepared for the day of rest. I think it is likely that young Edward Blinn and Nettie Youtsey had an understanding before he left Cincinnati to practice law in Lincoln. It was several years before he was in a position to marry. My great-grandfather was distressed to learn that his daughter was being carried off to the very place where he had been so offended by rowdy and drunken behavior, but he did not forbid the marriage.

When my grandmother came to Lincoln as a bride, someone gave a tea for her. The guests left, by twos and threes, and were raked over the coals. As the teaparty broke up, my grandmother said, "I stayed to the end so you couldn't talk about me."

She was homesick, and every summer, while court was in session and my grandfather was very busy, she went to Kentucky. When he could, he came and joined her there and they stayed on a while longer. One year, Annette said, he was much longer than usual in coming and she missed him so she was never homesick for Kentucky again—only for him.

While she was in Kentucky, my grandfather had a chance to buy, very reasonably, a house on Ninth Street that had never been lived in by anybody. The contractor had built it for himself, and changed his mind about living there. My grandfather sold the house they were living in, and he threw in the bedroom furniture with it, not knowing that my grandmother kept her engagement ring in a little bag tied to the back of one of the bedposts.

For a long, long time—for twelve or thirteen years, my grandparents had no children. One of my grandmother's brothers married a Catholic, creating a scandal, and they had six daughters, and at one point my grandmother wrote to her sister-in-law, whom she had become very fond of, asking if she would let one of the girls come and live with her in Lincoln because she was so lonely. The answer was, "I haven't one daughter too many."

My Grandfather Blinn's half-brother died, leaving a wife and three small children, and my grandparents took the youngest. They wanted to adopt her from the beginning, but her mother was of two minds about this. She spoke of taking the child back and didn't. Then she said they could have little Edith and a few days later wrote that they couldn't. In the end, by insisting that she take the child before they got any fonder of her, my grandparents were allowed to keep her. Shortly after that, they began to have children of their own. My mother was the oldest. Between Annette and my Uncle Ted, my grandmother lost a child, and it made her morbidly apprehensive. She held Annette responsible for my uncle's safety when they were playing together, and this heavy burden became a part of the fabric of Annette's dreams. Whether it was true or not, she thought that her mother didn't love her as much as she loved my uncle and my mother. But there was one person whose affection for her she was not in any uncertainty about. When my grandmother kissed my grandfather good-by at the front door, there, exasperatingly, was little Annette, sitting on the porch steps, waiting to give him the last kiss. In the evening, Annette went down to the end of the street in order to be the first one to meet him coming home. Once, she dressed up in her mother's clothes and stood waiting on the front porch to greet him. My grandfather tipped his hat to her, and it was too much. She ran into the house, crying, "Mother! He *doesn't* know who I am!"

My grandfather loved to bring people home with him for a meal, and extra leaves were always being slipped into the dining room table. The larder was like a store, with bins of potatoes, barrels of flour and sugar, and the shelves crammed with canned fruit and vegetables.

Ninth Street then was very much the way it was when I lived there, except that where two or three houses I knew stood there was an orchard, and every house had a barn behind it. The street wasn't paved, and so the children had the blackest imaginable mud to play in. When I was a child the sidewalks were of cement, but before that they were brick, and before that, wooden boards. When the wooden sidewalks were taken up so that the brick sidewalk could be laid, Annette said, the children followed the workmen in a body, finding all sorts of treasures that had fallen through the cracks between the boards.

In the texture of the Blinn family life in Lincoln there were both light and dark threads, with, as time went on, the darker ones becoming preponderant. When my mother was about nine years old, the barn behind my grandfather's house burned down, with my mother's Indian pony in it.

I grew up thinking that a man my grandfather had sentenced for some crime or misdemeanor had set fire to the barn, out of revenge, but my grandfather never sat on the bench of a criminal court, and what actually happened was that, for a prank, a boy poured kerosene over the hay in a manger and held a lighted match to it.

"We were out driving," Annette said, "and your mother was at home alone. Father saw the flames as he turned into Ninth Street, and said, 'I think that's our barn!' He tied the reins to the nearest hitching post and ran, but it was already too late." A neighbor had gone into the stall with my mother and thrown a coat over the pony's head. It was too frightened and totally unmanageable. My grandfather found out how the fire was started, but he did nothing, nor would he tell the children who had set the fire. All he said was that the boy's mother was a widow and having a hard time.

My Aunt Annette had mysterious fainting spells which they thought were caused by her heart. At that time the high school was on the third floor of a building that also housed the elementary school, and rather than have her climb the stairs she was tutored at home, which added to her sense of isolation. My mother went to a finishing school in Monticello, Illinois. My grandparents didn't hear from her at the usual time, and when a day or two passed and there was still no letter they began to worry. Then they had a letter from her roommate saying that my mother hadn't written because she hurt her wrist playing basketball. They went down and found her with a broken wrist untended to, and took her out of school. After that she was tutored at home with Annette.

Neither one ever had a friend who was as close to her as the three sisters were to each other, but Annette believed that when she went anywhere with my mother, people always spoke to my mother, never to her. They cannot have been unaware of Annette, because she was the beauty of the family, but my mother had a natural charm of manner, and people felt that she was aware of them, of what was

going on in their lives and in their hearts—as in fact she was
—and they responded to this concern for them, with the
result that Annette felt trapped and rendered invisible by
my mother's personality.

There are no antiquarians in my mother's family and
Annette is vague, and sometimes even mistaken, about de-
tails of family history. But not about the family life of the
Blinns at 301 Ninth Street.

"I had a kimona with red polka dots on it," she said. "I
was just wild about it. And one day Mother sent your
mother and me to see a woman who used to work for us.
They were very poor—her husband delivered coal. And
she was sick in bed and didn't even have a wrapper to put on.
Her two children were playing on the floor beside the bed,
and the sheets were dirty, and there were bags of coal in the
bedroom, and coal dust over everything. In those days our
dresses touched the floor and had trains, and when I saw
how dirty the place was, I gathered up my skirts. I couldn't
help it. But your mother walked right over and sat down
on the edge of the bed and took Nell's hand and began to
talk to her. That was the way she was."

The first time I heard this story it ended there. The next
time, years later, it had a different ending: "When we got
home Blossom burst out, 'Mother, I am *ashamed* of Annette.
She gathered up her skirts so they wouldn't touch anything!'
And Mother filled a basket with food and wine and clean
sheets, and said, 'Annette, since you behaved that way,
you can take this to Nell. And you can take her that kimona
you're so fond of.' "

This severity was never meted out to my uncle. It is, of
course, easier to perceive that a child is being spoiled than to
prevent it, but my grandfather tried. Where my Maxwell
grandparents quarreled over the bills that came on the
second day of January, my Grandfather and Grandmother
Blinn had words over Teddy. At some point, all unknowing,

my uncle had stepped into quicksand: he had discovered how much he could get away with.

My Aunt Edith (who was really my cousin once removed) was, on the other hand, not allowed to get away with anything. She was the oldest and that in itself would make for a stricter upbringing, but anyway, from things she said over the years, I have the impression that she nourished a number of grievances, and felt that my grandparents had distinguished between her and their own children. Annette says they didn't. If she had not loved my Grandmother Blinn dearly, or if my Grandmother Blinn had not loved her, would my Aunt Edith have taken such pride in setting before us my Grandmother Blinn's Thanksgiving dinner, from beginning to end?

She was like my mother and my aunt and not like them. Where they would open their arms to you, she would give you a peck on the cheek, and if you gave her a hug the response was only a fleeting smile. But such an eye for what made my brother and me happy! The magic lantern, the Peg-Lock blocks, and the Hollow Tree books that so occupied my mind and imagination all came from her. Never once did she forget to have our favorite dishes when we went to visit her, and she always managed to find out what we wanted to do and were afraid to ask for, and we got to do it. We allowed for what we thought was the difference and loved her as much as we loved my Aunt Annette but differently. It wasn't until I was grown that I discovered the power of feeling behind the peck, and the understanding and good judgment that illuminated her affection for us. She might have led a very different life and been rather a different person if my grandfather had believed in education for women. One of her teachers who was leaving Lincoln to take a job at Smith College wanted to take my Aunt Edith with her. My grandfather did not believe in higher education for women, and that was that.

My grandfather went back to St. Johnsbury every year, and the family with him. They usually stayed with his sister, after his father and mother died, but Annette remembers that one year her grand-uncle drove down from Canada and took them back with him. As they were crossing the border, he said, "Now, children, the horses are in Canada, the wagon is in the United States." His house had once been an inn, and there he and his sons and daughters and their families lived, each in a separate wing.

My grandmother continued to go home to Kentucky in the summer, only now the children went with her. When my mother and my two aunts spoke of their Kentucky cousins, their faces would light up. As a small child, I looked like my mother's cousin Wright, and sometimes, smiling at me, she would call me by his name. I felt it was an honor to look like Wright Youtsey. The Kentucky cousins played in a pack—in the house, down by the river, in the big hayloft. My mother's cousin Hugh Davis said that the attic was full of Civil War uniforms, which the boys used to try on, and there were also old guns, including a Kentucky long rifle and a beautiful twenty-eight gauge muzzle loader shotgun made in England. "Grandmother promised me one of those guns, but not being around when the house was broken up, I never saw it."

Along about the year 1890, they were all in Kentucky for a golden wedding anniversary. What my Aunt Annette remembers of this occasion is that her grandfather, knowing she loved bananas, took her into a storeroom where there was a huge bunch of them hanging from a hook in the ceiling and said, "Granddaughter, whenever you want a banana, come in here and get it." At some point they all came trooping out of the house and posed for the wet-plate photographer with his head under a black cloth. The grandparents are seated on a bench in the center of the picture. With his full and rather wild grey beard, my great-grandfather a little resembles the pictures of John Brown of Harper's Ferry, though he was not at all that kind of man. My great-grandmother has a long thin face and her hair, still black, is parted in the middle and brushed tight to her skull. She looks as if her life had turned out just the way she thought it would, and he appears to be in a state of mild shock at the realization of all they have lived through in the last fifty years. My grandmother's brothers look enough like my Grandfather Blinn to be his brothers, instead. George Youtsey and Aunt Sally and two of their children are in an open window directly above the bench. Tom Youtsey and his wife are standing, and so are my Great-aunt Ev's husband, Burch Davis, and my Great-aunt Sue's husband, Douglas Brown, with little Donald. And seated in chairs or on the ground are Howard Youtsey and Bertha (the Catholic, with a delicate pointed face and large gentle eyes), my grandmother's two sisters, Granny Blinn with my Uncle Ted on her lap, my Grandfather Blinn with Annette leaning against him (about this sort of thing the camera never lies), and a job lot of twenty-five beautiful children, my mother being among them. The young man who wrote that quietly self-possessed letter on the eve of the turning point of the Civil War is missing: He died young, of the hardships suffered on Sherman's march to the sea.

My Grandfather Blinn couldn't continue to worship in the religion he was raised in because there was no church of that denomination in Lincoln. He and my grandmother went to the Methodist church for many years, but they did not join it, because my grandfather felt that he could not subscribe to all of its tenets. Annette says that they stopped going to church because my grandfather was growing deaf. "One Sunday, walking home after the service, Mother asked if he had enjoyed the sermon and he replied, 'I didn't hear one word of it,' and she resolved not to put him through that any more." His deafness increased to the point where he had to have a trial suspended while he went to Chicago and was fitted for a hearing aid, so he could hear the witnesses.

On Sunday evenings he gathered the family together in the parlor and talked to them about the Bible. He said that there was no legal question that was not covered by some passage in the Scriptures.

He was the friend of every minister in town, and used to seek them out to discuss religion with them—particularly the Catholic priest. He had a very high opinion of all these men, my aunt says. Unless I am mistaken he also had a high opinion of Robert G. Ingersoll. When the old house across the street was emptied, the twelve volumes of Ingersoll's lectures and miscellaneous writings (*The Gods, Some Mistakes of Moses, Why I Am an Agnostic, Superstition,* and so forth) ended up in my father's den. Though they were not much read, they were looked at with respect, as if behind the glass doors of the bookcase we were keeping a king cobra. Voltaire would have served my grandfather's purposes better, but Voltaire was not accessible and Ingersoll was, is the simple truth of the matter.

The friend who was closest to my Grandfather Blinn's heart was Richard Oglesby. The two men were both of a speculative turn of mind, and among the things they loved to speculate on was the nature of life after death. They made a bargain that whichever one died first would make every effort in his power to inform the other of what he found. Since they were both lawyers, they also had that— they had the law in its theoretical aspects and as it was carried out in the courts—to argue about.

Though my grandfather's sympathies were easily touched, his social ideas would not be considered enlightened today. He defended the Chicago and

Alton Railroad in a suit brought against it by the destitute family of a man who was run over and killed while picking up coal on the right of way. Governor Oglesby took exception to this and said that if my grandfather had no other way to keep his wife and children warm, he'd do what the dead man did. My grandfather insisted that the man was where he ought not to have been: that it was not a question of the sacredness of property but of the sacredness of the law.

Oglesby's experience of life had been more varied than my grandfather's. He was born in Kentucky, and orphaned at the age of eight. He came to Illinois when he was twelve, was apprenticed to a carpenter, and then worked on a farm and read law when he got a chance. He fought in the Mexican War, as a first lieutenant, and took part in the gold rush of 1849. Then he came back to Illinois and went into politics. "He raised the second regiment in the State, to suppress the Rebellion," the *Logan County History* says, "and for gallantry was promoted to Major General." He fought under Grant at Belmont and Fort Donelson and was severely wounded at Corinth. He was elected governor of Illinois three times and between the last two times he served a term in the United States Senate. One of his speeches, a rhapsodic prose poem on the wonder and glory of corn, was considered a literary masterpiece. He married a sister of Miss Jessie Gillett, who brought that picture of Caerlaverock Castle to my Grandfather Maxwell. With small town people, every story is part of some other story.

Since he took exception to my grandfather's arguing the case for the railroad against the man who was killed picking up coal on the right of way, I feel free to question something he did—or, rather, something he didn't do. On the fourth of May, 1886, during Oglesby's third term as governor, a crowd of fifteen hundred people gathered in Haymarket Square, in Chicago, to demonstrate in favor of an

eight-hour working day. The demonstration was largely
staged by a small group of anarchists. The police tried to
disperse the meeting, a bomb exploded, and in the rioting
that followed seven policemen and four other persons were
killed and over a hundred were injured. Eight anarchist
leaders were arrested and tried. Shaw and Oscar Wilde
came to their defense, but Middle Westerners have never
been impressed by, or even interested in, the opinion of
foreigners. There was no evidence to connect any of the
anarchists with throwing or with making the bomb, so they
were convicted of inciting to violence. Oglesby was asked
—the appeal was signed by Ingersoll, among others—to
commute the sentence to life imprisonment, but he let the
sentence stand. Public feeling was aroused to such a pitch that
nobody wanted to be reminded that a man is legally innocent
until he is proved guilty. Whether my grandfather's belief
in the sacredness of the law held firm I do not know. Four of
the anarchists were hanged, one committed suicide in prison,
and three were pardoned by Altgeld, in 1893, on the ground
that the accused had not had a fair trial.

My grandfather was so fond of his friend that he built
a room on his house for him. The carpenters hadn't quite
finished when Richard Oglesby died, and so it was never
occupied by him. Neither did he report back to my grandfather how things were in the Afterlife. It was not his
fault; he was taken by surprise. He lay down for a nap in
the middle of the day and never woke up.

14

Though my mother had what is called pride of family, she was very much the same with everybody and let me discover for myself the broad categories that, in their ideas and manners, people tend to fall into. I would have had to be more than innocent, I'd have had to be exceedingly stupid not to be aware that her side of the family was totally different from my father's. And whether I should have or not, I made comparisons. The two sides of the family were different physically, and in the way they dressed, and in their habits and houses, and even in their speech. My father never said "he don't" but my Aunt Bert, who had an eye for beauty and some sense of what books are worth reading, did. My Grandmother Maxwell even went so far as to say "ain't" (which is, of course, not the solecism we were taught in fifth grade to believe it was, but just old-fashioned). What they talked *about* was also totally different. And what they ate. When we had steak at home it was ritually broiled over the coals of the kitchen range by my father himself, and two inches thick, and rare. At my Aunt Maybel's it was half an inch thick, fried in a pan, heavily peppered, dark brown, and tough. She served canned fruit and vegetables in the summertime, and no lunch or dinner was without a dish of pickles or some other form of relish.

The presents my mother's sisters gave me at Christmas and for my birthday always went straight to the mark and inflamed me with excitement and pleasure. I did not even

bother to thank them. I knew they knew. My Aunt Maybel's presents seemed meant for some other little boy, and
I was conscious of insincerity as I thanked her for the gold
ring that I did not like the feel of on my finger, or the
dollar bill that did not seem to belong in the category of
presents at all.

My Aunt Maybel was not indifferent to children, and
managed to capture the hearts of two of them. She used to
look at me with an expression that I am sure meant that she
knew I was not as fond of her as I was of my mother's sisters
but that, even so, I was her nephew and this was not something I was going to squirm out of.

On one occasion when we'd been fishing and had very
bad luck, I attempted a witty remark that brought my
father's wrath down on my head. The witty remarks of
nine-year-old boys are seldom greeted with applause, in
any case, and he was cross at not catching any fish. What I
said was, "That's what happens when you go fishing on
Sunday." And what he said was, "If that's the way you feel,
why don't you go live with your Aunt Maybel." I didn't
know then and I don't know now how he really felt about
her—whether he loved her but didn't like certain aspects of
her personality any more than I did, or just couldn't
bear her.

I don't remember my mother's ever being in the house
on Union Street, but of course she was. Politeness demanded it from time to time, and so did consideration for
my father's feelings. She appears in several of the photographs of family reunions in my grandmother's scrapbook, and is clearly and eloquently an outsider. I knew,
without having to be told, that my mother did not like my
Aunt Maybel, that my Aunt Maybel did not know this,
and that it was a cat that must never be let out of the bag.

I decided at rather an early age that the Christian Church
had something, or perhaps everything, to do with the way

my Grandmother Maxwell and my Aunt Maybel were. At children's parties I was not very good at pinning the donkey's tail on the place where nature intended it to be, but this time I was at least in the vicinity of the truth. And the truth itself was offered to me when my grandmother took me with her to the Willing Workers, a group of elderly women who met on Wednesdays in the bell tower of the church and, quilting together, helped pay off the mortgage as drops of water wear away stone. The gossip was of people I had never heard of, and when lunch time came, the old women astonished me by eating pie with their fingers. I didn't know you could do this, and I enjoyed it very much. I even tried to introduce the practice at home. Eating pie with your fingers was a custom of country people. The Christian Church has never been as strong in cities as in small towns and hamlets, and every one of those old women undoubtedly grew up on a farm, like my grandmother. No farmer's wife in the year 1912 would have found my Aunt Maybel's cooking in the least strange. Though my aunt and my grandmother lived in town, in their manners and at heart, and above all in the way they were so sure about things that are surely open to doubt, they were country people.

Lincoln itself was a farming community, and owed its prosperity to the rich farmland that lay all around it. It was also a place that successful farmers retired to when they were ready to give up farming and spend their declining years at the Elks Club, playing rummy. And there were a certain number of men in Lincoln who, like my father, owned land which they kept a careful eye on and from which they derived a substantial part or even all of their income.

On hot August nights without a breath of air stirring anywhere, people sitting on porch swings said placidly, "Corn-growing weather," and put up with the heat because sooner or later it meant money in the bank for everybody. The tenant farmers were certainly not exploited the way Mississippi sharecroppers are; they lived in decent if bleak two-story houses, and had enough to eat, and when the wheat and corn and oats and alfalfa were sold, tenant and owner split fifty-fifty. My father kept his same tenants year after year, and his relations with them were cordial, but they never came to our house to dinner, and I never got to know any of their children.

On Saturday nights the farmers drove into town in their buckboard wagons, and I saw them roaming the courthouse square with unsmiling faces when we drove downtown for an ice cream soda. At that period, rising in the world meant giving up working with your hands in favor of work in a store or an office. The people who lived in town had made it, and turned their backs socially on those who had not but were still growing corn and wheat out there in the country. What seemed like an impassable gulf was only the prejudice of a single generation, which refused to remember its own not very remote past.

With its roots deep in the country and its ingrained suspicion of all forms of innovation, how could the Christian church turn its back on the people who lived by the labor of their hands, as everyone had in the past? At any rate, it didn't.

On those occasions when I went to church with my grandmother, my Uncle Paul seemed to be rather conspicuously in charge of things. If he was, as I assume, an elder, then the other elders didn't have a very easy time of it.

Looking at the pictures my aunt and uncle had taken at the time of their marriage, I think how could he have asked her to marry him—for she was not only a big woman, bigger than he was, but physically forbidding. Even in her twenties she looked like a grade-school principal, with tight lips and a heavy jaw and a pince-nez. And then I look at his picture— at the high-crowned derby hat set square on his round head, and the badly tied necktie, and the amount of self-esteem concentrated in that face—and think how could she have accepted him? Couldn't she see that the one thing in the world he could never do was admit he was wrong about anything? And since she was the same way, how could they hope to live together under the same roof? They met when they were students at Eureka College, and I wonder if perhaps they were the victims of some oversimplification—could he have married her because she was not attractive and therefore couldn't be frivolous, and did she marry him because he didn't smoke or drink or play cards?

I didn't like him, but the dislike was not so strong that I was uncomfortable in his presence. I am tempted to say that he was a bigoted, bowlegged man from a very small town over by the Mississippi River and let it go at that. This snobbish statement is accurate as far as it goes, but it fails to do justice to my uncle's peculiarities, as my father called them.

The two men actively disliked each other, from the beginning. My father was a boy in knee pants the first time he laid eyes on his future brother-in-law, at a baseball game at Eureka College. My uncle was playing on the college team, and my father mortified his sister to tears by saying, in a loud voice, "Maybel, your beau has bowlegs." She wasn't the only one who was mortified; my father did not care to be related even by marriage to somebody with legs like that! With closer acquaintance he found other qualities he could object to more.

Since all people reflect to a considerable degree their original environment, it seems safe to say that some of my uncle's peculiarities would not have been considered peculiar in Augusta, Illinois, in the 1880's, but I have never been there and do not know what it is like. My uncle was unique in Lincoln.

He did not frequent the Elks Club or get involved

in heated political arguments, or belong to a foursome at the Country Club, or sing barbershop chords. Or tell stories that began, "There were two Irishmen named Pat and Mike, and Pat says to Mike, he says, 'Mike . . .'" Or swear. Or drink. The breath of scandal couldn't get within a mile of him. He had none of the amiable vices, and no friends, so far as I know.

His laugh was unpleasant, and the shoulders of his suit were flecked with dandruff. Where another man, finding himself socially uneasy, would feel in his coat pockets for his pipe or cigarettes, my uncle would take out his penknife and pare his fingernails. There was also something odd about his shoes: They turned up at the end, in a way that nobody else's did, and you could see the shape of his toes through the leather. He appeared to be perfectly satisfied with his own conduct, and did not hesitate to tell other people what he thought of theirs. They were invariably polite to him, realizing, perhaps, how cut off he was by the narrowness of his outlook. He remained in the same job for forty or fifty years. If he'd been incompetent he'd doubtless have been fired; and it must have been his unfortunate personality that kept him from being promoted.

My uncle did not invent the standards by which he so harshly judged people; they came down to him intact from the chief founder of the Disciples of Christ. Alexander Campbell's idea of the works of the Devil may have been devoid of subtlety and unduly strait-laced and in some respects even absurd, but it was shared by a good number of his contemporaries. My uncle did not have this excuse; nor was he well-educated or blessed with anything like the intelligence of the founders of his church. He was a dutiful son to his own parents, and I never knew him to be disagreeable to my grandmother, though he was, on occasion, very disagreeable to my father and my Aunt Bert.

He and my Aunt Maybel bickered continually about questions of fact—about whether it was on Tuesday or Wednesday that it rained. I was so accustomed to this it didn't occur to me (and anyway, it isn't the sort of thing children think of) that below the surface of the argument there was a more serious incompatibility. Though he called her "Babe," it appears, from things my father said over the years, that they did not like each other and that toward the end of their life together the dislike turned to hatred. I would be tempted now to conclude that the incompatibility was sexual except that it was a period in which the very idea of sexual compatibility was unthinkable, and people who indulged in it sooner or later had to leave town.

They made a curious-looking couple. My aunt had a grey streak running through her dark hair, which, like my grandmother, she wore in a pompadour. At home she went around in a not always clean Mother Hubbard. When she went out she was corseted in such a way as to give her a small waist and a high shelf-like bust, as it was called in those days. My uncle may have been responsible for this, since he insisted on going into the fitting room with her. I never see pictures of the women in Minoan wall paintings without thinking of my aunt. When they sold their horse and bought a Dodge sedan, she drove the car as if she was still driving a carriage and the steering wheel was the reins. She also habitually repeated remarks that didn't put any great strain on the hearer's understanding, as if repetition was a form of emphasis. Which it is, of course. But what was it she wanted to emphasize when she said, "I happened to look out of the window and saw you coming up the steps. I say I saw you coming up the steps"?

When I try to conjure up her face, the grim disapproving look has a tendency to shade off into a defensive expression, as if she were really a frightened woman. But is this something I am making up, because of the softening influence of time?

My aunt took very good care of my grandmother, but I sometimes heard a note of irritation in their voices when they spoke to each other—probably no more than the patient exasperation of two grown women shut up in the same house, with no one else's shortcomings to occupy their minds.

The outside world impinged so lightly on Lincoln in those days, and people had little to amuse them but the drama of personal relationships. Probably it was not altogether without malice that some woman—I don't remember her name and I hardly knew her—praised my Aunt Maybel to my mother's sister. It is not easy for children to maneuver grown-ups into a corner where they either have to speak the truth or lie, and I waited alertly for what my Aunt Annette would say. There was a long pause, and then she answered, without enthusiasm, "Mrs. Coffman is very frugal."

I realized that it was the worst thing you could say about anybody—and all within the bounds of politeness!

Perhaps they had to be frugal (as distinct from just being careful about money) but I doubt it. They kept a horse and carriage, and their house was not mortgaged, and they both owned stocks and bonds, and I think if they'd been really hard up, I'd have heard about it. What I remember, instead, is my father and mother smiling over the fact that when my aunt and uncle went to Augusta for three days they had a man come and turn off the electricity and the gas.

The three days a week that my uncle was on the road, my aunt and my grandmother ate bread and jelly for lunch, and bread and gravy for supper. When he got home they had meat again. Because my aunt had built the house with her money, she charged my uncle rent. She typed his business correspondence using two fingers and was paid at the going rate, and with the money she earned over the years she allowed herself several impressive extravagances. She bought a chest of table silver—twenty-four of everything, with her monogram. And she had a velvet dress made for herself. It took ten yards of the finest quality of black velvet.

When the state agents of the New York Underwriters met at some spa, my aunt invariably won the ladies' hammering contest. My uncle had taught her to drive a nail with short steady strokes instead of big feminine wildly aimed ones, and she never met her match.

My aunt left a self-portrait in the form of a travel diary that is more revealing than anything I could write about her. When my uncle went to the annual convention of the special agents of his insurance company, she always went with him. I think he needed her for protection, anywhere but in the ambiance of the Christian Church. And my aunt felt that she owed it to posterity to keep a record of what happened to her when she left home.

Talent is handed down in pieces, like other family traits, and unfortunately the pieces are not always in useful combinations. My father was naturally musical but he had no musical taste; that is to say, if he had been forced to sit through *Don Giovanni* or *Die Schöne Müllerin*, he would have acknowledged that they had a right to exist, and compared them unfavorably to Rodgers and Hammerstein. My Aunt Bert loved to read, but my Aunt Maybel got the literary ability. She is a master of the anticlimax, not all the humor is unintentional, and the style shows an affinity with Ring Lardner. Internal evidence suggests that this particular journey took place in the late winter of 1917.

Our Third Trip to New York

We left Sunday a.m. at 7:50 on the C. & A. R.R. for Chicago about forty minutes late, had a nice ride to Chicago, met Bert in the LaSalle Hotel and had dinner with her and we visited at the Hotel on the Messna * until 4:30 p.m. Very cold in Chicago such a terrible penetrating wind.

Went to Station at 5:00 p.m. and met the bunch waiting for our Special Car over the Pennsylvania R.R. and to my surprise I was the only lady in the bunch so they said they would have to adopt me as I was sure a good sport to go with that bunch alone. There was however one other lady in the car. We left at 5:30 p.m. a little late, supper was the first thing for all and we made for the dining car with a grand rush. No meats under a dollar, potatoes twenty-five cents, and all of us had strawberry shortcake with whipped cream at forty cents. We sure felt like we were eating money, Oh yes, bread and butter ten cents and a cup of coffee, individual coffee pot or tea either twenty cents. After supper we went back to our car where we found the Porter making up the berths, Paul visited with the men and as the motion of the car made me sea sick I retired at 8:30 p.m. to be jostled all night like the rest as we all put in one horrid night, no one resting but Mr. Tanner and the strange lady, so Tanner got it from everybody about his selection of a smooth railroad, we lost time all the way.

Up at 8:00 a.m. Tuesday † and we had a dish of straw-berries forty cents and toast fifteen cents and cakes fifteen cents, Paul had coffee but only had black tea so I drank water in preference.

Played cribbage with Mr. Tanner and he beat me two out of three games. Then Paul and I played pinochle and I beat him two out of three games, we had been over this road

* Mezzanine, perhaps?

† She means Monday.

before so the scenery was not quite so interesting as the first time.

Our dinner again showed the high cost of living. After dinner we tried a three handed game of Pinochle with Mr. Knop of Dakota and I won all of them.

The meals were only fair but the prices terrible, everybody had strawberries for supper again, expected to have supper in New York but our train was about three hours late and had part of our special fares refunded upon reaching New York City.

Conjestion or something wrong with Taxies when we reached New York, but the McAlpin Hotel being only a short distance we walked and the men had to wait awhile as there were about one thousand to take Taxies and then ran a bluff and got some one else car and made the Chauffer take them on when he discovered his mistake.*

We were soon settled in our room at the McAlpin on the nineteenth floor, nice room with a bath and beautiful Mahagony furniture but no rocking chairs in the Hotel or not in any of the rooms we have ever had there and you know how Maybel enjoys them, it would just suit Blossom.

It was too late for a theatre so we went out to a Film show near the hotel at twenty-five cents and it was fair, it was too cold to rubber any so we went back to the Hotel in a hurry and retired shortly it being 12 a.m., had a good nights rest and up at 7 a.m. Tuesday a.m. had baths and then breakfast at Child's Restaurant where things were not quite so dear but served in very small quantities if your turn ever comes. Paul took the elevated to the office and although cold I spent the a.m. looking at the beautifully trimmed windows of the stores, then walked up to Forty-Third Street about nine blocks to locate the Drug Store and theatre ticket office where

---

* Who had to wait and who pinched somebody's car and where the Chauffer took them and what he said when he discovered his mistake, the reader will have to decide for himself; it's beyond me.

*you get your tickets for the theatres at half price which Mrs.
Dux introduced me to last year. Back to Child's for my lunch
alone and to the room and was so tired and cold, took a nap,
then wrote Post Cards to my Sunday School Class, several
friends and some of the family, also a letter to Mother
Maxwell, Paul having mailed cards to both Mothers in
Chicago, also when we reached New York, after which I
dressed for dinner by the time Paul came back at 5:30 p.m.*

*We went to the Knickerbocker Hotel to dinner, both of
us had a turkey order and when it came it was hardly enough
for one,* after dinner we went into the parlor and listened
to the music, believe it was the largest room I have ever
been in used for that purpose, there must have been fifty
people in there and could hardly notice anyone was in the
room we occupied so little space, beautiful paintings adorned
the walls and many beautiful ferns in the room, all were
waiting for someone to take to dinner and two quite large
dining rooms were quite well filled, I went to the bathroom
and to my astonishment I saw two splendidly dressed women
I cannot call them ladies, in there smoking cigarettes, it was
bad enough to see nearly every couple that comes in the
dining room order drinks the first thing but to see them
smoking looks even worse. Shortly we went to the theatre
and saw "For the love of Mike", it was a musical farce and
not very good but beautiful costumes. Retired about 11:45
p.m. and rested well until 7 a.m.*

*Went down Broadway to Gunter's for Breakfast and on
to Grey's Drug Store for theatre tickets to "Cheating Cheat-
ers", for Wednesday night, it was pretty good, another farce
with a woman detective for the hero.*

*I spent the day again looking around through the stores,
Altman's is one of the modern stores and very substantial, I
purchased a waist there, they do not have their name on their
store as people seeing the store will investigate and find out*

---

* Big eaters, both of them.

for themselves. Mr. Altman died a short time ago and left bequests to many of his clerks he had had for a long time several received more than $2000. They said he did not raise salaries so often but was always doing something for his employees and seemed to get the very best out of them for his treatment.

Wednesday afternoon I went to Matinee alone, "Lilac Time", a drama with Jane Cowl as the leading lady and she was very fine, it was a war piece, or story. I was back to the Hotel ahead of Paul and we went to a swell restaurant, Wallicks, it was one beautiful room, mirrors, and paintings, adorned the walls and it was furnished with gold furniture. I had more turkey and Paul more beefsteak and had to pay the full price but it was the best cooked and served that we had had.

We were in a little earlier and retired about 11:30 p.m. as the theatre was some nearer the Hotel, rested pretty well and up at 7:30 a.m. baths and dressed and to breakfast at Gunters on Broadway. Paul left me to take elevated for office and I wandered down Fifth Avenue, two streets across, as stores do not open until 9 a.m. and close at 5 p.m. That is the street with the swell stores, Vantines, wonderful perfumes, toilet waters, japanese goods of all descriptions, Taylor and Lord one of the finest department stores, Bon Witt & Co. a beautiful dry goods store but on a smaller scale, and so many small shops of every description. Spring was very much in evidence in all the show windows and looked beautiful but the weather on the outside was below zero and warmer things felt better, the newest and most attractive things to me were the hand bags, girdles, and beads, they all ranged in price above ten dollars in fact that would purchase only a very plain one. Had my lunch alone as usual. I was always at the Hotel ahead of Paul so we lost no time in getting out to dinner as everything is soon crowded.

This was Thursday night and it was a bad snowy night, so

*we had our dinner at the McAlpin where we were staying,
and as the theater was a Complimentary from the Company,
which included the ladies and we had a long ways to go we
took a taxi and they held us up for $1.80 one way. It was the
grandest opera house of all and our seats were $3.50 each.
"My Century Girl" was the theatre, all spectacular, but
gorgeous, it was simply grand, costumes were exquisite so
far as they went, the light thrown on the stage were surely
beyond anything I ever saw. It was still snowing so we invited the Canadian delegate and his wife to ride back with
us to McAlpin and it was quite late or rather early.*

*We were up at 7 a.m. and I went to office with Paul, they
were all very nice to me. Mr. A. R. Stoddart invited me to
sit in his private office and I had quite a nice visit with him,
also Mr. Bennett, White, and others and saw quite a number
of the delegates who came East with us, all were busy men
with their personal troubles concerning their own field of
work. Mr. Grannatt went to lunch with us and we took a
little walk and then back to the office awhile. When Paul
was through we went to Wanamakers to look around but
both of us were so tired I purchased a pair of Golf shoes and
we walked up Broadway to the Hotel, seeing as we went, it
was about twenty-five blocks, but that is the way to see the
city, we past the Flat Ion* [sic] *building and were almost by
it when I remarked to Paul, I did not see that it was so
windy, and so many had told me that a lady had to almost
hold her skirts down or they would be over her head so
strong a wind all of the time, when my hat went sailing down
the street so I found the wind. When we reached the Hotel
we laid down and slept about an hour and both felt better,
you see that such late hours were hard on us not being used
to such. Time was too precious to lose much so soon dressed
and dined at a restaurant as every place was full and we
wanted to go to the Hippodrome, it also was spectacular but
poor however we saw the roller and ice skating that I had
heard so much about, their costumes were also beautiful*

and several hundred people on stage at once, which was also the case at the Century. Also Iren Kellerman * swiming.

Up at 7:30 a.m. packed and had breakfast and left over Michigan Central R.R. for Buffalo, a pretty ride along the Hudson River, but it was frozen over much of the way, they wanted us to take a boat but those who did said they had to constantly break the ice to get through. Rode all day and reached Buffalo about 8:30 p.m. settled in our room at the Statler and rushed out to see what we could of the business district, but found everything closed and looked quite small and shabby after those beautiful stores of New York.

Hotel Statler is a very nice Hotel although small but good service, their dining room represents a cave and is very artistic, lighted with unique lanterns. There is also a Statler in Detroit much larger and they are building one at the present time in St. Louis & N.Y.

After a good nights rest we took the train at 7:55 a.m. to Detroit, it was snowing hard when we left Buffalo. When we reached Niagara Falls, they stopped the train and let us get off for five minutes to see what we could of the Falls and they are wonderful but not as nice as when you go to them and are nearer. We were side tracked for all freights as passenger trains did not count when a freight was in sight and I think that every time we wished to see something in particular there was one passing us to shut out our view. . . .

They went on to Detroit, and saw a Japanese lady with a parrot that looked just like Polly, but I think we might as well take leave of them here, with the freight cars blocking the view, like a sequence from an old Mack Sennett comedy. They were, after all, of the same period.

* She means *Annette* Kellerman, I expect.

15

Family photographs are as subject to mortality as people are. You think, I remember that picture—I wonder where it can be? And the answer is, nowhere. It got thrown out, by somebody who said, "After I'm gone, who will care about these things?" Or by somebody who didn't even know who it was a picture of. The past is forever being swept away in the interest of neatness and order. It is unforgivable, or at least I don't intend to forgive it.

When I was a child there was a postcard sized photograph of my Uncle Ted sitting with his arm around a vivacious young creature, in the curve of the crescent moon. He was attractive to women, because of his looks and because he knew instinctively, and I suppose also by close observation, just how money should be spent. I had dinner with him once in the Pompeian Room of the old Palmer House in Chicago, and never have I seen anyone more secure in his dealings with a head waiter. At the time, my uncle was in his forties and working in the ticket office of the Illinois Traction System in Champaign.

My father blamed my Grandmother Blinn for the way my uncle turned out. He said that all my grandfather's efforts to discipline my uncle and make him realize that he was not a young Vanderbilt were frustrated by my grandmother's habit of giving him money behind my grandfather's back. What seems strange to me is that, caught in a familiar situation, people still go on behaving in the same predictable way, even though everybody knows that there is only one ending to it, and that unhappy.

The problem that occupied my uncle's mind when he was a young man was how to make money in other ways and in larger amounts than by, say, going to work as a teller in a bank or writing insurance. He leased a plane from the Wright brothers, with the understanding that if it went up he would receive a check for two thousand dollars from the town of Lincoln. Few people had ever seen an airplane, and certainly not up in the air. My father, with his strong interest in the future, wouldn't have missed it for anything, and he took me with him. The plane was sitting in a field at the edge of town from which the wheat had just been harvested. I remember the stubble pricking my bare legs, and the heat, and the endless waiting. Forty years later, my father said that while we were waiting in that wheatfield all afternoon, my Grandfather Blinn was pacing the floor of his office. Whether the plane went up or not, my uncle had contracted to pay the Wright brothers a thousand dollars he did not have.

Who brought the plane? Wilbur or Orville Wright? It couldn't have come by truck or by train and it was too big for a wagon. *It flew there.* It must have come down out of the sky with its wings spread, like a big hawk, and settled on that field of stubble. And it must have flown away again, quietly, when everybody's attention was on other matters. But what people remembered forever after was the day the airplane was supposed to go up and didn't.

Inevitably my uncle got into difficulties my Grandmother Blinn's skirts were not wide enough to protect him from. He persuaded my grandfather to buy an automobile—a Rambler, with carriage lamps for headlights, the canvas top held in place by leather straps, and the gearshift (or was it the emergency brake?) on the outside, above the running board. To blow the horn you squeezed a rubber bulb. It was the first automobile on Ninth Street. Would it had been the last anywhere on earth. Because my uncle was so knowledgeable, he was invited to go to Chicago with friends who had bought a car there and were driving back to Lincoln in it. The car went out of control and turned over. My uncle lost an arm in the accident. Nobody else was even hurt. Annette says that he was not driving at the time, and that the car was going forty miles an hour, which I had trouble believing until I remembered what the un-paved country roads of that period were like. It was probably muddy and the car went into a skid. My uncle may have reached for the steering wheel. He was found under it.

Overnight his life was changed. The jobs that are open to a man with one arm are not numerous, and he was suddenly the last thing in the world he had ever expected to be—an object of charity. Rising above this disaster, he became engaged to a charming red-headed girl from a good family in Lincoln. They were married after dark, in the Episcopal church, and I seem to remember looking out of the window of a hack, on my way to the wedding, and seeing snow on the ground. I was only four, and I may have superimposed this occasion on another, for I also remember being with my aunt and uncle when they were delivering Christmas presents.

Instead of moving on to some other family, disaster settled in for a visit of some duration. My Grandmother Blinn suffered a massive stroke when she was in her early sixties and was an invalid from then on.

Impatient with a grate fire that would not burn, Annette poured kerosene on it. In the explosion that followed, her hair and clothing caught on fire. She had the presence of mind to roll herself in a rug. I don't know where or when this happened. I only remember my mother's distress, and the scars on Annette's hands, where she had beat at the flames.

To keep down the rats at Gracelands my grandfather imported a ferret, and the ferret bit him on the ear while he was sleeping. This happened on the twentieth of October, 1912. On the fourth of November he appeared in public for the last time, at the funeral of a friend. The family doctor and various other medical men acted out a charade of treatment. There was no cure for blood poisoning in those days, and the center of infection was in the head.

The Christmas festivities were held upstairs in my grandfather's bedroom so he could be present, and when the door was thrown open I saw my grandfather sitting up in bed at the same instant I saw the lighted tree. My aunt says that he sat up in a chair briefly and then had to return to his bed. What the older generation remembered I don't remember at all—how my Cousin Peg and I rushed into the room, and she exclaimed "Oh see my rocking horse!" and I exclaimed "Oh see my dolly!" The point being that we had claimed one another's presents. I never thought this often-told story very amusing, because, for one thing, it impugned my masculinity, and for another, both the doll and the rocking horse, which was huge and covered with real horsehide, were, as it happened, hers.

In any event, we took our presents and spread out all over the house. Leaning over the bannister, I watched my brother and my new aunt playing with his racing cars in the long front hall. And my grandfather was left to his slow dying, which went on clear to the end of January. I don't know what I was told at the time. Nothing, probably. He was sixty-three. The funeral was on a Sunday afternoon and, the house being filled to overflowing, people stood outside on the porch or on the sidewalk. The day was so warm it was almost springlike. The minister of the Cumberland Presbyterian church offered a prayer, and one of my grandfather's lawyer friends eulogized him in a speech that was much admired at the time but that strikes me as windy and ambiguous ("Mr. Blinn was not understood at all by a great many people. He was not what you would call a mixer. He was not a man who desired an army of loose friendships. What he sought, and what he got was close, warm, personal friends . . . When his children were born, Mr. Blinn, his strong affections always on the alert, reached out and encircled them all, and he bestowed on his wife and family such a rich heritage of affection as I never have known before . . . So it is a mistake, a great mistake, for anyone to think that E. D. Blinn was a heartless man . . ."), as if some legal defeat still rankled.

I was a middle-aged man before my father told me that my grandfather died a most horrible death, in agony, with his head swollen to twice its normal size.

"Life is a narrow vale between the cold and barren peaks of two eternities," Ingersoll said. "We strive in vain to look beyond the heights. We cry aloud—and the only answer is the echo of our wailing cry. From the voiceless lips of the unreplying dead there comes no word."

In the case of my Grandfather Blinn there was word, or so his family believed. They believed that he came back after he died, with a message for them. They thought he was gone, and he opened his eyes and said—There are two versions of what he said. My mother's version was that he said, "Heaven is a providing place," and died. I know I am not inventing or misremembering this. I hear the sound of her voice saying the words. Annette says that his dying words were "United . . . hereafter." She is given to unconscious mimicry, and as she was telling me about my grandfather's death she opened her mouth and made her hand move in front of it in a gesture so authentic my hair stiffened. After that, nothing could shake my mother's or Annette's belief that there is a life without end.

My grandmother waited about a year and then joined him in the cemetery. During the last months of her life a Mrs. Eliot, who had come to Lincoln as a bride at the same time my grandmother did and later moved away, was persuaded to come back and live with her. The two elderly women, sitting on either side of the cannel coal fire in the back parlor, passed the days talking about people they had known, and pleasant times, and the way things used to be. And about their husbands, and their children, and Kentucky.

My Grandmother Blinn was there, and then, abruptly, she was not there, and strangers were living in the house across the street.

From observing my own two children and what they do or do not remember, I have come to the conclusion that until the age of five the camera shutter remains open, producing a single long time-exposure. Then, mysteriously, something happens—not to the negative, which is indestructible, but to the print, and all that is left is a few torn-up scraps that might have been found at the bottom of a wastebasket.

My own earliest memories are all of details in the house of my maternal grandparents. Exhibit A: the street number, etched in frosted glass over the front door and read in reverse as I am sliding down the bannister; B: a peculiar chair that has no back but, instead, two arms at right angles to each other; C: the taste of a particular slice of raw potato tucked in my mouth when I wandered out to the kitchen. And the black marble Victorian fireplace in the back parlor where Granny Blinn sits, and where the family congregates around her. And Annette lying on the floor of this same room, with her eyes closed, giving off emanations of un-happiness. When I bend over and kiss her, there is no response.

In these earliest memories, the figures are frozen in some act or attitude, and I am the only person that moves. But not long ago my brother made me a present of one of his memories—Christmas dinner at my Grandfather Blinn's, with the same figures released from their immobility and conspirators in a practical joke. I am there too, even though I have no recollection of it, and am not one of the con-spirators because I would certainly have given the joke away. They are all talking and telling familiar funny stories and passing their plates up to the head of the table for more turkey and cranberries and oyster stuffing. Except my mother, who is sitting quietly, saying nothing. My father gave Annette the same present he gave her, and she is trying not to show that her feelings are hurt. Now that people have all but stopped playing practical jokes on one another, it is hard to see why they were ever tolerated. To find them uproarious you have to ignore, or to take pleasure in, the fact that the one necessary ingredient is a touch of cruelty. On the other hand, people filled with more love than they know what to do with sometimes bungle things. In the middle of Christmas dinner, a groom appeared out-side the dining room window with a riding horse, my father's real present to my mother.

Both my maternal grandparents were dead by the time I was six, and in that dense Tolstoian family life I don't suppose I was ever much alone with either of them. The values and assumptions of that household I took in without knowing when or how it happened, and I have them to this day: The pleasure in sharing pleasure. The belief that it is only proper to help lame dogs to get over stiles and young men to put one foot on the bottom rung of the ladder. An impatient disregard for small sums of money. The belief that it is a sin against Nature to put sugar in one's tea. The preference for being home over being anywhere else. The belief that generous impulses should be acted on, whether you can afford to do this or not. The trust in premonitions and the knowledge of what is in wrapped packages. The willingness to go to any amount of trouble to make yourself comfortable. The tendency to take refuge in absolutes. The belief that you don't have to apologize for tears; that consoling words should never be withheld; that what somebody wants very much they should, if possible, have.

How much of this comes from my Kentucky grandmother I cannot say, but the prevailing atmosphere of her house and of ours was, I think, Southern, though I have never been very far south of the Mason-Dixon Line and have to imagine what Southern family life is like. My grandfather, being a New Englander, must have inherited Puritan genes, and he had a New England upbringing, but Puritanism didn't predominate and in fact wasn't even apparent in his character. He was profoundly attached to his family and his friends, and his pleasure in having people around him was as much a part of him as his largeness of mind. He was not without a sense of the mystery that surrounds human life, but he took a skeptical view of the revealed truths and doctrines of formal religion, and put his faith in reason—a thing it is now, of course, no longer reasonable to do.

The lawyer who spoke at my grandfather's funeral said that because my grandfather rarely went to any church and did not belong to any particular congregation, a good many people got the idea that he was an atheist, but that he was not; that he believed in "a conscious infinity, an intelligence that was the Creator of it all. That was Mr. Blinn's God"; that he believed also that the laws regulating and governing the universe are finished—none ever were or can be added, from the moment of Creation—and that they are also immutable; that our act or the reflex of our own act is what gives us happiness or misery; that we are punished not by God but by the emotional consequences of our wrongdoing —by our regret and shame; that human happiness is the highest good, and we can be happy only by being concerned for the happiness of others; that there is a destiny that makes us brothers, and so no one goes his way alone; that Heaven and Hell are not places but mental conditions.

How much of all this is what my grandfather actually believed and how much is the embellishment of Mr. Timothy T. Beach is the question. My grandfather had thought and read a great deal on the subject of religion, and I suspect that he approached the eternal verities with a more humble mind than this funeral eulogy would suggest.

In their unconscious assumptions and attitudes, my mother's family was hardly Christian at all. But neither were they pagan. I don't know what they were. I do know, really, but it is a question of what name to put to it. When Annette was forty, she had a son, now a grey-haired man, who bears a physical resemblance to my (and of course also his) Grandfather Blinn. But the resemblance is more than merely physical. What I am aware of in him, and found in my mother and Annette and my Aunt Edith and my older brother—the family trait they all have in common—is the pure feeling of the heart. I hesitate to say that it was their religion, but it is what they lived by.

16

When my mother was painting china, I stood beside her, watching. She painted odd-shaped Art Nouveau tea sets and dresser sets and vases decorated with pale pink or yellow roses and violets and daisies for her sisters and her friends, and nursery plates for their children. The smell of turpentine always brings it back to me. The cotton dabs covered with silk cloths were to soften the outlines, so that the flowers were more natural. As she squeezed the paint from the tube she said, "This is duck green . . . This is rose madder . . . This is alizarin crimson . . ." and I saw the color emerging and was in love with its name and smelled the turpentine and felt her presence beside me all as a single happiness. In the same calm matter-of-fact way that she taught me the names of colors, she also taught me to kneel beside my crib in the dark and say, "Now I lay me down to sleep," and, when I was older, the Lord's Prayer.

It was a rule of my Grandfather Blinn's house that when he and Governor Oglesby were discussing religion, the children could stay up until they fell asleep. Annette says that her religious convictions came much more from being present on those occasions than from attending Sunday school, though she and my mother did that too. As grown women they believed in God but felt no guilt about not going to church; apparently He had excused them from it. The God my mother believed in (plainly modeled on my Grandfather Blinn with perhaps a touch of the grandeur of Governor Oglesby) was large-minded and just and affectionate toward His family, who lived in the hollow of His hand—where else would they live? Heaven was an actual place. And the dead were not all shuffled up together but moved freely among their families and their friends. (When Dr. Donald died, Annette said, in a letter, she was glad that after so much suffering he could go on to the people of his time.)

Without at all understanding the consequences, my mother put an Old Testament fear in me by telling me that God did not love little boys who did something that, as it happens, all little boys do. Since she knew every thought that passed through my mind without my even having to tell her about it, there was good reason to suppose that He also knew what I was up to. But this also meant that He was in all insufficiently lighted places (the back stairs, the long hall upstairs between the bedrooms and the bathroom) shielding me from the unnamed terrors of the dark.

The reason my brother and I didn't go to the Christian church Sunday school was that my mother was afraid to have us cross the railroad tracks. My first exposure to the New Testament ideas came when I was presented with the Beatitudes, printed as a little book, with bright-colored illuminations. It was given to me by an old woman who came to the door at tactful intervals with Boston brown bread and potholders, and it enlarged my expectations of life, for if people who hardly knew me gave me presents when it wasn't even Christmas or my birthday, at any time I might have an agreeable surprise. It also made me think. My brother was four and a half years older than I was, and as an object for teasing I was irresistible to him. When he had nothing better to do he played with me the way a cat plays with a chipmunk or a mole, hoping to produce signs of life, which usually came in the form of temper and tears. That the meek would inherit the earth and the pure in heart see God was just what I had been hoping to hear.

When my Grandfather Blinn died, the house across the
street was sold to a retired farmer. There were three boys
in the family, and my brother and I were drawn to them
like nails to a magnet. They went to the Presbyterian Sunday school, and so we asked my mother if we could go with
them. Though, historically speaking, the Presbyterian
Church belongs among the more rigid and orthodox forms
of Protestantism and its adherents have been notable for
their excitability and rancor, neither the minister nor the
congregation of this church appeared to be in the least concerned with proving that what Jesus had in mind was the
Presbyterian Church and no other. Those adults I remember
individually were cheerful, complacent, and full of kindly
feelings. There was never any talk of hellfire and infant
damnation, or any mention of the fact that everybody
wasn't subject to redeeming grace. No one was outside the
pale except the heathen Chinese and Japanese, who were
fast being converted and brought into our midst by missionaries. We recited the Lord's Prayer and the Apostle's
Creed, and we sang fervently, Sunday after Sunday, the
same few rousing hymns—"Ring the Bells of Heaven"
and "*Bless*-ed sur-*render* so *hap*-py and free . . ." and
"Jesus wants me for a *sun . . . beam*, a *sun . . . beam*,
a *sun . . . . . beam . . .*" as if the only thing in the
world that mattered was our enthusiasm. I went to Sunday
school with Bennie Irish, and learned about Abraham and
Isaac, and Joseph's coat of many colors, and how God made
the world in six days and on the seventh rested, and how the
Red Sea parted, and the Disciples couldn't stay awake in the
Garden of Gethsemane, and Nebuchadnezzar ate grass. The
man who led the singing had a V-shaped notch in one ear that
was sufficiently interesting to draw my wandering attention
back from the old lady whose knees wouldn't stay still.
Every so often, some child with a birthday would be invited
to come up in front of the Sunday school and deposit in a

glass fishbowl seven pennies if he was seven years old. Or a missionary would tell us about the work of converting the heathen, and show us beautiful embroidered kimonos and tiny shoes that, hard as it was to believe, Chinese women wore on their feet. And when Jesus said *Suffer little children, and forbid them not,* he was talking about me.

Like all old people, my Grandmother Maxwell sighed without knowing that she was doing it, and our going to the Presbyterian Sunday school was undoubtedly the cause of some of those sighs.

She never reproached us—at least not directly. But she would announce, as if it were the continuation of an argument she and I had been having, that Jesus wasn't sprinkled. "You won't find a word about sprinkling in the New Testament," she would say, looking at me severely. "I don't care what the Presbyterians say, He went down *under* the water and He came up *out* of the water!"

I had not been either sprinkled or immersed, but I knew that my grandmother loved me, and I could not believe that so obedient and gentle a child as I was would be consigned to the flames. On the other hand, I do not think that my grandmother said that merely for the pleasure of hearing out loud something she believed in in the innermost recesses of her being. She must have hoped that the words would sink in, and that, when I was older, I would be moved to act upon them.

I don't suppose she would have wanted my brother and me to be brought up without any knowledge of religion, but by not going to the Christian church we broke the chain that went back through five generations and a hundred years— through my father to her, and through her to, on one side, Charles Turley and his father, Charles Turley the pioneer, and on the other to her mother, Louisa England, and her grandfather, David England, who swung his scythe three days for three bushels of wheat, and her great-grandfather,

Stephen England, who chose this land of milk and honey for his descendants to live in, and formed the first Christian church in central Illinois, and preached the gospel sitting down when he could no longer stand.

On Sunday morning I would stand in front of my father, waiting for him to put down the paper and fish around in his trousers pocket for a dime for me to put in the collection plate. At that moment Mr. Irish was struggling with a stiff collar and putting on his best blue serge suit so he could walk to church beside Mrs. Irish, but my father placidly returned to the Chicago *Sunday Tribune*. Without his ever having to resort to explanations, I knew that he was finished forever with going to church, but that he didn't mind my going to the Presbyterian Sunday school, if that was what I wanted to do.

I don't know what made him stop, except that what he did not believe in he would have nothing to do with. He was perfectly tolerant about every religion except the one he was brought up in. He almost never spoke of "the Christian Church"; he said "the Campbellites"—clearly with a derogatory intent. They were intolerant, narrow-minded, hide-bound, backward-looking, and impervious to reason. Barton Stone's name must often have been mentioned in sermons my father had to sit through, but I wonder if he knew anything whatever about Stone's life and saintlike nature. In any case, my father was not speaking entirely from prejudice; the atmosphere of the Christian church in Lincoln *was* self-righteous and censorious.

Until I came upon it in print, in a yellowed newspaper clipping in my grandmother's scrapbook, I did not know that my mother had ever been a member of the Christian Church. Annette says she did it to please my Grandmother Maxwell. I don't know when she stopped going, or why. But surely my mother wouldn't have gone off to the Christian church on Sunday morning without my father, so he must have continued to go to church after he was a grown man, and after he was married, and probably as long as my Grandfather Maxwell was alive.

But my mother took the Bible quite as literally as my grandmother did—sometimes even more literally. There was a very bad cyclone in Mattoon, Illinois, and when my mother heard about it, just as we were about to sit down to supper, she took all the food off the table and wrapped it in a tablecloth, and had my father take it down to the interurban station, where there was a freight car waiting, and we went to bed hungry.

For a time, during the First World War, my mother went to the Presbyterian church with us, until one Sunday when the minister made some patriotic statement that was greeted with applause by the congregation. She never went back. Her objection was to handclapping in the house of the Lord, not to the assumption that He took sides, for which there is ample warrant in the Scriptures. She used to say fervently that it was not the English who defeated Napoleon Bonaparte, nor the Austrians, nor the Russians, but God Almighty. She was quoting Victor Hugo. She loved sentimental ideas just as she loved sentimental music, and so did everybody else.

In a way that is as mysterious and fascinating as the imitative disguises of moths and butterflies, children manage to resemble now one and now another member of the family they spring from. There was a period during my adolescence when I looked quite a lot like my Uncle Ted, making my father uneasy. With reason. He did his best to teach me that money is something you hang on to, but I couldn't help noticing the confident way my mother spent it. She was extravagant with her own money, but not with my father's. And if it hadn't been for my father she wouldn't,

I think, have had any money to be extravagant with.

When my Grandfather Blinn died it was assumed that his estate would be considerable, but he did not leave anything like the amount of money people expected. His obituary says that he was a public-spirited man, and the large fees he received in important cases were invested in local improvements such as the Lincoln Street Railway and the Central Illinois Telephone and Telegraph Company—both shaky enterprises that required fresh capital again and again before they were finally on a secure footing. Young men who went to him for financial help usually got it, and his indifference to money seems to have extended to large sums as well as small ones. In the midst of a busy life, he often didn't bother to put in writing the loans he made. When his partner remonstrated with him, saying, "Why do you loan money like that when you know you'll never see it again?" my grandfather said simply, "I knew their fathers." Lame dogs do not always find it convenient to remember just how they were helped over the stile, and the same goes for men who are no longer young and halfway up the ladder.

In my grandfather's will all four of his children were named as executors. I don't know what my uncle did that he shouldn't have—probably he signed his sisters' names on the back of certificates of one kind or another so that he could cash them. My mother and my aunts became alarmed and appealed to my father to step in and protect their interests, which he did. But by that time a good deal of money had simply vanished.

My mother's share in my grandfather's estate came to $8000. It was carefully husbanded by my father, and not washed away in the Depression. The interest paid half of the college education of my two brothers and me. The principal was then divided, thirty years after my grandfather's death, and my share became the down payment on a small house in the country. Though I did not buy it for nostalgic reasons, I took a certain pleasure in the fact that the exterior had been treated with a creosote stain like the cottage my father and mother built at the Chautauqua grounds when I was about three years old.

We moved out there soon after the Fourth of July and stayed until school started in September. Four big oak trees shaded the roof, keeping it cool. They were also an invitation to lightning, and my mother dreaded the August thunderstorms. Sitting on the porch in the evening, we burned punk to keep the mosquitoes and gnats away, and passed the citronella around. The katydids were deafening.

At the beginning of the Chautauqua season, tents sprang up and cottages were opened and aired, and we no longer had the place to ourselves, but my father and mother, foreseeing all this, had picked a lot on the extreme outer edge of the Chautauqua grounds, far away from the big cone-shaped open auditorium, and William Jennings Bryan, and the string quartets, and the Anvil Chorus; away from the cooking classes, and the wading pool, and the afternoon baseball game; away from the log-cabin museum crammed with objects very much like the things that were auctioned off when my Great-great-grandfather Turley died, except that the metal they were made of was now green and mysterious with age; away from the tent stakes that were so easy to trip over, and the invitations you could not say no to—away from *people* is what my father and mother had in mind, but Jimmy Hoblit and his wife came and settled down right beside them.

Twice a year, in the fall and again in the spring, the sewing woman paid a visit to the house on Ninth Street. It lasted a week, and all ordinary affairs were put aside until she left.

Her name was Effie Seyfer, and she was neither a servant nor a friend of the family, but something more intimate than either, and I wished that she would live with us forever. Any page of cutouts I found in her fashion magazines was mine for the asking, and sometimes out of an excess of gratitude I put down my scissors and went and hugged her. What she was like, to me, was the odor of cookies baking in the oven. But she was a woman of character. Her father was a drunkard, and she had him put on the black list, which meant that no saloon would let him have any liquor. While admitting that there was nothing else for her to do, people wondered that she could do such a thing to her own father.

One day, hearing a bustle in the upstairs hall, I went to see what was going on. Annette had pulled my mother's dressmaking form out there and she and my mother and Effie Seyfer were dressing it up in a coat and a fur neckpiece and a big-brimmed hat pulled down so that you couldn't see there was no face. The front door opened. I heard my father's footsteps as he hung his hat and coat in the closet under the stairs and then took two or three more steps before he stopped. "Anybody home?" he called out, and they motioned that I was not to answer. Then without a sound the women retired behind the guest room door. At the turn of the stairs he saw the strange lady and, all his gallant feelings rising up in him, said "How do you do?" politely. Tittering behind the closed guest room door. To think that people were once so innocent.

When I was six years old, my father and mother went to Cincinnati to visit Youtsey cousins on both sides of the Ohio River. They were gone two weeks and I did not know what to do with myself or even how to get from one minute to the next. Each day was a hundred years long. Talking about this visit when he was an old man, my father said with amusement, "Your mother wasn't satisfied with looking up relatives who were close at hand. Nothing would do but we must go see one old aunt who lived out in the country far from anywhere, and when we finally found her she was sitting on the porch of her cabin, barefoot, and smoking a corncob pipe." Though he liked my mother's cousins individually, he had rather had his nose rubbed in that Kentucky family.

In a fishing camp on a lake, my mother had seen a set of Copeland willow china, of a rare shade of light cobalt blue. It was being broken at the rate of a cup and saucer a day, and when she got back to town she said, "Aunt Sally, how can you let that happen?" The answer was "If you want it, take it." My mother supplied the fishing camp with a set of china from the ten cent store, and the Copeland willow was shipped to Lincoln.

When they came home from this visit they were in the grip of a mania: They had played golf. My father promptly joined the country club in Bloomington. In February, with the snow lying deep on the ground outside, he cut circles out of white typewriter paper and practiced putting on the moss-green carpet of our long living room. He also set to work and raised the money to buy the land for a nine-hole golf course, across a ravine from our cottage at the Chautauqua grounds, and to put up a clubhouse in the style of a Swiss chalet. With woods on either side of the fairways and a great many sand traps and some quite steep hills, the course was considered very sporty. My father got a set of clubs for my brother and another for me, and we all four took lessons from the coach, a young Scotsman named Walter Kennett. He was quoted in our house morning, noon, and night—what to do with the right shoulder, where to place the hands on the club, with the thumbs overlapping. And the proper stance. And the follow-through.

During the week we played with my mother, and on

the way home to our cottage would stop and eat rasp-
berries from a big square patch that the mowing machine
had left in the middle of the fairway on the fifth hole.
Weekends I caddied for my father, for twenty-five cents a
round, and prayed that he wouldn't play eighteen holes. We
were locked in an Oedipal conflict about where I should
stand when he teed off. I could see where the ball landed
only if I stood behind him, but he insisted that I stand on
the fairway seventy-five or a hundred yards ahead of where
he was. Time after time I saw the ball rise high into the
white air and never come down. Then would follow a for-
lorn searching in the rough grass, and being scolded, and
more often than not *he* found the ball, and squared off
grimly for his next shot.

The game was new to everybody in Lincoln, and people
had not yet learned to take reasonable precautions. Absorbed
in keeping his right shoulder down and his left arm straight,
my father followed through correctly and stretched the
piano tuner out cold on the ground beside him.

Having done so much more than anybody else to bring
the club into being, my father expected, not unreasonably,
that he would be elected its first president, but when people
are too entirely beholden to some one person for something
exceptional they get tired of being grateful. I am afraid my
father's personality also had something to do with what happened in that election. What he thought about something
was usually expressed in a firm clear voice and in language
that did not always allow for a divergence of opinion. Also
he would walk down the street lost in his own thoughts and
not know that somebody was speaking to him, and fail to return the salutation. So they wouldn't have him. Instead, they
elected as president a man who was interested in preserving
our native songbirds and who had had nothing whatever to
do with creating the country club, and they elected my
father *vice*-president.

My mother was heartsick. I can hear her voice saying to Annette, "How can they do that to my Bill?" They could and they did. Two of my father's friends sat up all night drinking whiskey with him, and when daylight came he was a different man. They had succeeded in convincing him that —though I think this is open to question—he had brought it about himself. He set to work to change his habits and his personality. Tact did not come naturally to him but he learned to be tactful, even so. And since he was never insincere, people forgave him when the effort he put into being tactful was apparent. He learned not to walk down the street lost in thought, and to allow room for a diverging opinion. And he went out of his way to be affable with people he hardly knew. It worked, of course, but I liked better the way he was before.

The willow china appeared on state occasions, but the fishermen had broken so many plates that my mother could use only single pieces—a large platter or the soup tureen. So one Christmas my father gave her a barrel of English bone china, which (God knows how) he managed to unpack and hide all over the house without our knowing it. Where she was concerned, he was capable of flights of fancy that were not matched by anything in the rest of his life. We spent the whole of that Christmas day searching for china, and at twilight my mother emerged triumphantly from the coat closet under the stairs with the last missing piece in her hand.

She found some cretonne that matched the Indian Tree pattern of the china, and made doilies, which she used for the first time on a night when the Rimmerman girls were invited to dinner. As always, they all three talked at once, ignoring, or adding footnotes to, or correcting one another's remarks, and my father had a one-track mind. It was too much, listening to them and having to carve. He neatly deposited a slice of steak on the doily in front of him instead of on a plate. The three old maids were delighted. It was the proof of fallibility they needed to love him more.

My brother got an air rifle that same Christmas and two days later, just as my grandmother was saying, "It's the empty gun that kills people," it went off, just missing the toe of my Uncle Paul's queer-looking shoe and making a hole in the living room carpet. It was the sort of thing he had been doing all his life, but even so my grandmother and my uncle were both upset. The one took it personally and the other didn't like guns.

Another mania, of a less agreeable nature than golf and more widely shared, was already visible on the horizon. My mother spent certain days of the week rolling gauze bandages, in a white uniform, her black hair covered by a white scarf with a red cross on it. My father drilled with a group of local businessmen. Our class at school saved prune seeds, out of which gas masks were to be made, by a process not explained to us. And I was taken to see a movie called *The Beast of Berlin*. The title must have referred to the Kaiser, but what made an impression on me was the fate of the captain of the U-boat that sank the *Lusitania*. He went mad from remorse, and his distorted face—the eyes round with remembered horror and all his teeth showing—appeared at the window of a cottage where a simple peasant family was saying grace with folded hands before their evening meal. When I grew up I discovered that with a certain amount of hard work I could learn Latin, French, Italian, and Greek, but every German word remained unrecognizable to me no matter how many times I looked it up in the dictionary.

My older brother says that by joining that drill group my father had made himself eligible for the draft, and was on the point of being called up when the war ended. My mother drove the car in the night parade on Armistice Day and my father sat astride the bonnet, smiling and waving to everybody. I thought he was just very happy that the war was over and I was pleased to see him that way, because he was usually rather serious. I'm sure he wasn't the only drunk in that parade, but anyway, in his relief at not having to leave us and go fight in the trenches, he had tied one on. My brother says that he had to be put to bed.

I was aware that I had lived through an important moment of history. I know now but I didn't know then that the less people have to do with history the better. Our whole family came down with Spanish influenza during the epidemic of 1918—my mother and father in a hospital in Bloomington, where my mother had gone to have my younger brother, and where she died three days after he was born. My father told me, toward the end of his life, that it had been arranged that Annette was to stay with my older brother and me, and at the last minute she announced that she had to go to Chicago. I think probably what happened— I have never quite been able to bring myself to discuss it with her—was that she had received an urgent communication of some sort from her husband. She was separated from him at the time, and everybody would know if she went to see him in Lincoln, or he came to see her, so he had asked her to meet him in Chicago. There was nothing to do, my father said, but hurry us off to my Aunt Maybel's.

It was not a place either of us would have chosen to be sick in, but I learned from this visit that my Aunt Maybel's sense of custodianship extended to more than toys. On Christmas Day my brother and I both came down with the disease that was raging everywhere around us. In her cotton nightgown, with her hair in a braid down her back, she appeared beside my bed every three hours during the night. Without speaking but with, nevertheless, a look of concern on her face for which I was grateful, she held out a glass of water and the pills the family doctor had left for me. A rock doesn't have to be congenial if it is the only one there is to cling to. Sometimes it was my uncle who came, instead. And they were also, of course, taking care of my brother, who was in the big brass bed in the spare room. Time passed by in jerks. I woke to a grey winter light, in that little room with my uncle's desk and typewriter and all the grim-faced ancestors looking down on the progress of my fever, and remembered things I had overheard my aunt saying on the telephone downstairs in the dining room, and was fright-ened, and closed my eyelids for a second to shut out thoughts I couldn't deal with, and when I opened them again it was black outside the windows. If only people would say to children when something unbearable happens, *Now you are growing up . . . This is how it comes about,* it might help, I think. It might have the same alleviating effect that being able to recognize the fact that you are dreaming does, when you are in the grip of a nightmare.

One morning the telephone rang quite early, before my aunt brought my breakfast to me, and I heard enough to know that she was talking to my father in Bloomington, and that there was something he wanted her to do for him. A little later she called my brother and me into my grand-mother's room. It was the first time I had seen him since we were taken sick, and we hardly looked at each other. We were in alien country. My aunt sat down in a low rocking chair and took me on her lap, and I knew when her eyes filled with tears what she was going to say, but it had to be put into words and she did that too. What had to be done she could be counted on to do.

17

What I can remember of my childhood (which came to an
end at that moment) all lies in the framework of seven or
eight years, during which I was much more aware of the
seasons than I was of the calendar, though I made several
of them in school and brought them home to my mother to
use. Sometimes it seems as if everything happened in a
single long day that can be unwound inch by inch like a
Chinese scroll. And I do not so much remember things as
see them happening. In much the same way that my Aunt
Bert saw Mary Edie setting out with a baby in her arms
to find her husband, I see a man and a woman—both young,
in their early thirties—and a little boy, fishing on the
Illinois River. The river is very wide at this point, and the
man does not like the look of the sky. He puts his fishing
pole away and begins to row. The oarlocks creak in a slow
steady rhythm. The rowboat sits low in the water. The
resort where they are staying is a long way, around a bend
in the river. The wind is blowing now, and the sky is
getting blacker and blacker. *Creak. Creak. Creak.* The air is
green. The sky is split open by forked lightning and this is
followed by a massive clap of thunder. There are whitecaps
on the water. When the man tells the little boy to get down
in the bottom of the boat, the little boy hears in his voice
that his father is afraid. He turns and looks at his mother, in
the stern of the boat. She, too. The little boy now knows
something he didn't know before: It isn't true that nothing
bad can happen to them. The knowledge is remote as, lying

in bed at home, he smells the snow that has fallen in the night. But it is nevertheless permanent.

Kneeling beside his crib in the dark he says, "If I should die before I wake . . ." The rest of the words say themselves while he considers the possibility of what he has just said. Words are real to him; all promises binding. And in the night, with everybody in the house asleep and the gas nightlight in the upstairs hall at the head of the stairs to show the way, anything can happen. Anything at all. Fatalistically he accepts the woman's goodnight kiss, and a few seconds later, when she has left the room, he bravely lets go, knowing that children have died in the night on this very street, even on the very same side of the street.

The woman and the little boy have the same large brown eyes. (So does my younger daughter.) When he touches velvet he thinks of the sound of her voice. He puts his head in the hollow of her neck and finds there unfailing comfort and the immediate renewal of self-confidence. Which is his self and which is her? When she withdraws for any reason, he has no choice but to go looking for her.

The man's eyes are a clear blue. The cheek the little boy kisses at bedtime is scratchy. The man smells of cigar smoke and his own agreeable self. He wears stiff collars, and combs his hair with water.

They are in a sleigh—a cutter—and they have a plaid carriage robe over their knees, and the silvery sound is the horse's bells shaking. It is very cold. Bundled up in woolen scarves, with his stocking cap pulled down to his nose, the little boy is in an ecstasy at being out after dark on a starry night, between his father and mother.

In the early spring the palms are brought from the greenhouse and placed one on either side of the front walk. The sidewalk is thrust up in places by tree roots, and the curb is higher than is usual nowadays so that people can descend without awkwardness from the metal step of a carriage.

The little boy gets down on his hands and knees, searching in the grass for spring beauties. He comes on the discarded shell of a locust and wonders if he shouldn't preserve it. The trouble is, everything is worth preserving. The brick driveway is littered with tree flowers and seeds with wings attached to them. On the Kuhls' front lawn there are buckeyes lying about which the Kuhls don't seem to want. Behind the Kennedys' house there is a mulberry tree. And behind the Harts's house more violets than it is possible to pick, but he always asks first, and old Mrs. Harts says, "Go right ahead." She has a bad back and wouldn't dream of bending down to pick violets.

On Easter Sunday the two boys leap from their beds and run down the stairs and outside, where they start searching for what the Easter Rabbit has left for them, in nests of green paper straw, in my father's hats. (But when did she do this? We woke up terribly early. Also he was very particular about his clothes, and yet every hat he owned was out in the yard where it could have been rained on. Did she take them without asking, or was it that he trusted her with everything he had, including his hats?)

On the Fourth of July, American flags hang from all the front porches, ashen-colored snakes curl up out of the cement sidewalk, and the little boy takes firecrackers out of their red Chinese wrapping paper and lights them. The older boy doesn't bother with this kind; he sets off cannon crackers, while unheeded adult voices cry *Be careful!* In the evening, sparklers leave their seraphic calligraphy on the eye of the mind.

Now they are in that cottage under the oak trees. By the back porch there are morning glories climbing on strings. It is the territory of the mourning dove and the bobwhite and the whip-poor-will. The ground is carpeted with the umbrella-shaped leaves of the May-apple, and there are trees that do not grow in town, red-haws and honey-locusts. The cottage smells of kerosene lamps and the fireless cooker. The walls are thin, and the distinction between outdoors and indoors is felt mostly when it rains. Mice and squirrels ignore it. In the middle of the night, the two little boys sit up in bed, in the yellow lamplight, watching the woman chase a flying squirrel with a broom. From the rafter it swoops to the top of a curtain. She swings and when the broom lands, the flying squirrel is somewhere else.

The thumping of radiators all over the house in town means that summer is over. Old Dyer comes night and morning to tend the furnace, and the washing goes off to Mrs. Dyer in an express wagon pulled by one of her grandchildren and comes back clean and beautifully ironed and smelling sweet.

In the evening, after they have left the table, the man stands holding a double sheet of the Lincoln *Evening Courier* across the upper third of the brick fireplace in the library, which does not draw properly until it is warm. The woman is sewing. When the doorbell rings, he goes to the front door and they hear him say, "Why, good evening, Mrs. Kennedy. Come in." Mrs. Kennedy is dignified and handsome, and has grey hair. She lives two houses up the street, and at a certain season of the year the little boy is often in the Kennedys' backyard, eating mulberries off the ground. He doesn't have to ask permission.

Taking his hand now, his mother leaves his father and Mrs. Kennedy in the library, and settles herself in the living room, on the big divan. It is understood that Mrs. Kennedy has come to talk to his father about her troubles—that is to say, about Mr. Kennedy. Mrs. Kennedy is a lady and Mr. Kennedy is not a gentleman, and it was a mistake for them to marry. Her difficulties are of a kind for which there is no remedy. Her voice is never free from sadness and the little boy has never seen her smile. Since she cannot bring herself to talk about the thing that is really weighing on her heart,

she talks about something else—about her life shut up in a
silent house with a husband who is not courteous or well-
mannered but angry with her, for reasons it would never
do to go into in the year 1915. She says that Mr. Kennedy is
angry at her because she cannot control her feelings. She says
her life is at a standstill and she has to go on as if nothing
had happened. She asks the little boy's father if he believes
in God. He does and he doesn't believe. He has read
Thomas Paine and Ingersoll, but he still doesn't rule out
the possibility of a divine order in the universe. He considers
that Mrs. Kennedy is a highly intelligent woman, and talking with her is like talking with a man. The little boy strains
to hear what is being said in the next room. Some time back—
perhaps only a few years but at any rate before he was old
enough to remember, though he seems to sense, just out of
reach, a faint glimmer of something, so perhaps it was when
he was very small—the Kennedys lost their only child, a
daughter, a happy and radiant girl of seventeen. She had an
orange and a glass of milk before she went to bed, and died
in the night. It won't stand as an explanation now but it did
then. From this tragedy Mrs. Kennedy cannot extricate herself. There are circumstances in which such behavior might
be criticized, but no one criticizes her. Except Mr. Kennedy,
whom nobody likes. And if it is true that people are not
entirely dead, until they are no longer remembered or spoken
of, then the beautiful Linda Kennedy still has a place, a
life, on Ninth Street, which at this period is thickly populated with children. In the living room, the woman bites off a
thread and then, with her hands idle in her lap, stares past
the head of the little boy, who has fallen asleep. Interesting
though the conversation in the next room was, it is his
bedtime and he had no choice. The woman is not jealous
of Mrs. Kennedy's friendship with his father. He will tell
her afterward, as they are undressing for bed, what Mrs.
Kennedy came to see him about.

When the little boy has the earache he goes to his father and says, "Will you blow smoke in my ear?" and the man obligingly draws on his cigar and then puts his lips to the little boy's ear and the earache goes away.

In a white corduroy suit that Effie Seyfer made for him, white stockings, and white shoes, he walks down the aisle of the Episcopal church, totally unconscious of the bride in his wake. And he doesn't drop the ring. Later, sitting on a gold chair where his mother put him, he watches the footmen come and go with trays of champagne. He is forgotten by everybody. Just when he is about to give up all hope, his Aunt Edith appears with a plate of ice cream for him, and he feels the way people do who have survived a shipwreck.

His aunt and uncle come down from Bloomington for the night and early in the morning he rushes into the guest room and gets in bed between them. Something in the quality of their laughter tells him how welcome he is. But what about their own children? No children.

On summer evenings, to escape the heat or for a diversion, the man hitches the horse up to the high English cart and they go driving. Often they take the Donalds with them. The dog goes too, uninvited, but on the other hand, nobody turns and shouts "Go home!" When they overtake some ordinary buggy or farm wagon they congratulate themselves on being above the dust. (The cart was made for a Chicago millionaire, who decided that he didn't want it after all, and through the maneuvering of Dr. Donald my father got it very reasonably.) The landscape through which they are moving is as flat as a chessboard. The squares are marked off by high hedges of Osage orange. If it is July, the grain is cut and stacked in the fields. If it is August, they may see the yellow chaff pouring out of the snout of a threshing machine. The horse's tail goes up and the little boy is in a good position to observe what happens next, and it is all so interesting, and nobody takes any notice. The courthouse clock, floating in the sky, shows them the way home. It doesn't necessarily follow that the cart will stop in front of the ice cream parlor as they pass through town but sometimes this happens, and when it does the little boy is terribly happy.

In the middle of the week, when the man is away, they cannot go driving to cool off and at night the woman and the two boys wander from room to room downstairs. When they find a doorway with a slight stirring of air, they put their comforters down and fall asleep there. The man sits in some bleak, airless hotel room, wiping the trickle of sweat from his neck and wondering what they are doing at home. Two or three of his traveling acquaintances knock on the door and ask if he wants to go with them to a house they know about, and he puts on his tie and coat and straw hat and goes with them. But when the others go upstairs with the girls, he remains behind, nursing his beer. (I have his word for this.)

On Sunday morning he waits at the curb until the front door opens and the woman comes out of the house and down the steps, wearing a long riding habit with a divided skirt. She rides sidesaddle. If people have ever seen a woman riding astride they do not talk about it. The little boy tells everyone that when he is six he is going to have a pony. On the afternoon of his sixth birthday he stands at the front door collecting tribute—a baseball glove, dominoes, a box kite, and so forth. Later the children play games. They run around the yard keeping huge colored tissue-paper butterflies in the air with fans. They play London Bridge Is Falling Down. It falls on the little boy and he is caught fast in the arms of an enchanting young woman with red hair. (I have been told that she was not absolutely sure she wanted to marry my uncle, but then he lost his arm in that accident and how could she decently back out of it? Within five years they were divorced, and I never saw her again.)

The patients sit fidgeting in the waiting room of Dr. Young's office in Bloomington while the little boy watches the circus parade—as it leaves the circus grounds and then, after the calliope has passed, the Model T shoots across town and they see the whole thing over again. The little boy is quite sure that in his uncle's eyes he has no faults, and that his uncle will never disapprove of him or be offended by anything he does. (I was mistaken: He never forgave me for growing up.)

And there is no Shetland pony in the barn of the house on Ninth Street because there is no barn. When the carriage horse ran away for the third time, leaving the woman and the little boy stranded at the Chautauqua grounds, the man sold it. Also the English cart—though how he managed to bring himself to do this I do not understand; it was his pride. The barn was torn down and in its place there is now a garage and they go on much longer drives, in a seven-passenger Chalmers, and have flat tires, and get stuck in mud up to the axles.

The older boy announces that on the twenty-fifth of March he is going to be twelve, not eleven, as everybody thought. The woman grows tired of arguing with him about it, and when his birthday cake is brought into the dining room there are twelve lighted candles on it. He blows, and eleven go out.

In the school yard he exchanges marbles and baseball pennants and contagious diseases with other boys. Red measles, German measles, mumps, whooping cough, chicken pox—he brings them all home and the little boy catches them from him. They sit up in bed working puzzles and keeping each other company and scratching. There is a quarantine sign on the front door. When it is removed and they are allowed to go back to school, formaldehyde candles will burn all day in the sealed-off, empty bedroom.

In the house next door there was a little girl who was

just the age of the little boy, and who caught spinal menin-
gitis and died. Ethel Kiest. Mrs. Kiest's lace curtains are
more interesting (deer and landscapes) than the little boy's
mother's, and whereas the furniture in his house is walnut
or mahogany, the furniture in the Kiests' house is golden oak.
On the big round dining room table, Mrs. Kiest keeps all the
china and silver that will be used for the next meal, under a
white cloth with a lace edge, grouped around the highest
object—the silver sugar bowl with a domed top. Anything
that reminds the little boy of circuses—and the dining room
table is very like a circus tent—he admires. He would like it
if his mother followed this custom. On top of the roll-top
desk in Mr. Kiest's den there is a stuffed prairie dog, which
the little boy stands and stares at. In the parlor there is
a very large book of photographs of the Columbian Exposition. He is allowed to look at it. If it is the time of
year when the windows are open, and Mrs. Kiest is baking
bread or coffee cake, the air brings this interesting fact to
the little boy's attention and he stops playing with his lead
soldiers and pays a call on the house next door. He is even
more transparent than most children. "Would you like
some coffee cake?" Mrs. Kiest asks, and he always remembers to say thank you as she hands him a sizable piece, still
warm from the oven. Mrs. Kiest and the little boy have
something that binds them together besides his love of eating
and her pleasure in watching him do it. He and Ethel Kiest
did not always play amicably, but when they quarreled he
could get up and go home, safe in the knowledge that the
next time he saw her it would be forgotten, and now he
misses her. He remembers her very clearly, and so does Mrs.
Kiest. She had blue eyes and very fair skin and blond hair
and a slight limp, noticeable only when she ran.

The redbird is singing in the rain. There is a rooster in
the back yard of a house on Tenth Street, and a squirrel is
scolding. Somebody is beating cake batter in the kitchen,

and a rug just got shaken in the back yard of the house next door. Again: *snap*. The iceman's pick is descending through a two-hundred-pound cake of ice, a horse and buggy is going by, and the older boy is playing "Goodby Maw, Goodby Paw, Goodby Mule with Your Old Hee-Haw" on the piano when he should be practicing scales. Wild geese fly over the house on their way south for the winter, and at the first sound of their honking he pushes his chair back from the dinner table and rushes outdoors. He is a throwback to William Higgins, whom he has never heard of, and all in the world he wants is to be a hunter or trapper. Sighting the geese along the barrel of an imaginary gun, he takes aim and fires.

Awakened by a splash of gravel on the windowpane, the little boy watches him get up and dress and then he and Harold Irish go off together before daylight, in the searing cold, to see if there are any muskrats in the traps they have set along Brainerd's Branch.

Now the snow is gone and it is summertime. The woman is sitting on the plaid carriage robe, on the bank of Kickapoo Creek, dreaming about I wish I knew what. The yellow leaves drift down, they float downstream, past her cork. (So much of what I remember from this period of my life is touched with a bloom, a golden dust, but especially those all-day fishing expeditions, which I didn't even particularly enjoy at the time. Now they are seen in the slanting light of something that has not yet happened, and so are a great many other things. As if it were continually late afternoon.) When the cork bobs sideways, she gives a jerk with her pole, and the little boy, sitting with his behind in the roots of a tree nearby and the end of his pole in the water, observes that she has caught another sunfish.

Pioneer instincts have survived in both of the boys. The older boy throws the little boy's hat up in a pine tree at the country club and it is one teasing too many. The little boy picks up a midiron and starts after him. Murder is what he is bent on, but he is prevented from it. Walter Kennett runs out of the caddy house and grabs him.

Saturday nights he falls asleep listening to the music that floats across the ravine from the clubhouse.

The summer is gone and the snow lies deep on the ground. It is morning. There are white tropical forests and Chinese pavilions and volcanic islands with palm trees on the window-pane. In the warmth of his bed and half asleep, the little boy waits for the woman to come in and close the window and turn on the radiator.

In this house there are no folding doors to shut the Christmas preparations away from sight, and the little boy knows the tree is there, in the alcove of the living room. Each time he goes upstairs he has to turn his face away. Just before dark, it happens. He doesn't mean to look but on the way upstairs he loses control of his eyes. The bicycle is there. And it's blue! In a delirium of guilt and joy he goes on up to his room.

("This house is like an empty shell," Walter Kennett said after my mother died, and he never came to see us again. Neither did Mrs. Kennedy. What I don't understand is how we could have taken that happiness for granted and not sensed that there was a time limit to it and that each day was bringing us closer to the folding chairs and the grey casket in the dining room and the reek of too many white flowers and the ministerial voice intoning, "I am the resurrection and the life . . ." Apparently she did sense it, or why did she say to Annette, "I made Happy promise that if anything happened to me he'd break all my cut glass. I don't want some other woman to have it." She told the wrong child; cut glass was not real to him the way muskrats and rabbits and quail and pheasants were real, and he forgot, and now some other woman has it, but not the woman she had in mind. She would not have objected to a daughter-in-law's using it. So great was her longing for a little girl of her own, she would even, I think, rejoice in the idea. But with what confidence one speaks for the dead —that they would have liked this and they would not have liked that—when the living are so unmanageable, when it is so hard to marshal or maneuver them even toward something that is obviously for their own good that one never dares promise anything in their name. She also said, "When I am gone nobody will know how to do my hair.")

Nobody thought to tell the little boy that it is better to learn to ride a bicycle on level ground. He has almost mastered the wobble, but not the principle of the coaster brake. The bicycle is gathering speed and he doesn't know how to stop it. He and it are about to end up in a heap at the foot of Ninth Street hill.

Equilibrium is not his strong point. Far too often he takes refuge in tears. Even trivial things set him off, and this exasperates the man. Their relationship is neither simple nor always the same. It includes both love and dislike. The man is not interested in hearing explanations for failure—not even legitimate ones. "No alibis!" he says and turns away.

The little boy knows when his father is angry with him, and that the anger is controlled. What he doesn't know is what would happen to him if his father's anger weren't controlled. Would he be annihilated? (Actually, it was my own anger that was of the annihilating kind.)

The little boy has a kind of druidical love for the white lilac bush that grows by the dining room window. During a thunderstorm in May, when it is covered with white blossoms, a big branch snaps. The weight of the wet blossoms was too much for it. The little boy rushes out into the wind and the rain and, weeping, tries to put it back. At the same time he is aware of the faces at the dining room window, sober with concern—not for the lilac bush but for him, for what will happen to him when he grows up and has to face the things that sooner or later happen to everyone.

The dog is getting old. White hairs on his muzzle, and on winter mornings he is so stiff that the woman has to lift him from the piece of carpet where he sleeps and carry him out onto the back porch. One day when the little boy comes home from school, the dog is not there. The woman explains that it did not hurt when the veterinary put him to sleep, and Old John was not frightened of him: He walked over to him and greeted him. The little boy believes her but he is confused and distressed, even so, to think that he will never again feel that cold nose against him, and the house seems queer without the dog. The older boy takes his tears off where nobody can see them.

The man is standing in water up to his thighs, and his hand is under the little boy's stomach. The little boy feels as slippery as a fish. He is afraid he will get water in his mouth. Also of he doesn't know what. He is shivering with the cold, and his lips are blue. His father is explaining what to do with his arms and that he must kick hard. "I won't take my hand away," he says, and the little boy knows that what the man says he won't do he won't do. The little boy moves his arms, kicks, gets water in his mouth, and keeps on moving his arms and kicking. Supported by the hand he thinks is there, he is swimming, but he doesn't know it, until he looks around wildly and sees that his father is twenty feet away, smiling at him.

18

My Aunt Edith took my little brother home from the hospital after my mother died, and wanted to keep him, but my father said that he intended to bring up his own children and keep his home.

We had a series of housekeepers. I don't know how my father stood it; it was hard enough to be a child and sit across the dinner table from them. Where there had been only us there was now this stranger, whose remarks were prepared for by a silence and brought on another, during which I was aware of the scrape of knives and forks on plates.

The light bulbs did not give off enough light, the food had no taste. My father walked the floor with his hand on my shoulder, and spoke hopefully about the future, but his face was the color of ashes and his soul was not in his body. My brother and I did not attempt to comfort each other, though we slept in the same room and could have said things in the dark. And I made endless trouble for my father by repeating something I shouldn't have. Though I was only ten years old at the time and I have had fifty years in which to forgive myself, at the recollection of it I am once more deeply ashamed. The evening of the day my mother died, I was lying on the horsehair couch in the sitting room, under the picture of Caerlaverock Castle, when old Mrs. Stokes came over from next door to pay a visit of condolence to my grandmother. They sat talking in the parlor. I was exhausted from weeping, and unable to think, because an event of the utmost importance had taken place without my consent, so when I thought at all it was to try and make it *not* have happened, and periodically even that impulse gave way. My eyes were closed and I could not lift my hands from my side. To all appearances I was asleep. I was asleep but not asleep. I heard everything that was being said in the next room. After the two women had praised my mother, my grandmother settled down to the subject of my mother's family, about whom she had a great many things to say that were news to me, and I did not always even understand what they meant. For example: ". . . so Mr. Blinn went to Dr. Young and told him he had to marry Edith."

I managed to keep all this gossip bottled up inside me for about three months, until one evening as Annette and my brother and I were coming up the driveway of our house, I found myself telling them. I knew immediately by Annette's intense interest and the look on my brother's face that I should have kept on keeping that conversation to myself, but by then it was too late. The two sides of the family stopped speaking to each other, and my father's burdens were made heavier. They were already quite heavy enough. All he ever said was, "Did you have to do that?" and I suppose the answer (though I hung my head and didn't say anything) was yes. My grandmother continued to treat me the way she always had, but I was no longer as comfortable with her.

On July 26, 1919, my father sat down at his desk and wrote a letter to Annette, who was in Mackinac Island:

Things have been happening fast and furious this week. Mrs. E—— taken sick last Tuesday, in the hospital ever since, some indication of Lung trouble. With the two boys at Ediths have had to leave Blinn with Mother and Maybel —lock up the house and just quit. Talked with the woman you mentioned—thinks she would like to come but knows nothing about children—especially babies—and for that reason afraid to take responsibility.

Am going up to talk with Edith about it today and will probably see her then. If you were only here to talk it over with would be so glad—This being a mother and father both is over my head but trying to keep fighting on. Blinn fine and weighs over 18 pounds. One consideration at least as I sit and write to you. The atmosphere of my home is at last free from the strain and unpleasantness so long existent. And by the love of Mike, it is going to have a housekeeper of some kind interested enough in me to keep it that way.

The next housekeeper brought her grandson with her, and my father hoped he would be company for me, but we quarreled childishly over nothing—over the top of a cracked crockery teapot that he found in my sandpile and that I recognized as a part of something that had belonged to my mother.

Annette and her family were in the habit of spending the winter in Florida, but the first Christmas after my mother died she sent my Uncle Will and Peg off without her so that she could be with us. "When I walked in, on Christmas Eve," she said, "there were red roses everywhere. In vases, in bowls, in anything that would hold red roses. I looked questioningly at your father and he said, 'They're my Christmas present to Blossom.' "

I sort of remember those roses.

The housekeeper developed ear trouble which was diagnosed as erysipelas and the family doctor told my father that he must let her go because she shouldn't be around the baby with it. After she left, she wrote poison pen letters, unsigned, about my father and Annette, to my Grandmother Maxwell, which upset her (she had had very little experience with malice as passionate as this and didn't know what was expected of her) but did no real harm, and to Annette's husband. My uncle was jealous of Annette's affection for my father, and even of her affection for my older brother and me. After the letters, he stopped Annette from coming to our house. Since she was the nearest approximation anywhere on earth to my mother, this was very hard on all of us, and also, of course, on her.

The third housekeeper was easy-going and slatternly and addicted to reading movie magazines, and she had a dog that looked like her. She also had a peroxide-blonde niece whom she hoped to marry off to my father. I don't know whether he considered marrying her or not. His life was insupportable as it was, and he always tended to see women through rose-colored glasses, so perhaps he did toy with the idea. He took her—the niece—to see Annette, who was in the hospital at the time, and when my father lingered a moment to say good-by, Annette said from the pillow, "Bill, she won't do." My father said, "What do you mean?" and Annette said, "I mean she won't do!"

My Aunt Bert had begun to travel up and down the state with two big black suitcases full of samples, and on weekends she would be with us.

Though I have no trouble in conjuring up my mother's hand, with the pen moving slantwise between the second and third finger, almost the only specimen of her handwriting that I possess is a letter to my Aunt Bert. It had been decided in the family that they would not exchange Christmas presents any longer, and my mother was writing to say that affection had impelled her to go against the agreement and send a small present.

Some of the things that made the house on Ninth Street so pleasant when I was a child—Oriental rugs that I knew the pattern of by heart, a carved Victorian walnut sofa, a mahogany dresser and its mirror—belonged, I found out a long time later, not to us but to my Aunt Bert, who had left them with my mother.

I often heard Annette and my Aunt Bert described, by their contemporaries, as the two most beautiful young women in Lincoln. They were also friends. After my Aunt Bert came home with her baby and was divorced, Annette said, a man who had been in love with her before she was married and who was still in love with her applied to my father for permission to court her. He had the reputation of being a rounder, and my father turned him down. Afterwards he married, and was a very good husband. This cannot have been her only chance for happiness. I think she followed the dictates of her heart, as always, and that there was nobody she loved enough to marry.

At the time I am speaking of, my aunt was a handsome, strong woman with a kind of physical radiance. The gaiety she brought into the house made it habitable again. She teased my older brother and hugged me and dandled the baby on her knee, and perhaps saved my father's sanity. The color came back into his face, and he was more like himself. He began to accept invitations and to go to the Country Club dances. The social life he returned to was changed beyond recognition from anything he and my mother had known, for the Twenties had arrived, and Prohibition. The clubhouse being closed in winter, the Country Club New Year's dance was held in town, in Bates's Academy, and gave rise to scandal. People—nice people—were drunk in public.

One day my father came up the back stairs to the empty maid's room where I had built the city and palace of Montezuma and was re-enacting the conquest of Mexico and sat down in the only chair, and took me on his lap—a thing he hadn't done in years—and told me that he was going to be married.

I was not faced with the prospect of living with a stranger, or with someone who wouldn't understand how I felt about my mother, for when I was four years old the pretty young woman who was going to be my stepmother used to gather up all the children on Ninth Street and walk them downtown to a kindergarten run by two elderly women, and until my father told me that he was going to marry her I had thought of her as someone who belonged to me.

My father sold the house on Ninth Street and most of the furniture with it. He very sensibly didn't want to begin a new marriage in a place that had so many associations with his first one. For a year, while he was building a new house, we lived on an unpaved street in a rented house with nothing to recommend it except that it was a block away from Annette's. At first it took a certain amount of courage for me to go there, for I didn't know my uncle or even what to call him. I had never heard him referred to at home except by his full name or sometimes, scathingly, by his initials, "W.B." So I called him "Mr. Bates," politely; until my Cousin Peg asked her mother why I did this and Annette spoke to me about it. With a considerable grinding of gears I managed to say, "Yes, thank you, Uncle Bill," when he asked me if I would have another piece of steak, and he accepted the change without a flicker of expression. Though he was a surveyor, he spent his whole life watching over the farms he had inherited from his father. He went every morning to the country, and when he came home and found me there, he would pass through the living room, nodding to me and making some remark to Annette that maintained the proper degree of tension between them, but never making an issue of my presence, though I always expected him to.

Sometimes I would find another displaced person there: my Uncle Ted. For varying periods of time and in a way that must have been totally without hope (for his face gave off no life and at family dinners when he smiled it had a dampening effect on the occasion) he managed to earn a living. Between jobs, when he was hard-pressed he would turn to Annette for help. It had to be given surreptitiously, and sooner or later made trouble between Annette and her husband. My Uncle Ted was very fond of my Cousin Peg and of my older brother. I was uneasy with him, and aware always of the immovable arm ending in a grey kid glove.

So far as I know, Annette never quarreled with her husband about my being there. I rather think it wasn't a serious issue between them. He loved his own children, and probably treated me as he hoped somebody would treat them in my circumstances.

But the bitterness and unforgivingness of those small-town family feuds! I can hardly believe this now, and yet I know it is true because I saw it happen: On the morning of my mother's funeral, he came to our house—a thing he had not done since I was old enough to remember—and my father shut the door in his face.

In the hospital, with the terrible clairvoyance of the dying, my mother said to Annette, "I don't want the Maxwells to have my baby."

I don't know what Annette said to my father at the time, but many years later he said, in such a way to cast doubt on the story, "I was in the hospital too, and she never said anything to me about it."

Was it because they were both so ill? Or to spare his feelings? It would never have occurred to me that it needed saying, but possibly I knew (because it is the kind of thing children always know) how she felt about that household better than he did. It may have been the one thing she kept from him. Out of love.

From the time he was about a year old, my little brother

spent one day a week with my grandmother. And then gradually, since he had no mother and the housekeeper was glad to be relieved of the responsibility for him, the one day stretched out to three or four.

Long before this, when my mother was alive, my father had a chance to give up the road and take a much better job in the Chicago office of the insurance company he worked for, and my mother said no, it was not a good place to bring up children. The offer was repeated when he was in his middle forties. This time, tired of lugging that heavy grip from one small town to another, he said yes. When we moved to Chicago he had every intention of taking my younger brother. But my grandmother threw herself on her knees before him (this scene I have no difficulty whatever in imagining) and cried, "Will, if you take that child I will die, it will kill me!" And since he loved her, he couldn't do it. He thought the moment could be postponed. And of course it could. There is nothing that cannot be postponed. It is the only act of his life that I ever heard him express serious regret for. In the end, what it meant was that my younger brother was brought up by my Aunt Maybel and my Uncle Paul. They both idolized him. Until then, my Uncle Paul's life had been made up of the Christian church, the New York Underwriters, and his family in Augusta. He became so fond of my little brother and he displayed this fondness so openly, by hugging and kissing, that my father's sense of propriety was offended.

I used to wonder if it was possible for my little brother to love someone who was so different from my mother as my aunt was. Until I heard that, coming home from school one winter day, he had slipped and fallen on the ice, and got a slight concussion. In telling about it, my aunt said, "I had been watching for him, and he came up the street calling my name." Then I knew.

· · ·

The failure of Prohibition is, for me, the point at which the 20th century becomes distinct from the preceding ones. The essentially Puritanical Protestant churches have been losing steadily ever since the power to bring ordinary human life into relation with eternity.

The Puritan believes that his own understanding of things is the only possible one, and therefore must not be departed from. But it was departed from, successfully, in Darwin's *Origin of Species* and in all the scientific thinking that grew out of it. Man took his place in the animal kingdom, instead of being but little lower than God.

At about the same time, light thrown on the New Testament by Biblical scholarship made it questionable that when (in the words of Thomas Campbell) the Bible spoke, anybody had, in some instances, understood what it said. In my childhood, the barrier between one Protestant church and another seemed permanent and necessary, though I never asked myself what purpose it served. The congregation of the Presbyterian church acted as though they didn't even know about the Cumberland Presbyterian church, just across the street from them. But the strong sense that all Protestant denominations had of their separate identities is now steadily giving way. The Unitarians have merged with their next of kin, the Universalists, the Congregationalists with the Christian Church, and this organization in turn with the Evangelical and the Reformed Churches, and so on. In the spring of 1970, ninety delegates from nine Protestant churches voted in favor of a proposal that would merge their membership of twenty-five million members in an organization called the Church of Christ Uniting. After which they rose and sang the doxology. And elected as their first chairman a representative from the Disciples of Christ. It doesn't look to me like the forward surge Thomas Campbell imagined but, rather, the response to a threat which they are not strong enough to stand up to individually—that, in the words of Barton Stone, the power of religion has disappeared and even the form of it is fast waning away.

I joined the Presbyterian church in Lincoln as soon as I was old enough, and when we moved to Chicago I started going to another Presbyterian church there, until one day I brought home from the school library a copy of Mark Twain's *The Mysterious Stranger.* I was a very priggish adolescent and I wanted to test the strength of my religious convictions. They were not, it turned out, very strong. But I was not content with saying that I did not and could not know whether there was a divine order in the universe, which was my father's position for most of his adult life; I didn't stop short of atheism. Perhaps not atheism. My father's is a rational position, mine simply an unbelief. A negative. If you could only develop a print from it you would have saving faith.

I would like to believe in God but not all that much is, I sometimes think, the simple truth of the matter. When I am thoroughly frightened, I do more than half believe in Him. Other people's inability to believe troubles me just as much, because it has altered the world I live in.

Reading *The History of the Disciples of Christ in Illinois,* I came upon a paragraph about a man named John F. M. Parker, and in it were these two sentences: "Within eleven months he lost a son, a daughter, his farm and his wife. But then he said: 'I know whom I have believed, and am persuaded that He is able to keep that which I have committed to Him against that day.' "

It makes me hang my head in shame.

Where the understanding of other men differs from ours there is just as good a chance that we are in the presence of truth as of opinion. Therefore a new kind of enlightenment ought to have resulted from the respectful and unemotional consideration of one man's understanding against another's.

Instead it seems to have produced a new kind of darkness, with little choice, actually, but to wait for what time brings. The providing place that my Grandfather Blinn had a glimpse of prematurely is not in the firmament, as people once thought.

"Let us weigh the gain and the loss in wagering that God is," Pascal said. "Let us consider the two possibilities. If you gain, you gain all; if you lose, you lose nothing. Hesitate not, then, to wager that He is." It is not very persuasive. I think I prefer my Grandmother Maxwell on the subject: *If the universe was a machine, it would have said so in the Bible. Come here and let me take a washrag to your ears. I declare, you could grow carrots in there.*

She went to her rest in the Twenties. After the funeral they all went back to the house on Union Street and my Aunt Bert and my Aunt Maybel quarreled so bitterly that they were never on friendly terms again. Among other things, my Aunt Bert accused her sister of coming between Max and her. If my Aunt Maybel was indeed a child stealer, then the attic of the house on Union Street was full of toys for the same reason that the witch's house in *Hansel and Gretel* was made of candy.

Someone remarked once to my father that it was a pity his sister never had any children, and he said, "I happen to know she could have had them." There was no use asking what he meant by this statement; if he had felt it was proper to say more, he would have.

My Aunt Maybel died of a heart attack in 1939. She was sixty-five. She died away from home—not in her own bed, with her own things around her. Not even in a hospital, but among people she didn't care for. I try to imagine what it was like, but I cannot get over my astonishment at her dying in Augusta, Illinois. And they brought her body home, to a house without gas and electricity. How grand and mysterious life is!

Though my Uncle Paul was living at the time, she left everything she owned to my younger brother. The chair my uncle had drawn up to the dining room table for thirty-seven years, the knife and fork he ate with, the brass bed he slept on, were no longer his. My brother was in college, and from college he went into the army, and he did not claim his embarrassing inheritance. My Uncle Paul asked my Aunt Bert, who was still stuck in that coal-mining town in southern Illinois, to give up her job and come and keep house for him. She threw out the turbanned plaster heads of Europe and Africa, the parrot's eggs, the bulldog, the peacock feathers, the starfish, and the seahorse, and a great many other things, and after that the house was nothing like so gloomy. But it also no longer had the look of immortality about it. My father kept his fingers crossed, knowing how quick-tempered and tactless my aunt could be, and for a time the arrangement seemed to be working, but it was only an accommodation, like that between the Campbellites and the Baptists, and the deep underlying differences finally declared themselves. One night my father was wakened from his first sleep by the ringing of the telephone. "Yes?" he said, preparing himself for bad news, before he knew from where. "Come and get your sister," my uncle said. "All right," my father said. "I'll be over in the morning." "You won't come in the morning," my uncle said. "You'll come and get her right now!" So my father did. He never entered the house on Union Street again. Nor, since he asked me not to, have I.

My father set my Aunt Bert up in a small but quite comfortable apartment, where she lived out the rest of her life in the passionate enjoyment of doing as she pleased. At last she had her own furniture and rugs about her, and all the family pictures, and my grandmother's beautiful patchwork quilts, and there was no one to object if she read until three in the morning—no one but my father, who thought people shouldn't stay up late reading.

She complained about the physical indignities of old age. And after Max died, his suffering haunted her. She had only one grandchild to squander her affection on, and to occupy her lonely imagination. But they did not see each other often, and her granddaughter was not on anything like the easy terms with her that my two brothers and I were. When I wrote her that I was getting married, she wrote back, "Happiness is our birthright, and now you have come into your own." This statement strikes me as a triumph of love over experience.

Because he had taken care of his sister for so long, my father made her sign a paper stating that on her death everything she owned was to go to my stepmother (who was younger than my father and could be expected to outlive him). He did not put money above morality, but neither did he treat it purely as a medium of exchange. It was like a person in that it had rights which must be respected. With two farms and the securities in his safe-deposit box, he had enough so that if he should die, my stepmother would be amply provided for. And my aunt's possessions were not very valuable. But apparently he felt that by helping her he had diminished the value of his estate in a way that must be compensated for. I knew my aunt was not happy about this arrangement, but I also knew that my father did not welcome opinions about his conduct that he hadn't asked for. I needn't have worried; the arrangement was never carried out—I assume because my stepmother talked my father out of it, but he was quite capable of seeing for himself that it was improper in that it did not leave his sister free to dispose of her own possessions, and that it was only natural she should want to do this.

When my aunt died, in 1957, my father told Max's daughter to take whatever she wanted, and derived considerable satisfaction afterwards from the thought he had done this. A small quantity of old furniture that had had good care and been much loved was in this way saved from ending up at the Salvation Army. But one thing my father did hold back on that occasion.

I have no idea how much people in Lincoln knew about my Aunt Bert's first marriage. I tend to think that in small towns people know everything. My Aunt Bert didn't tell Max the truth about his father. Instead, undoubtedly because it was believed to be for his own good, they—she and my Aunt Maybel and my grandmother and my father—all lied to him. He grew up believing that his father died shortly before he was born. And this is what he told his daughter—thus perpetuating the lie that was passed off on him. Not until after his death did she begin to suspect, from certain remarks my Aunt Bert made, that she had not been told the whole story. Indirect intimations, mostly. The cat struggling to get out of the bag. My aunt never said anything specific; it was rather her absolute refusal to talk about Max's father that finally aroused her granddaughter's curiosity.

At the time of her death, my Aunt Bert left a sealed envelope, with written instructions that it was to be burned unopened. My father was her executor, and he carried out these instructions before Max's daughter arrived in Lincoln for the funeral. Characteristically, he told her what he had done.

When he introduced her to old friends as Max's daughter she sensed that he was proud of her. (He would never have introduced any woman slightingly, in any case.) He was the only member of her father's family who was acceptable to her mother. She told him that Max had admired him very much and my father looked surprised and said, "I didn't know."

He might have guessed. I remember the respectful way that Max looked at my father, and spoke to him. When Max was dying and my father took my Aunt Bert to Cincinnati, he asked my father to play the piano for him.

Max's daughter questioned my father about her Grandfather Fuller, but all my father would say was that he "was not a very honest man." It seemed as if all sources of information were permanently closed to her.

Later, when she began going through Max's records, she learned that her grandparents were married on April 2, 1898; that the marriage license stated that he was "of Chicago"; that Max was born on January 5, 1899, at which time Louis E. Fuller was described as a newspaper man; and that he died on February 4, 1900, in Springfield, Illinois.

She wrote to the Bureau of Vital Statistics in Springfield, hoping to learn the cause of her grandfather's death from the death certificate, and was informed that there was no such certificate. Letters to twenty other counties near Springfield also failed to turn up a record of his death.

Finally, she wrote for photostats of the probate papers of her great-grandfather, Galusha E. Fuller, who lived, as I have said, in Waukesha, Wisconsin, and from these she discovered that her great-grandfather's will, written on June 6, 1901—a year and some months after Louis Fuller was supposed to have died—mentioned him as a beneficiary: "To my son, Louis E. Fuller, I give and bequeath the sum of One Dollar ($1.00), having heretofore advanced to him what I consider to be his just share of my estate." Furthermore, she found that a settlement of her great-grandfather's estate on May, 1905, listed among other heirs, Louis E. Fuller of New York City.

The clerk of the Circuit Court of Cook County produced a copy of my Aunt Bert's divorce papers in which it was stated that she and her second husband were married on June 25, 1905—little more than a month after the settlement in which Louis E. Fuller was said to be alive and residing in New York City. Unless my Aunt Bert's marriage to Max's father was in some way illegal to begin with, the only reasonable conclusion anybody could come to was that she had divorced Max's father as well.

My cousin applied to the clerk of Logan County for the papers concerning her grandmother's divorce from Louis E. Fuller. From them she learned the facts I have already given in chapter nine.

Though my aunt was brought down in her first flight, she had been so brave. Defeat that comes about through timidity is final. The person who has acted bravely is sustained by the recollection of that moment when he could have acted with caution and chose instead to throw caution to the winds. Having lived through so much, and had such a good view of the seamy side of life, my aunt had earned the right to be rash if she felt like it.

Max's daughter still did not know where and when her grandfather died, whether he had ever remarried and had other children who would be her half-aunts and -uncles, or exactly what the trouble was that led her grandmother to guard her secret so long and so carefully. She thought of everything it could be, including bigamy, and suspected that it was nothing so dramatic as most of the possibilities that occurred to her. From the wording of her Great-grandfather Fuller's will, her grandfather must have been, to say the least, irresponsible about money. Regardless of what he did, he was her grandfather and she wanted to know about him. And her knowing would certainly harm no one now.

A further search among her father's papers uncovered

the name and address of a first cousin on the Fuller side, Louis Fuller's sister's son. She wrote to him and got a letter back, saying that he had known her Grandfather Fuller very well. He was the victim of a domineering father. As a boy he had dreams of becoming an inventor, but his father had other plans for him, and he had to hide his inventions under the floor of the barn or his father would find them and destroy them. As a grown man he drifted from one job to another. Before him at all times was the vision of untold wealth that would come to him as the reward of his inventions. Dreamers, as my father often pointed out to me, are inclined to get into financial difficulties. On several occasions Louis Fuller's father bailed him out, and then he said, "No more." Unable to get money any other way, Louis Fuller committed a forgery and served eighteen months in prison. I can see him saying to himself as he dipped the pen in the ink, *They would never put me in jail for $118. He wouldn't let them do it.*

He came home to Waukesha when his father died, learned that there was nothing coming to him from his father's will, and returned to New York without waiting for the funeral. He married again. His second wife was a Roman Catholic, and she was a very good wife to him. During the latter part of the First World War, this same nephew was stationed nearby, and used to visit Louis Fuller and his wife every weekend, until he was mustered out of the army. He developed an affection for both of them.

During the Twenties, Louis Fuller was trying to patent a dry stencil and wanted an affidavit from his nephew, which was supplied, though not promptly. He then wrote to thank his nephew for sending it. The letter begins: "Your letter and affidavit received. It is very satisfactory and will probably be of material assistance to me. I would like to have a supplemental affidavit setting forth in a few words the facts as to the delay which must be accounted for if possible. Something like this: That you first heard from me about an affidavit as to your knowledge of my possession of the invention about November 1924; that the import of it did not occur to you at the time, but that you intended to take up the matter later but through inadvertence did not do so at once, thinking that you would do it in your next regular letter to me; that having heard from me again on or about June 1925, asking for the information, you have made an affidavit showing your knowledge as to my possession of the invention. You might also state in this affidavit, that you saw me take a piece of gun cotton, place it on an ash tray and ignite it and that it burned at once with a flash and a large flame, that this was seen by three other persons present beside myself, and you (Ryan, Nichols, and Aunt Elizabeth). Do not mention the names. . . ."

On the second page of the letter this sentence occurs: "It seems to be my job in this world to lick rascals. But worms do not lie on their backs forever." There is also a terribly touching postscript: "I am remembering about Samson. He did not pray God to thrust the pillars asunder, but that he, Samson, be given the strength to do it. And so it happened. Also, 'He goeth forth clothed in the Armor of righteousness, and who can withstand him?' But every day I see evil triumph and good dragged in the dust; the wicked prosperous and happy and the good poor and miserable. Solomon states that this was one of the greatest mysteries which he had ever contemplated. But if this Objective Reality is in fact a place of trial to train the Soul, and She profits by it, all is well. I have a deep conviction that the wicked, rich man has got something to learn. But if God's infinite mercy saves him, what of His infinite justice? You cannot say one is greater than the other."

And what about Max? When his cousin called on him in his office in Cincinnati, in the year 1935, and he learned about his father at last, did he go home and tell his wife what he had learned? The answer is he did not. Then or ever. His daughter was only nine years old at the time, and only seventeen when he died, and until the day before he died he was expecting to recover. In his place I think I too would have decided to wait until my daughter was a little older. "What saddens me now," Max's daughter says, "is that I was so often in New York when my Grandfather Fuller was alive, and could so easily have looked him up, and may even, who knows, have passed him on the street." There is reason to think that Max did look his father up, on one of his trips to New York—perhaps the very one when he had dinner with me in the Village.

Before Max died, he completed the line of descent of the Fullers, going back to a Robert Fuller who came from Southampton and landed in Salem in 1638, in the ship *Bevis*. In writing to his cousin about genealogical matters, he says, "I suppose you think this is a lot of useless nonsense, but once worked out, it may be valuable to someone someday."

One of the mysterious innuendoes that my Aunt Bert made in speaking to her granddaughter was that before Max's father died she had gone home to her family, and one night he tried to kidnap Max, then a baby. From this Max's daughter deduced that for a time at least her grandfather must have cared a great deal for his son—though I think, considering how little he had seen of that baby, it is also possible to regard it as the act of a heated imagination. I have even wondered if this could be the true story of the Dickensian burglar who was trying to get into the house on Kickapoo Street. My grandmother would certainly not have felt like going into my Aunt Bert's marital difficulties with a child of four, and with that unbroken run of bad luck Louis Fuller would be bound to place the ladder under the wrong window.

19

Searching through books and papers for information that is usually not there, I often ask myself why I was so incurious about my forebears. Most of the things I would like to know, my father could have told me. If this kind of curiosity is one of the aspects of oncoming age, then my lack of it earlier was natural. But there is another possible explanation. My father had a number of stories that he liked to tell of an evening before dinner—the adventure of the copper-toed shoes, the adventure of the bellboy in the lobby of the hotel in Ohio, how he borrowed the money from Tim Hardin, how Professor Hieronymous met with his comeuppance, how my grandfather said to my father, "If you'll just put aside a thousand dollars," and so on. He did not like to be interrupted in the middle of his narrative, and by the time he got to the end I would have forgotten what it was I wanted to ask him. So I didn't ask the questions I might have asked, and now there is no one to ask them of. Here and there, digging, I bring up some small piece of archaeological information.

The *History of Logan County* says that my great-great-grandfather's brother, John England, who was bored by the whole idea of money, was fatally injured at Cornland in November, 1884, but not what happened. Apparently everybody knew, and so there was no need to record it.

Facing the Christian church in Lincoln, across that little park with a bandstand in the center of it, was the white clapboard mansion of the Honorable Robert B. Latham. I remember it as a very beautiful old house with slender posts supporting the upstairs porches, shutters at all the windows, wooden balustrades here and there, and a cupola. Having laid out the town of Lincoln, he devoted the rest of his life to making it amount to something. The *Logan County History* does not even attempt to list the enterprises and institutions that were brought into being by his energy and influence, but lumps them all together in a formal expression of gratitude.

Speaking at a meeting of the Old Settlers' Association, in 1876, he said that there was scarcely a forty-acre lot in Elkhart woods but what he had chased a wolf over. His father, James Latham, was the first white settler in Logan County, and the first Probate Court, in 1821, was presided over by him. From his photograph Robert Latham could be a religious prophet or, equally well, a gun-runner in a novel by Joseph Conrad.

The second generation of his descendants went through their inheritance so fast that gossip could hardly keep up with them, and in the early 1920's his house was sold to a real estate developer, a golfing companion of my father's, who tore it down and put up a row of semi-identical bungalows. A real estate developer, with rather different ideas and dealing with a different situation, is just what Old Man Latham was, and I don't suppose he fell asleep when the conversation got around to money. And if one wanted to grieve, one could also regret that quarter-section of unbroken prairie the town was originally—trees skirting the streams, a sea of grass and wild flowers reaching out in every direction to the horizon, at night the howling of wolves, in the early mornings of spring the thrumming of prairie chickens, a country of foxes, raccoons, wildcats, and great herds of deer.

One can grieve over all the water that has ever flowed over the dam.

The Latham house, which ought to have stood for generations, is gone. So is the Donalds' house next door to where we lived on Ninth Street. It burned down in the night. But by that time they were both dead. During Dr. Donald's last illness my father took my wife and me to call on him. We had only been married a few months, and had come home on a visit, and my wife was being introduced to all the old family friends. Dr. Donald was sitting up in bed, in what used to be his den and was now converted into a downstairs bedroom, and his first concern was for my wife—that she should be made comfortable and feel liked. As I look back, I realize that what he did was give our marriage his blessing. At the time I was only aware of the fact that he approved of the girl I had chosen to marry, and of me, and that there was something about his approval that had made us both suddenly very happy. Everything I said seemed to fit in with his conception of what I was likely to think or feel. It was as if, going about his business, he had kept an eye on me. Perhaps he had. It was the first time I had ever really talked to him. We moved away from Lincoln when I was fifteen, and during the latter part of his life he was in Chicago—carrying on his business affairs and I suppose keeping out of reach of Aunty's tongue—much more than he was in Lincoln, so we didn't often see him when we went there. I find it very strange indeed that, though we lived in Chicago too, he never once came to see us, and nobody expected him to. He must have passed through the Looking-Glass into some other world that at no point touched the one we were living in. Or perhaps some friendships are attached to the place they flourished in, and have no existence anywhere else. Anyway, I discovered, too late, that he was a marvelous storyteller and that I loved him. At one point he took my hand in his and held it, resting on the counterpane, and said, in that soft Scottish voice, "My boy, I remember so well the day you were born. It was a terribly hot day in August and . . ." All the rest went out of my mind instantly, as if I were in the presence of something it was dangerous for me to know.

After my Grandfather Blinn died, my mother transferred her veneration to Dr. Donald, and so did Annette. But they weren't the only ones. When people had something weighing on their heart, they went and talked to him. He told Annette once that my father had been to see him, and had talked about my mother.

The Dyers' house is still there, at the foot of Ninth Street hill: a frame shoebox covered with green roofing paper. How on earth did they keep warm? A scraping sound in the cellar of our house meant that Old Dyer was shoveling coal into the furnace and fiddling with the drafts and the damper. Sometimes in the dusk he and I met in our driveway. He was a big man, in clothes so old that they had no shape but fell in folds. His daughter had worked in our kitchen and he must have known a good deal about all of us. All I knew about him was what I perceived in the fading light—that the voice that said "Evening," was at least an octave lower than any other human voice I knew, and that his steps were heavy and slow. On hearing a quotation from the Bible he knew instantly where it came from. He was the son of a freed slave who came to Springfield from Richmond, Virginia, and drove his horse and wagon at night, taking runaway slaves from one station of the underground railroad to the next. Mrs. Dyer was born in slavery, the property of the wife of (so mixed up are the elements of history at the time it is happening) a general of the Union Army. Her father and mother ran away but were caught and returned, and the general sold her father somewhere down South and he was never heard from again. William Dyer, Old Dyer's son, put himself through medical school and was practicing in Kansas City. This everybody knew about and considered remarkable.

For a decade and perhaps more, the lives of our two

families were closely entwined in mutual dependence. After we moved away from Lincoln, my father never failed to call on Mrs. Dyer once or twice a year, for as long as she lived. Usually my brothers and I went with him. They made—Mrs. Dyer and my father made polite conversation. At the back of their minds they both must have been thinking of my mother, but her name wasn't mentioned. It wouldn't have been tactful, since he had another wife, for Mrs. Dyer to speak for my mother, and for my father to do this would have been to run the risk of embarrassing Mrs. Dyer by being too intimate. When he got up to go, he would take out his wallet and present her with a new ten-dollar bill.

My Great-grandfather Youtsey's house in Cold Spring, Kentucky, is also still standing. One of my mother's cousins—that same Wright Youtsey that she used to say I looked like—drove me out from Cincinnati to see it, in the 1930's, at which time it belonged to a farmer, who was off somewhere in the fields. It looked like any yellow brick farmhouse. While my Kentucky cousin talked to the farmer's wife, I put my head in the door of two or three downstairs rooms, which seemed bare and unloved, and went outside again. I told myself that I was looking at my mother's childhood, but there was nothing anywhere that supported this idea in any way. I said, "It must have been very different in my great-grandfather's time," and my mother's cousin smiled and said, "Grandfather kept his wheat in the drawing room."

My Grandmother Blinn's first cousin, Henry Youtsey, was charged with the murder of the governor of Kentucky.* Actually there were two governors. The Republican candi-

---

* There is no thorough account of this crime. For the background and most of the facts I am indebted to Dr. Bennett H. Wall of the History Department of Tulane University.

date, William S. Taylor, had a plurality of the votes cast in the election of 1899, and was inaugurated, on the twelfth of December, but the Democrats controlled the state legislature, and the legislative committee on elections decided in favor of the Democratic candidate, William E. Goebel. In short it was a steal. On the other hand, there had not been one honest state election in Kentucky since the Civil War. The campaign of 1899 was an effort on the part of the Democrats to wrest the state from the grip of the Louisville and Nashville Railroad.

Behind this struggle was another, between the old families in the rural districts and the German immigrants who settled in the cities. With few roads or bridges connecting them, only the railroad, the various counties were politically independent of each other and of the state government through their isolation. This situation lasted well into the 20th century, until about 1930. Within the county boundaries, the men who controlled the county did as they pleased. It was no problem to buy a jury or get a man killed. And Goebel himself had been tried for murder. He is an interesting figure. *The Dictionary of National Biography* says that Goebel was four times in the Kentucky Senate, and that during this entire period of legislative service he encountered bitter opposition from within his own party. "This political animosity resulted, among other things, in his killing John Sandford, a prominent banker and politician in Covington, in April 1895. On his examining trial he pleaded self-defense and was released, the grand jury subsequently refusing to indict him. He identified himself with the reform element, and is generally credited with the passing of much of the reform legislation of the period, particularly that relating to taxation and the regulation of the railroads. . . . In 1899 he was a candidate for the Democratic nomination for governor, and secured the nomination . . . by a series of shrewd political maneuvers which greatly increased the number of his enemies and divided his party. . . . Goebel was not an orator but had a talent for vituperation and biting speech. He was taciturn and reserved, and had practically no friends outside his own family. He owed his success to unusual skill as a politician and to a courage that seemed to have no limit."

He was on his way to the Senate, at ten minutes past eleven on the morning of January 30, 1900, when he was shot by a man standing in the window of the third story of a brick building immediately east of the state capitol. Goebel was carried into the Capitol Hotel, and the brick building was surrounded. A man came rushing down the stairs—a farmer named Whittaker, from Taylor's own county—and was found to have five revolvers on his person, two in each side pocket of his overcoat and one in a side pocket of his trousers. He was arrested and denied the charge. There were no empty chambers in any of the revolvers. The legislature was in session at the time, and someone rushed into the hall and shouted, "Goebel has been shot!"— producing confusion. The legislators poured out of the building, bareheaded, many of them with their hands on their revolver pockets. Hundreds of people rushed to the scene of the tragedy, carrying a revolver in *each* hand, and the state of Kentucky was on the verge of civil war. Goebel was sworn in on his deathbed, and died a few days later. Taylor fled the state to escape the charge of murder. He had his office in the building from which the shots came, and for a week before the assassination forty people had been sleeping in the upper part of the building. Nobody knew their names or where they came from.

My grandmother's cousin was a fine-featured, slight man in his early thirties. My mother always said that he was convicted on circumstantial evidence, the evidence being that Goebel was shot from such a distance that there was only one man in the state of Kentucky who could have done it. And separating the marksmanship from the use it was put to, the family took a certain pride in this accomplishment. But it is pure fiction. Dr. Wall says there were at least a hundred men in Kentucky at that time who could have shot Goebel from that window and who had an interest in doing it. Henry Youtsey got into trouble chiefly because he talked too much. For twenty-four hours, everybody talked; after that they shut up and never talked again. They had discovered that there were a dozen groups who were trying to kill Goebel and they didn't know but what one of their men might have done it.

No fair—or even rational—investigation of the murder was possible. The trial dragged on for eight years. With a change of administration, most of the defendants were set free. My grandmother's cousin was one of the three men who were not. He was a stenographer in the State Auditor's office, and closely associated with Caleb Powers, the Secretary of State, who was charged with being "accessory before the fact to the willful murder of William Goebel." There was testimony to the effect that Henry Youtsey had a key to Powers' office, from which the shot had been fired, and also that he had exhibited a box of cartridges and said they were for Goebel. He spent nineteen years in jail, and then was pardoned, after talking some more. One of my mother's cousins met him shortly after he was freed, and said indelicately, "Now that it's all over, tell me, Henry, did you do it?" and the answer (which I believe) was "No, I didn't."

Henry Youtsey held public office in Cold Spring after he was released from prison. Caleb Powers served a term in the United States Senate.

It is not true that the dead desert the living. They go away for a very short time, and then they come back and stay as long as they are needed. But sooner or later a time comes when they are in the way; their presence is, for one reason or another, an embarrassment; there is no place for them in the lives of those they once meant everything to. Then they go away for good.

When I was in college I was wakened out of a sound sleep by my own voice, answering my mother, who had called to me from the stairs. With my heart pounding, I waited for more and there wasn't any more. Nothing like it ever happened to me before, or since.

There is a Chinese proverb that says every piece of good luck is in the end a misfortune, and every misfortune is cause for congratulation if one could only read the future. One of the two business associates whose names figure in the unconfident letter from my father to my Grandmother Maxwell became his only enemy—Charlie Higley, who by the Twenties had become a millionaire, having made a fortune for himself and another for the insurance company by playing the stock market. Money made him overbearing. He was elected president of the company and moved on to the New York office. He managed to retain the title of head of the Western Department (which would otherwise have passed to my father) and the salary. My father put up with this patiently, but there was more. Mr. Higley began to show a pronounced preference for the opinions and the company of a younger man in the office, whom he could easily have advanced over my father—a humiliation my father was not ready to accept. For the first time, he began to look old. The thing he was afraid of didn't happen. My father's enemy died suddenly, and was replaced by someone who was well disposed toward my father. He was put in charge of the Chicago office and made a vice-president of the company.

Eventually the presidency was offered to him, and he decided not to take it. It would have meant moving East, leaving all their friends, and dealing with all manner of situations and pressures that he was not experienced in, and he was happy where he was. He retired from business prematurely, in his early sixties, because of a detached retina, and he and my stepmother moved back to Lincoln to live.

The Lincoln *Evening Courier* ran a piece about him. My Grandmother Maxwell's clock is mentioned. He must have pointed the clock out to the reporter who came to interview him. And also talked about his boyhood, for the article speaks of his posting bills for the theatrical engagements at the old Opera House, and of the fact that he played the violin with the High School Society orchestra. Here, for a few seconds, the whole house of cards I have so patiently been constructing threatens to collapse. All it takes is one slippery card. Have I misremembered? Was it the school orchestra he composed that schottische for? Was the Christian church in Lincoln opposed to instrumental music?

Perhaps it doesn't much matter, except that it casts doubt on other things that I thought I had right. But what do I do about the unused cards—all those ancestors I have tried to steer clear of because it is just too much? And because so little is known of them, of the women particularly. Only their names: *Anna Harper*, who married Stephen England. And *Agnes Kirby*, my great-great-great-grandmother, who married James Turley and lies buried in Carlyle Cemetery, near Mt. Pulaski, Illinois. And *Elizabeth King*, Jemima Keepers' mother. And *Rosannah Yocum*, whose mother died when she was a child and who was brought up by her sister and took her sister's husband's name and married William Higgins. And *Deborah Lee*, my great-great-great-great-great-grandmother, who was the daughter of John Lee. And *John Lee*, whose will begins, "In the name of God Amen, I John Lee, of the County of Goochland, being very sick and weak though thanks to God in perfect senses and memory do think it proper to make and ordain this my last will and testament . . ."

And *David Cheatham*, my great-great-great-grandfather, who lived in Virginia, in the Blue Mountains, and in his will left his son John a Negro named Frank, his son Leonard a Negro named Joseph, his son James a Negro named Squire (but freed an old Negro woman named Patty), and left his wife, Barbary, "choice of furniture, her loom, her trunk, her side saddle, my cupboard and its contents, a farm of forty acres during her widowhood, and one choice milk cow with corn meet to support her for twelve months."

And *William Keepers*, my great-great-grandfather, whose newly dug grave, in Mt. Hope Cemetery, filled with water from the "spouty ground," and it was necessary to weigh his coffin down with stones to keep it from floating like a rowboat.

The drinking water in Lincoln comes from an underground river millions of years old. Until it was buried by glaciers it flowed in the light of day. Its source was near Blowing Rock, North Carolina, and it ran northwest across the middle of the continent, much of the time at right angles to the Ohio, which did not then exist. From a point just beyond Fort Wayne, Indiana, its course was due west, to Lincoln, where it was joined by the Mississippi. Their combined waters flowed south into a bay of the Gulf of Mexico, which at that time extended northward to within a few miles of St. Louis.

The thing about a house of cards is that it cannot be left standing. Even if it doesn't collapse suddenly, you say to yourself *It's finished*, and make it fall, and gather the cards in and put them away in a desk drawer.

The Christian church in Lincoln is, I believe, still very much as it used to be, and flourishing. Attached to it is a training school for preachers, also flourishing. Some time ago the congregation detached itself from the main body of the

Disciples of Christ, which had become too progressive for it. Mulish like my grandmother, the church in Lincoln preferred not to move with the times, and, instead, allied itself with half a dozen churches in Illinois and Missouri to form what is now known as the Uncoöperative Branch.

Family history is like a kaleidoscope in that you can keep shifting the essential elements and coming up with new patterns and combinations, but it is never-ending, and so I will present the reader with one more turn and stop. When I was in my forties, and married, and living in Westchester County, my father and my stepmother came for a visit. It was October, and cool enough for a fire in the fireplace. Before dinner I made a round of drinks, and my father and I sat on either side of the fire, talking, with our glasses on the floor beside us, and suddenly a suspicion crossed my mind, for the first time. I don't know why it took me so long to ask this question or why it never occurred to my father to tell me without my having to ask. I picked up the poker and rearranged the logs and then, leaning back, said, "Am I like your father?" and he said, rather crossly, "Of course."

Toward the very end of his life, he suffered from shortness of breath and also, like many old people, from a tired mind. And, either because he didn't realize what he was doing or because it saved time and trouble, he telescoped his narrative in such a way that it only took him a couple of minutes to run through the entire repertoire, getting everything quite wrong but having the satisfaction of telling once more the stories he loved to tell. He celebrated his eightieth birthday and then he began to fail rapidly and after a slight heart attack ended up in the hospital. He and the Episcopal minister had become friends at Rotary Club meetings and when the minister appeared in the door of my father's room he threw up his hands in delight. By his own choice he had a Christian burial service and lies in consecrated ground.

NOTE ON THE TYPE

This book was set in a modern adaptation of a type designed by the first William Caslon (1692–1766), greatest of English letter founders. The Caslon face, an artistic, easily read type, has had two centuries of ever increasing popularity in our own country—it is of interest to note that the first copies of the Declaration of Independence and the first paper currency distributed to the citizens of the newborn nation were printed in this type face.